WHERE
THEY NOW ?

(Life after Soccer.)

Compiled by
Andrew Pringle

Best wishes
Andy Pringle

Runnymede Publications
Romsey, Hampshire.

A RUNNYMEDE PUBLICATIONS BOOK

First Published in 1995 by
Runnymede Publications
a subsidiary of
Runnymede Estates Ltd,
Romsey, Hampshire,
England.

A catalogue entry for this book is available in the British Library.

ISBN 0 952 5428 0 3

Printed and bound by The Ashford Press, Gosport, England.

To: Geraldine, Hannah-Louise,
and Sarah-Jayne, who will be so glad
*that the "**Bloody book**" is finally finished.*

ACKNOWLEDGEMENTS

This book would not have not been published without the help and patience of an enormous number of people (listed below) to whom I offer my sincere thanks.

NEIL "Monster"FISLER:

Whose contribution deserves particular praise (and whose telephone bill will now no doubt be considerably reduced!)

Lyn at Acclaim Business Services; Richard Arnwell (Stockport County); Mike Blackstone (Exeter); Tony Bugby (Oldham Chronicle); Dennis Bundy Promotions; Peter Creed; Mike Davage ; Tom Finney O.B.E.; Ford Graphics; Terry Frost; Dave Goody; Johnny Haynes; Duncan Holly; Graham Hughes (Wolves); Inside Information (who saved this project from being eaten by the computer on more than one occasion!); Mike Jones; Peter Jones; Tony Matthews; Peter Osgood; Richard Owen; Andy Porter (Spurs); Mr & Mrs Poynter; Mick Reid; Roger Wash; Sid Woodhead (Grimsby Town); The staff at all of the League and Non-League clubs who helped; The many Newspapers and photographers who supplied information and photographs, and finally a special thankyou to all the former players who co-operated to make this publication possible.

WHERE ARE THEY NOW ?

Thankyou for buying this book (if you are currently browsing in a book shop, this will take you far too long to read, so please proceed immediately to the cash desk and hand over a meagre £9.99 so that you can enjoy it in the comfort of your own home!)

I sincerely hope that you will be entertained, amused, and sometimes surprised to find out what has happened to your favourite players since they retired from playing. Every effort has been made to avoid embarrassement, in fact many more interesting stories had to be left out for fear of prosecution (or worse!) - the tales of crime; drugs; prison; and strange sexual preferences; will have to wait for a braver author than me !

As you can imagine, keeping up to date with every former player is an impossible task. Even with so many people helping there are bound to be errors and ommisons. Please would you be kind enough to forgive any mistakes that you find, and if possible drop me a line to ensure that the inaccuracy is not repeated in any future re-print - thankyou.

Andy Pringle

PRINGLE, Andy. *Dusthole Diddlers, (1970's).* Like many youngsters, was scorer of many crucial match winning goals for both club and country. However, during waking hours, the closest he got to professional football was occasionally sharing the same muddy school playing field with Steve Foster (Brighton & England), and then finally being offered a trial by Peterborough United whilst compiling this book. (Their error may have been spotted, if the 37 year old with an executive waistline, had turned up at their training ground with his boots on the designated day!). Now that "Where are they now" is published, the property developer/entrepreneur/author will be at a loose end and open to any sensible and legal offers of ways to help pay his bills.

AAS, Einer. *Notts F (1980-81)* Played 20 games for Nottingham Forest in the early eighties after joining them from Bayern Munich. Now lives in his native Norway where he works in a bank.

ADAMS, Chris. *Tottenham, Norwich, Watford, (1951-1955)* Ex-Spurs outside left now works as a painter & decorator, living in Romford, Essex

ADAMS, Micky. *Gillingham, Coventry, Leeds, Southampton, Fulham (1979-1994)* Experienced former Leeds United and Southampton full back who seems to have found the knack of scoring goals whilst combining his playing role with that of coaching at his current club, Fulham.

ADDISON, Colin. *York, Notts F, Arsenal, Sheff Utd, Hereford (1957-1973)* Joined West Brom as assistant to Ron Atkinson, then followed him to Atletico Madrid in 1988. Has also held posts at Hereford Utd (twice); Durban City (South Africa); Notts County; Newport Co (twice); Derby Co; Celta (Spain). In October 1994 Colin became Merthyr Tydfil's fourth manager in 15 months. His stay was brief, ending in the following February. Now lives in Hereford and acts as a scout.

AHERNE, Thomas. *Luton (1948-1956).* Full back who played both for Northern Ireland and the Republic. Settled in Luton after playing 267 League games for the Hatters, and worked locally for Vauxhall for many years until his retirement.

AITKEN, Charles. *Aston V (1960-1975).* Aitken was one of Aston Villa's all time greats. He spent 17 years at Villa Park playing a total of 561 games. Charlie quit in 1976, moving to New York Cosmos in the States. Returned to start a jewellery and antiques business in Birmingham.

AIZLEWOOD, Mark. *Newport, Luton, Charlton, Leeds, Bradford C, Bristol C, Cardiff, (1975-1995)* Well travelled Welsh international (33 caps) now player/coach at Cardiff City FC.

AIZLEWOOD, Steve. *Newport, Swindon, Portsmouth (168-1983)* Strong full back who made over 400 league appearances, has returned to his home town of Newport in Gwent where he trained, and now practices as a Chartered Surveyor.

Len Allchurch minding his Sheepskin Shop. *(Courtesy: South Wales Evening Post)*

ALCOCK, Terry. *Port V, Blackpool, Bury, Blackburn, Port V, Halifax, (1963-1977).* Now Licensee at the Bull public house in Burscough.

ALEKSIC, Milija. *Plymouth, Luton, Tottenham, (1973-1981)* Goalkeeper who upon retiring from the game in 1982, emigrated to South Africa in 1982. Now works as a sales representative selling photocopiers and fax machines, having previously spent ten years selling golf equipment.

ALEXANDER, John. *Millwall, Reading, Northampton. (1977-1981)* After retiring in 1981, John stayed in the game to utilise his administrative skills as Secretary at Watford Football Club.

ALEXANDER, Keith. *Grimsby, Stockport, Lincoln, (1988-1994)* Lanky forward who joined the professional game at a relatively late age, but has now progressed into track-suited roles: firstly at Lincoln City as Manager, now in his current role as player coach at Mansfield. Also turns out for Ilkeston Town Vets in the Umbro Vets League.

ALLARDYCE, Sam. *Bolton, Sunderland, Millwall, Coventry, Huddersfield, Bolton, Preston, WBA. (1973-1989).* Played for eight League clubs as a reliable defender and had a spell in America with Tampa of Florida before moving into management. Currently boss at Blackpool.

Ivor Allchurch *(Pic: S.Wales Eve Post)*

ALLCHURCH, Ivor. *Swansea, Newcastle, Cardiff, Swansea, (1947-1965)* Brother of Len, made 68 full appearances for Wales. Awarded the MBE in 1966 for his contribution to soccer. Lives in Swansea and is now retired, having worked driving a van for several years, prior to which he had worked as a coach for a local Leisure Centre.

ALLCHURCH, Len. *Swansea, Sheff Utd, Stockport, Swansea. (1950-1969)* For some years was a hotelier, but now runs a successful leather goods business, the "Len Allchurch Shoe, Leather, and Sheepskin Centre" in Swansea. Enjoys his golf which he plays off an eight handicap and still occasionally turns out for charity soccer matches.

ALLCOCK, Terry. *Bolton, Norwich. (1952-1958)* Played 334 games in 11 years at Norwich, scoring 84 goals. Now a garage owner in the City.

ALLDER, Doug *Millwall, Orient, Watford, Brentford. (1969-1979)* Now lives in Hersham and works in the building trade, but considering taking a full time job at London's Heathrow Airport.

ALLEN, Jimmy. The British transfer record was smashed in 1933 by Jimmy's move from Portsmouth to Aston Villa, for a fee of £10,750! He died at home in Southsea, in February 1995.

ALLEN, Keith. *Portsmouth, Grimsby, Stockport, Luton, Plymouth. (1962-1970)* Still lives in Plymouth and works as a car salesman.

ALLEN, Les. *Chelsea, Tottenham, QPR. (1956-1968)* **Former England Under 23 goalscoring forward. Now lives in Hornchurch and is a professional model maker. Father of Clive and Bradley, who now play for Millwall and Q.P.R.**

ALLEN, Peter. *Leyton O, Millwall (1965-1978.)* Lives in Brighton, practices as a Solicitor.

ALLEN, Ronnie. *Port V, WBA, C Palace. (1946-1961)* Won 5 England caps and scored over 200 goals in his 400 plus games for West Brom.He then managed Wolves, Atletico Bilbao, Sporting Lisbon, Walsall, WBA, Panathinaikos in addition to a spell coaching in Saudi Arabia. Most recently back at the Hawthorns as Assistant Manager.

ALLEN, Tony. *Stoke, Bury (1957-1971).* England international left back, winning three caps, who was a regular for Stoke for over a decade. Still lives in the City where he is now a licensee.

ALLINSON, Ian. *Colchester, Arsenal, Stoke, Luton, Colchester. (1974-1989).* Winger who rose to fame with Arsenal, but began and ended his league career at Colchester United, before becoming player/manager at Baldock Town. Now manages Stockfield FC in the United Counties League.

ALSOP, Gilbert. *Coventry, Walsall, WBA, Ipswich, Walsall (1929-1946).* **Prolific scorer for Walsall in two spells during the 30's and 40's. Went on to work for on the ground staff for twenty years. Died in 1992, and had a stand in the new Bescot Stadium named in his honour.**

ANDERSON, Peter. *Luton, Sheff Utd, Millwall (1971-1982)* Midfielder, served three English clubs interspersed with spells in the States with Tampa of Florida. Now back home working as a Sportswear representative, based in Newcastle.

ANDERSON, Terry. *Arsenal, Norwich, Colchester, Scunthorpe, Crewe, Colchester. (1961-1975).* England Youth international who played over 200 games for Norwich City. Became a publican in Caistor, Norfolk, but died in 1980 at the age of 36, drowning after taking a training run.

ANDERSON, Trevor. *Man U, Swindon, Peterborough. (1972-1978).* Won 22 caps for Northern Ireland as a player. Now working as Manager of Linfield, who swept the board, winning the League, Irish Cup, League Cup and Budweiser Cup competitions in Ireland in 1993-4.

Viv Anderson

ANDERSON, Viv. *Notts For, Arsenal, Man U, Sheff Wed, Barnsley, (1974-1993)* Joined Nottingham Forest as an apprentice having briefly worked as a printer before deciding to pursue a footballing career. Solid performances at full back established Anderson as one of the best in the country, and prompted big money moves to Arsenal, and then Manchester United. He made 30 full international appearances, and was the first black footballer to play for England. Also played for Sheffield Wednesday and was player/manager at Barnsley, before joining his old United pal, Bryan Robson, at Middlesborough FC, as his assistant.

ANDERSON, Willie. *Man U, Aston Villa, Cardiff. (1963-1976)* Played over 300 League games in his thirteen year career in England, 229 of them for Aston Villa. Now works as an executive with a radio station in Oregon, USA.

ANSELL, William. *Northampton (1947-1951)* Northampton's goalie for several post war years. Now retired and living in Bletchley, Northants.

(Courtesy: East Fife Mail)

ARCHIBALD, Steve. *Tottenham, Blackburn, Reading (1980-1991)* Scottish international striker, joined Tottenham from Aberdeen in 1980. 58 goals from his 128 games in Spurs colours led to his move to European giants, Barcelona. Later he had two brief spells back in the English League, firstly with Blackburn (1987), then with Reading (1991). Steve has now returned Scotland where he is manager of Manager of East Fife FC.

(Picture courtesy Clive Lewis of GCL Photography, Hale Barns)

ALLISON, Malcolm. *Charlton Ath, West Ham U (1949-1957).* Former West Ham centre half who became a flamboyant manager ahieving incredible success with Manchester City in the 1970's, as well as bringing colour to a number of other clubs. Malcolm now lives near Middlesborough and his last League post was as Manager of Bristol Rovers in 1993, ironically the year that he celebrated 50 years in the game. Believed to have suffered a substantial loss as a result of the collapse of the B.C.C.I. bank. 1995 saw him embark on a nation-wide tour as half of a double act with Tommy Docherty.

ARDILES, Osvaldo. *Tottenham, Blackburn, QPR, Swindon, (1978-1989)* Argentinian internatinonal who gained fame during the 1978 World Cup finals, and by joining Spurs shortly afterwards. Appointed Manager of Swindon Town in August 1989. Managed Tottenham Hotspur until November 1994, then in March 1995 became an advisor to a London Law firm specialising in sports contracts, before setting off to take up a coaching post in Mexico with Guadalajara.

David Armstrong *(Pic: Southampton Echo)*

ARMFIELD, Jimmy. *Blackpool (1954-1970)* An eye-catching defender who played for Blackpool between 1954 and 1970. After a brilliant display in the 1962 World Cup finals in Chile, was voted best "Right-back in the World". Played 43 games for England. At one time, making 37 consecutive appearances. After playing almost 600 games for Blackpool, went on to manage Bolton, and Leeds. He still lives in Blackpool, works as a journalist and can often be heard on Radio sports programmes. In 1993, was appointed 'technical consultant' by the F.A. and he played a major part in Terry Venables'selection as England manager.

ARMSTRONG, David. *Middlesboro, Southampton, Bournemouth. (1971-1987)* A full England international and former Under 23 player. Made over 350 appearances for Middlesborough before his transfer to Southampton in 1981. Finished his career at Bournemouth but still lives just outside Southampton. Joined Waterlooville FC as General Manager in March 1995 having previously spent a number of years as an officer for Football in the Community, latterly at Reading.

(Courtesy of Worthing Herald)

ARMSTRONG, Gerry. *Spurs, Watford, WBA, Chesterfield, Brighton, Millwall. (1975-1986)* Won 63 Northern Ireland full caps. His last club, Brighton took him to the South Coast, where he went on to manage Worthing & Crawley in the Beazer Homes League. Appointed assistant manager of the Northern Ireland national side in 1994.

ARMSTRONG, George. *Arsenal, Leicester, Stockport (1961-1978)* A left winger who signed for Arsenal in 1961. Armstrong went on to give the Gunners sterling service in over 500 league games, before joining Leicester City in 1977. He won England Under 23 honours, and was part of Arsenals 1970/1 Double winning side. Gained experience at Aston Villa (coach); Fulham (coach); Enderby Town (manager); Middlesborough (coach); Narvik (Norway, coach); Kuwait (coach) before becoming reserve team coach at Highbury.

ARMSTRONG, Ken. *Chelsea (1947-1956).* **Joined Chelsea from local league side, Bradford Rovers in 1946, played 362 league games and won one England cap in 1955. Emigrated to New Zealand, where he became National Coach. Died in 1984 and his ashes were then strewn over the pitch at Stamford Bridge.**

ARNOLD, Jim. *Blackburn, Everton, Preston, Port V (1979-1986)* Was England semi-pro keeper with Stafford Rangers, prior to joining Blackburn Rovers. Now lives back in Stafford and works as a Recreation Officer for the local Police Force.

ASHCROFT, Billy. *Wrexham, Middlesboro, Tranmere (1970-1985)* Played over 300 league games for his three clubs. Had a spell in Holland but now runs the "George" pub in Southport.

(Courtesy: Cumberland newspapers)

ASHMAN, Alan *Notts F, Carlisle (1948-1957)* Very experienced manager, who prior to his retirement held posts both home and abroad. Probably best remembered in charge of Carlisle and for his four years with West Bromwich Albion when they were in the first division. Now works as a part time scout from his home in Walsall.

ASKEW, Billy. *Middlesboro, Hull, Newcastle, Shrewsbury. (1979-1994)* Made his name with Hull (247 league appearances). Has since played for a number of non-league clubs, Workington Town being his most recent port of call.

ASTLE, Jeff. *Notts Co, WBA, (1959-1973)* **Started his career at Notts County scoring 32 goals in 103 games, this persuaded West Brom to buy him in 1964. At the Hawthorns he became a popular and deadly goal scorer, especially good in the air. Played five games for England, without scoring, however his record of 137 league goals more than made up for this. Won a League Cup winners medal, followed by scoring the deciding goal in the 1958 F.A. Cup final against Everton. Now lives in Ashby-de-la-Zouch and runs his own industrial cleaning business. His vocal talents have also recently been exposed to the nation through his regular appearances as resident singer on BBC's cult programme "Fantasy Football" with Frank Skinner (Baggies fan) and David Baddiel.**

ASTON, John. *Man U, Luton, Mansfield, Blackburn. (1964-1981)* Played 346 league games, won Championship and European Cup winners medals with Manchester United. His father, John senior, also played for the Reds, between 1946 and 1953. Retired from football in 1981. Now runs his own pet shop, Pet World, in Stalybridge.

(Courtsey: Pete Norton, Northampton)

ATKINS, Ian. *Shrewsbury, Sunderland, Everton, Ipswich, Birmingham, Camb U (1974-1993).* Appointed manager of Northampton Town in January 1995, having previously held posts at Cambridge, Birmingham, and Doncaster Rovers.

(Picture courtesy : Raymonds Press Agency)

ATKINSON, Ron. *Aston Villa, Oxford (1956-1971)* Born in Liverpool, but brought up in Birmingham, Ron has become one of the really big names in Soccer, but started his illustrious career in the Birmingham Works League, for B.S.A. Tools. His first Managerial post was with Kettering in 1971, after making 383 League games for Oxford United. Spells at Cambridge United , West Brom, Manchester United, Atletico Madrid and Sheffield Wednesday followed before finally returning to Villa Park, where he had previously played as a youngster. Despite a poor run of results, it was still a surprise to most people, Ron included, when he was dismissed in November 1994. However, it was not long before he was back in League Management, with Coventry City - where he immediately won the Manager of the Month award, in record time, only 44 days !

ATYEO, John. *Portsmouth, Bristol C (1950-1965)* 315 goals in 597 games earned international recognition by way of six England caps. He retired in May 1966 and qualified as a schoolteacher. He taught in Warminster, before suffering a fatal heart attack at his Wiltshire home in 1993.

AULD, Bertie. *Birmingham (1961-1964)* Illustrious career with Celtic which included the famous 1967 European Cup win. Played for Birmingham City between 1961 and 1964. Had spell as Manager of Partick, but after 18 months left the game. Returned briefly, to manage Dumbarton. Recently, Bertie was a licensee in Glasgow.

AUSTIN, Terry. *C.Palace, Ipswich, Plymouth, Walsall, Mansfield, Huddersfeld, Doncaster, Northampton.* Terry's career covered seven clubs and over 300 league appearances. Now works as an Insurance Broker in the Mansfield area.

AYRE, Billy. *Hartlepool, Halifax, Mansfield, Halifax, (1977-1985)* Experienced Central defender (over 300 league appearances), who managed Blackpool, then Scarborough Town until December 1994. Took over as manager of Vauxhall Conference side Southport in April 1995.

BACUZZI, David. *Arsenal, Man C, Reading (1960-1969).* Despite being a qualified printer, former England youth international David, now works as a travel agent in Dublin. (His father, Joe, was also a player for Fulham and England.)

BACUZZI, Joe *Fulham (1936-1955)* Fulham full back who played 283 League games during his time at Craven Cottage which spanned almost twenty years from 1936, then after the war until 1955. Died in February 1995 at the age of 79.

BADGER, Len. *Sheff U, Chesterfield (1962-1977).* Long serving Sheffield United defender and England Under 23 cap, Len is now licensee of the Fox & Goose in Old Brampton, Chesterfield.

BAILEY, Gary. *Man U (1978-1986)* **Born in Ipswich, son of Roy, (Crystal Palace & Ipswich), Gary, an England International goalkeeper, has spent much of his life in Johannesburg where he now works as an anchorman for South African TV's version of Match of The Day.**

BAILEY, John. *Blackburn, Everton, Newcastle, Bristol C. (1975-1990)* Made his name with Blackburn Rovers before joining Everton for £300,000 in 1979. Won deserved representative honours with the England "B" . Became Youth Coach at Everton until 1993, and is still keen to find himself another appointment in the game.

Mike Bailey *(courtesy: Portsmouth News)*

BAILEY, Mike. *Charlton, Wolves, Hereford. (1959-1978)* Won two England Caps and made over 500 League appearances for his three clubs. Managed Hereford United, Charlton Athletic and had a spell as player-coach to Minnesota Kicks in the U.S.A. Sacked by Terry Fenwick, as reserve team coach at Portsmouth in February 1995.

BAILEY, Ray. *Gillingham, Northampton,. (1966-1971)* Wing half, who also played Cricket for Northants - now works for them as the groundsman at their County Ground, Northampton.

BAILEY, Roy. *C Palace, Ipswich, (1949-1965).* Father of former Manchester United goalkeeper, Gary, Roy won First Division championship medals in 1961 and 1962 with Ipswich under Alf Ramsey. Emigrated to South Africa and died in Johannesburg in April 1993 at the age of 61

BAIRD, Henry. *Man U, Huddersfield, Ipswich. (1936-1951)* Northern Ireland international wing half, was a Man Utd player before the war, then made 200 appearances for Ipswich after the hostilities had ended. Died in 1973 aged 60

BAKER, Alan. *Aston V, Walsall. (1960-1970)* Went into the Leather trade but now lives in Walsall where he works as a Castings Inspector.

BAKER, Graham. *Soton, Man C, Soton, Aldershot, Fulham (1976-1991).* Southampton born, Graham, won two England Under 23 caps while playing for his home side. Three moves later, including a return to the Dell, he hung up his boots to set up a driving school, which he now runs in the area around his home in Cheam, Surrey.

BAKER, Joe *Arsenal, Notts F, Sunderland. (1962-1970.)* As a centre forward, scored an incredible 93 goals in 144 games for Arsenal. Won three full England caps, although he had played for Scotland schoolboys as a youngster. Ended his playing career at Raith Rovers, before taking over as their manager in 1974. He later ran a pub in Craigneeuk, and worked in the building trade. However, he is now recovering from a heart attack suffered a couple of years ago, and spends his time doing after dinner speaking and some coaching in the Motherwell area for the S.F.A.

BAKER, Peter *Tottenham (1952-1964)* Played 299 league games for Tottenham Hotspur at right back. When he finished playing, Peter emigrated to South Africa, where he runs a sports centre.

BALDERSTONE, Chris. *Huddersfield, Carlisle, Doncaster. (1959-1975)* **Chris was an inside forward who made over 500 League appearances, 369 of them for Carlisle. But also played Cricket for Leicestershire and Yorkshire and on one occasion batted until 6.30 p.m. in the evening, was then driven away to play soccer for Doncaster Rovers an hour later, returning the next day to complete a century. He is still involved with cricket, but these days dons the white coat as a qualified umpire !**

BALDWIN, Tommy. *Arsenal, Chelsea, Millwall, Manchester U, Brentford. (1964-1977).* England Under 23 international, who was a part of the Chelsea "glory years" team of the seventies, which won the F.A.Cup and European Cup Winners Cup. Now lives in Fulham, and enjoys his life which consists of playing lots of of golf.

BALL, Alan. *Blackpool, Everton, Arsenal, Soton, Blackpool, Soton, Bristol R. (1962-1982)* Tenacious midfielder, Alan has made no less than 72 appearances in the full England team, a record that includes his key performance as a member of the team that won the World Cup in this country in 1966. He became player-manager to Blackpool and also tried his luck with Vancouver Whitecaps. His varied life as a coach has also included service with Bristol Rovers, Portsmouth, Stoke City, and Exeter City. Appointed team manager at Southampton in 1994, but after only one season, accepted an offer from his old friend Frannie Lee to take over at Manchester City in July 1995.

Alan Ball

BALL, Keith. *Walsall, Port V, Walsall. (1958-1972)* Port Vale's first choice goalie between 1968-1971, who also had three spells with his home town club, Walsall. He still lives there today and has a job working for the Local Authority.

BAMBRIDGE, Keith. *Rotherham, Darlington, Halifax. (1955-1965)* Now a draughtsman, living and working in Rotherham.

BAMFORD, Harry. *Bristol R (1946-1958)* **A full back who notched up close to 500 league appearances for Bristol Rovers. Once caused a stir when it was discovered that he practised ball control by dribbling around the racing pigeons that he owned. Died 1958 aged only 38.**

BANJO, Tanji. *Leyton Orient (1977-1981).* One of the forerunners to today's League contingent from Africa. Tanji only played 20 League games but was a full Nigerian International. Last seen working as a bus driver in the North of London.

BANKS, Gordon. *Chesterfield, Leicester, Stoke (1958-1972)* **Gordon is acknowledged as one of the Worlds greatest ever keepers, whose playing career was ended prematurely following a car accident in 1972, but he will be remembered as one of the England World Cup winners in 1966. Spent two years in America, where despite having lost one eye, was voted best goalkeeper in the NASL. After a spell managing Telford, Gordon went into commerce. Became self-employed in the sports promotion business, when the corporate entertainment's company he worked for went bust.**

Gordon Banks *(Pic: Raymonds Press Agency)*

BANNISTER, Bruce. *Bradford, Bristol R, Plymouth, Hull. (1965-1979)* **Played over 500 league games, now runs a sports shop, Sportshoes Unlimited, in Bradford, which it is claimed is the largest sportshoe retail outlet in the World.**

BARKER, Richie. *Derby, Notts Co, Peterborough (1967-1971)* Has had spells as Assistant Manager at Wolves, and Manager of Shrewsbury and Stoke City. Most recently was assistant manager to Trevor Francis at Sheffield Wednesday.

BARLOW, Colin. ***Man C, Oldham, Doncaster (1957-1964).*** **Scored 78 goals in 179 games during his five years as a player at Maine Road, then went on to become a successful businessman running his own import/export company which has offices in Milan and Prague. His love of the club encouraged him to become a key figure in the consortium which took control in 1994 and is now City's Chief Executive.**

BARNARD, Mike. *Portsmouth (1953-1958)* Inside forward who played 116 games for Portsmouth between 1953 and 1958. Also played cricket for Hampshire. Can now be heard on BBC Radio Solent's local sports programmes.

BARNES, Ken. *Man C, Wrexham (1951-1964)* Wing half who played over 250 games for Man City, and won representative honours with the Football League XI. Father of former Manchester City and England winger Peter, Ken was Chief Scout for the Maine Road Club until late 1994.

BARNES, Peter. *Man C, WBA, Leeds, Coventry, Man U, Man C, Bolton, Port V, Hull, Bolton, Sunderland (1974-1988)* A full England international winger who was born in Manchester and made his name with Manchester City. Transferred from the northern club, who groomed him through their apprentice ranks, to West Bromwich Albion in 1979. Went on to play for a number of league clubs before ending with a spell in America. Came back to the UK. in 1991, and turned out for Mossley. Returned to Maine Road to help out in the Social Club, but now helps coach the youngsters at the Club's Platt Lane complex. Also works for Piccadilly Radio as a Matchday summariser.

BARNWELL, John. *Arsenal, Notts F, Sheff U. (1956-1970)* John served Peterborough as Coach before taking over the managerial reins in 1977. Resigned in November 1978 to take the helm at Wolverhampton Wanderers. Was Manager of Northampton Town until December 1994.

BARRETT, Les. *Fulham, Millwall. (1965-1977).* Won England Under 23 honours whilst with Fulham - for whom he made over 400 league appearances. Then spent eleven years as a British Telecom engineer, but now runs a garden centre with his wife in Earlsfield, South West London.

BARRON, Jim. *Wolves, Chelsea, Oxford U, Notts For, Swindon T, Peterboro U. (1961-1980)* Moved into non league football with Cheltenham Town after a successful career keeping goal for six different clubs. Then worked with Ron Atkinson at Aston Villa as his assistant manager.

BARRON, Paul. *Plymouth, Arsenal, C Palace, WBA, Stoke, QPR, Reading. (1976-1986)* Goalkeeper, whose seven club career spanned ten years. Paul now lives in Egbaston, West Midlands and is working in Sports management.

BARRON, William. *Charlton, Northampton. (1937-1950)* Also played Cricket for Lancashire and Northants. Now retired, living in Northampton the town where he played most of his career.

BARROW, Graham. *Wigan, Chester. (1981-1994).* Experienced midfielder was appointed manager at Wigan Athletic in 1994, having taken Chester City to promotion the previous season.

BARTLEY, Tony. *Bury, Oldham, Chesterfield (1958-1966)* Now lives in his home town of Stalybridge where he works as a Sports Centre manager and is a fully trained sports coach.

BARTON, John. *Everton, Derby. (1978-1983)* Now lives in Derby and works as a P.T. instructor at Burton College. Managed Nuneaton Borough from May 1993 until March 1994 when he was appointed boss at BHL League side Burton Albion.

BARTON, Tony. *Fulham, Notts F, Portsmouth. (1953-1966)* A former England Youth winger, Tony gained experience as coach at Portsmouth, before becoming Manager at Aston Villa managing the team that won the European Cup. His coaching skills also took him to Southampton, Portsmouth and Northampton. Suffered a heart attack during his time at Northampton and died at his Southampton home in August 1993.

BARTRAM, Sam. *Charlton. (1934-1955)* Bartram must be the greatest goalkeeper never to be capped for England. In his younger days he was an outfield player, but took up goal keeping while working in the pits, when the Colliery's regular keeper was injured. He went on to keep goal for Charlton for over 20 years. Died 1981.

BASON, Brian. *Chelsea, Plymouth, C Palace, Portsmouth, Reading. (1972-1982)* Former Chelsea apprentice, but played most of his league soccer for Plymouth. He still lives in the West Country, currently managing an hotel in Truro.

BASSETT, Dave *Wimbledon (1977)* Dave was a distinguished non-league player, winning ten caps for England as a semi-pro, before becoming professional; Assistant manager, then Manager at Wimbledon. In six very colourful years, he guided them from the fourth to first division and establishing many "stars" such as Wise; Beasant; Curle; and Vinnie Jones, along the way. Leaving on a high (sixth in the first division), "Harry" decided to accept a new challenge and has been manager of Sheffield United since January 1988.

BASTIN, Cliff. *Exeter, Arsenal (1927-1946)* Played 350 games for Arsenal between 1929 and 1946, during which time he won 21 England caps. By the age of 21 had won League Championship, FA Cup winners medals and a full England cap. Became a licensee in Devon, but died aged 79, in an Exeter hospital after a short illness in 1991.

BATES, Don. *Brighton, (1957)* Now teaching at a school in Moulescombe, Brighton, Sussex.

BATSON, Brendon. *Arsenal, Camb U, WBA, (1971-1982)* Born in the West Indian island of Grenada, England 'B' cap Brendon, became deputy secretary of the P.F.A. in 1984/5, now holds the position of Chairman for the organisation.

BAXTER, Billy. *Ipswich, Hull, Watford, Northampton. (1960-1972).* Long serving centre half, veteran of over 400 games for Ipswich Town. Now lives in Dunfermline, Scotland, and has been a British Telecomms engineer for over 20 years.

(Picture courtesy: Scottish Daily Record)

BAXTER, Jim. *Sunderland, Notts F. (1965-1968)* Played for Scotland at Under 23 level and 43 times for the full national team. Started his career at Raith Rovers, then Rangers. Moved south to Sunderland in 1965 for £85,000 and then on to Nottingham Forest in 1967 before finishing his career back at Rangers. Retired in 1970 and became a publican in his native Glasgow.

BAXTER, Mick. *Preston, Middlesboro, Portsmouth. (1974-1984).* Mick made his name in 200 plus games for Preston before going on to play a further 100 games for Middlesborough. Tragically died of a heart attack in 1989 aged only 32.

BAXTER, Stuart. *Preston, Stockport (1972-1976).* **Although not as well known as a player, Stuart achieved incredible success as a manager in Japan, guiding Sanfrecce Hiroshima to the Suntory championship title in 1993.**

BEAL, Phil. *Tottenham, Brighton, Crewe. (1963-1979)* Defender who progressed through the youth ranks at Tottenham, and went on to play 330 league games for them. Now splits his time between his home in Devon, and Surrey where he currently runs a car hire business in West Drayton.

BEAMISH, Kenny. *Tranmere, Brighton, Blackburn, Port V, Bury, Tranmere, Swindon. (1965-1981)* In a sixteen year professional career, Kenny played for seven clubs and has now returned to one of them, Blackburn Rovers, where he is manager of their Commercial department.

BEARDSLEY, Don. *Hull, Doncaster, Grimsby. (1966-1974)* Became a partner in an Estate agency before leaving to set up on his own.

BEATTIE, Kevin. *Ipswich, Colchester, Middlesborough (1972-1982).* England international defender (9 caps) whose career was dogged by injuries. After almost a decade with Ipswich, went on to play in Sweden, then became player/coach to Kongsberg, the Nybergsund in Norway, before returning to England to run a pub. Unfortunately was taken ill and has not worked since 1991, but is keen to find a coaching job.

BECK John. *QPR, Coventry, Fulham, Bournemouth, Cambridge. (1972-1989)* Experience gained from over 400 league games with five clubs enabled John to move into management and was 'Manager of the Year' in 1990/1 while with Cambridge. Managed Preston until December 1994.

BEDFORD, Brian. *Reading, Southampton, Bournemouth, QPR, Scunthorpe, Brentford. (1954-1966)* **Had a terrific goal scoring rate throughout a career that took in six clubs. Upon retiring from the game, took up tennis, becoming a registered professional, and qualifying as an L.T.A. coach in 1972. Coached at I.L.E.A. sports centre 1968-1972, and was pro at Richmond Lawn Tennis Club 1980-1985. A knee injury forced him to give up in 1986, when he became Stadium Manager at Q.P.R.'s Loftus Road until he was made redundant in 1992**

BEECH, Cyril. *Swansea, Newport (1949-1956)* **Cyril has been acting as scout for Luton Town for over fourteen years, and is responsible for discovering players such as Mark Pembridge, Ceri Hughes and John Hartson among others.**

BELL, Colin. *Bury, Man C. (1963-1978)* Started at Bury before being transferred to Manchester City for a then record fee of £45,000. In a particularly successful four year period he was a key member of the City team that won the Football league, European Cup winners cup, and League cup. Played over 400 games before having to retire early due to injury. Ran his own 80 seater restaurant in Manchester until 1989, but is now back at Maine Road as Youth Development Officer.

BELL, Graham. *Oldham, Preston, Huddersfield. (1974-1986)* Well travelled midfielder who saw active service with six northern clubs is currently working in the Insurance industry.

BELL, Harold. *Tranmere (1946-1959)* Made a record 401 consecutive league appearances in nine years. Played a total of 595 matches before retiring in 1959. Lived in Sefton and worked as a club steward before his death in 1994, co-incidentally on the same day as the great Bobby Moore.

BELLAMY, Arthur. *Burnley, Chesterfield, (1962-1975)* Started as a junior with Burnley, signing pro terms at the age of 19. Now back at Turf Moor, where he works as the club's groundsman.

BENNETT, Albert. *Rotherham, Newcastle, Norwich (1961-1970)* Forced to quit at the age of 26 after a promising start to his career which included winning Under 23 honours. Ended at Norwich, where he now runs the Bricklayers Arms.

BENNETT, Dave. *Man C, Cardiff, Coventry, Sheff W, Swindon (1977-1991)* Former FA Cup winner with Coventry, was forced to retire from full time game through injury. Made a comeback with Nuneaton Borough in 1994/5.

BENNETT, Peter *West Ham, Leyton O. (1963-1978).* **Midfielder who played almost 200 league games for Orient, now works as a carpenter. Recent interesting contracts have included a five month stint in Moscow. His son is a talented golfer, who was the top amateur in the 1994 British Open Golf Championship.**

(Picture courtesy of Bournemouth Evening Echo)

BEST, George. *Man U, Stockport, Fulham, Bournemouth. (1963-1982)* One of the greatest ever individual players of all time. Made his debut for Man United at the age of seventeen, and played his first game for Ireland before his 18th birthday. In 1968 became both British and European footballer of the year. Won two League championship medals and a European Cup winners medal. After brief spells With Fulham and Bournemouth, played in America League, before ending his competitive playing days, many believe far too early. Now makes his living though public and media appearances, both home and abroad. Recently toured the country with Rodney Marsh in a popular stage double act.

BENNION, Stan. *Wrexham, Chester. (1959-1963)* Now Senior payments officer at Cheshire County Council. Lives in Newton near Chester.

BENSON, John. *Man C, Torquay, Bournemouth, Exeter, Norwich Bournemouth. (1961-1978)* Full back who played most of his league football for Torquay. Managed Bournemouth (1975-1979) and is now a member of the backroom staff at another of his former clubs, Norwich.

BENTLEY, Bill. *Stoke, Blackpool, Port Vale. (1965-1979)* Spent eight years in the Tangerine colours of Blackpool in the seventies. Bill is now self employed, living in Stoke on Trent.

BENTLEY, Dave. *Rotherham, Mansfield, Chesterfield, Doncaster. (1966-1979)* Made almost 250 League appearances for Rotherham, became Assistant Manager at Leeds. Now a Football Community officer based at Mansfield Town.

BERNARD, Mike. *Stoke, Everton, Oldham. (1965-1978).* Took a pub in the Dee Valley after he was forced to quit the game due to a knee injury in 1979. Lives near Swindon and makes his living by mending lawnmowers and gardening.

BERRY, George. *Wolves, Stoke, Doncaster, Peterborough, Preston (1976-1991).* Only the second coloured player to appear for Wales, made his debut for them against West Germany, ironically, the country where he was born !! A real character, who at one time had his own programme on the local radio station. Currently commercial manager and player for Stafford Rangers.

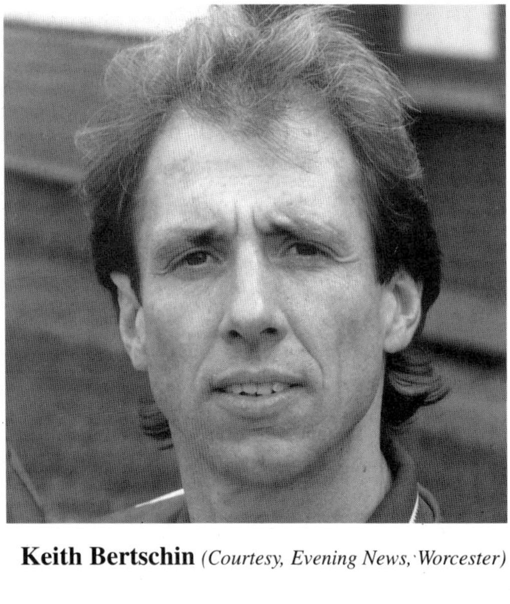

Keith Bertschin *(Courtesy, Evening News, Worcester)*

BERTSCHIN, Keith. *Ipswich, Birmingham, Norwich, Stoke, Sunderland, Walsall, Chester. (1975-1990)* Well travelled former England Under 23 forward. Now works as a financial advisor in the West Midlands, and is still knocking in the goals, currently for Hednesford Town in the BHL.

BERTOLINI, Jack. *Workington, Brighton (1952-1965).* Moved down from Stirling in to join Workington in 1953, then progressed further South to Brighton five years later. Now runs a pub in nearby Shoreham, also in Sussex.

BEST, Clyde. *West Ham (1969-1975)* Only the second ever black player to appear for West Ham when he made his debut against Arsenal in 1969. Played 178 league games as a powerful centre forward, scoring 49 goals. Clyde had become a Bermudan international by the time he left Upton Park to play in America firstly for Tampa Bay Rowdies, and then Portland Timbers. After a spell in Holland with Feyenoord, Clyde ended up back in Portland, Oregan, when he is now a successful entrepreneur running a dry cleaning business.

(Courtsey: Bournemouth Echo)

BEST, David. *Bournemouth, Oldham, Ipswich, Portsmouth, Bournemouth. (1960-1975)* The only time that goalkeeper David, played in the First Division was with Ipswich, and it was at Stamford Bridge against Chelsea that the amazing goal that never was occured, the ball passing through the side netting, was awarded against Best and the East Anglians. Managed Dorchester Town for a spell, now lives in Wareham and is Manager of Wareham Rangers in the Dorset Combination.

(Courtesy: Cambridge Newspapers Ltd.)

BILEY, Alan *Camb U, Derby, Everton, Stoke, Portsmouth Brighton, Camb U. (1975-1986).* Much travelled, Alan is now back in the Cambridge area, after a career scoring goals for a number of clubs and big money moves. Spells in Ireland and Greece preceded his return to manage Ely in the Jewson League. However business commitments which include running his own gym and health club "Bileys"in Biggleswade, forced him to quit, although he does now turn out for local league side, Potton United.

(Courtesy: Raymonds Press Agency.)

BIRCHENALL, Alan. *Sheff U, Chelsea, C Palace, Leicester, Notts Co, Blackburn, Luton, Hereford. (1964-1979)* England Under 23 international forward who played for eight clubs during a sixteen year career. After a two and half year stint as manager of Trowbridge Town, became Public relations officer at Leicester City, a post that he has now held for fifteen years. Alan's commercial interests include owning a village pub and running a ladies foootwear import business. He also helps local charities with his annual end of season run around the Filbert Street pitch.

BINGHAM, Billy. *Sunderland, Luton, Everton, Port Vale. (1950-1964)* Won 56 caps for Northern Ireland, before a broken leg ended Billy's playing career. Went into management in Greece, and later was manager of Everton in the 70's. Managed the Northern Ireland side until 1993. Was awarded the M.B.E, and is now a Director of Blackpool

BIRD, John. *Doncaster, Preston, Newcastle, Hartlepool. (1967-1984)* Solid central defender remained in the game as manager of Hartlepool, then York City, before taking over at Halifax Town.

BIRTLES, Gary. *Notts F, Man U, Notts F, Notts Co, Grimsby. (1976-1993)* Lives in Nottingham, and sells fish from Grimsby! Does occasional promotional work and radio commentaries on Radio Nottingham. Signed for Ilkeston Town last season, but also turns out for their Veterans side.

BLACK, Alan. *Sunderland, Norwich (1964-1973)* Moved south to join Sunderland, but after six years at Norwich returned to Scotland, and his native Dumbarton where he now drives a taxi.

BLACKLAW, Adam. *Burnley, Blackburn, Blackpool. (1956-1970)* Scotland international who guarded the goal for Burnley for over a decade. Still lives in Lancashire and is a publican.

BLACKLEY, John. *Newcastle, Preston. (1977-1981)* Moved from Hibs to Newcastle in 1977 for £100,000. Returned to Scotland to play for Hamilton Academicals. Became their Player/manager for a few months before being appointed Assistant Manager at Hibernian in 1983, then Manager from October 1984 until in 1986. Currently on the staff at St Johnstone FC.

BLACKWELL, Kevin. *Scarborough, Notts Co. (1987-1989).* Goalie who gained league experience late in his career after many years in non-league soccer is Youth Coach at Huddersfield.

BLAIR, Andy. *Coventry, Aston Villa, Wolves, Sheff W, Aston Villa, Barnsley, Northampton. (1977-1988)* After an eleven year league career continued playing for Kidderminster. Now extremely busy building up a variety of business interests including selling sportswear; owning a playschool. Can be heard on local radio in the Midlands covering Aston Villa matches.

BLAIR, Ronnie *Oldham, Rochdale, Oldham, Blackpool, Rochdale (1966-1982).* Northern Ireland international defender who played the bulk of his 450 plus league games for Oldham Althletic, now runs a printing firm in nearby Shaw.

BLANCHFLOWER, Danny. *Barnsley, Aston Villa, Tottenham. (1948-1963)* Barnsley paid Glentoran £6,500 in April 1949 to bring Danny across the water, and to launch a glittering career. He won the Player of the Year award twice, (1957 and 1961). Skippered Spurs through their glory years, winning many honours including the famous double in 1960/1. retired in 1963/4 for a new career in journalism, which he maintained until his death in Chobham, Surrey in December 1993, having suffered from Altzheimers disease.

BLISSETT, Luther. *Watford, AC Milan, Bournemouth, Watford.* Powerful centre forward who was one of Watford's star's in their exciting 'Elton John/ Graham Taylor' years. Two of his three spells at Vicarage Road were separated by a million pound move to Italian giants A.C. Milan. He is still knocking in the goals, at the age of 37, for Fakenham Town in the Jewson Eastern League.

BLOCKLEY, Jeff. *Coventry, Arsenal, Leicester, Notts Co. (1967-1979)* Steady performances in defence for Coventry prompted a £200,000 move to Arsenal in 1972. During his two years at Highbury he won One England cap, before ending his career with Leicester and finally Notts County. He still lives in the East Midlands where he now runs a successful engineering business.

BLOOMFIELD, Jimmy *Brentford, Arsenal, Birmingham, Brentford, West Ham, Plymouth, Leyton O. (1952-1968)* Although remembered as a successful manager at Leicester and Orient, Jimmy was a player for sixteen years and served seven clubs. Died in 1983 at the age of only 49. His son David is head of sponsorship at the F.A.

BLOOR, Alan. *Stoke, Port Vale (1961-1978).* Although he ended his playing days at Port Vale it was at nearby Stoke City that Alan played for over fifteen years. Still lives in the Potteries where he runs newsagency in his hometown of Stoke.

BLY, Terry. *Norwich, Peterboro, Coventry, Notts Co. (1956-1964)* One of the most prolific goalscorers in the lower divisions. Terry started at Norwich, but it was in his first season with Peterborough that he set a post war scoring record by netting 46 times from 52 games. Now owns a sports shop in Grantham, Lincolnshire.

BLYTH, James. *Preston, Coventry, Hereford, Birmingham. (1971-1982)* A Scottish international goalkeeper who in 1978, was a member of their World Cup squad. Now coaching at Coventry City.

BLYTH, Mel. *Scunthorpe, C Palace, Soton, C Palace, Millwall (1967-1980)* Strong central defender who made his name at Crystal Palace, won an FA Cup winners medal in 1976 with Southampton. Although an electrician by trade, Mel became a driving instructor before setting up his own building company in South London.

BOAM, Stuart. *Mansfield, Middlesboro, Newcastle, Mansfield, Hartlepool. (1966-1982)* Played 320 games for Middlesborough, and was a member of the team that won promotion to the first division in 1973/4. After a career of over 500 league appearances, he briefly went into management at Mansfield, but now lives in Kirkby in Ashfield and works for Kodak Photographic Co .

BOERSMA, Phil. *Liverpool, Wrexham, Middlesboro, Luton, Swansea. (1969-1978)* Started his career with Liverpool as a junior before moving on to Middlesborough for £72,500 in 1975. Retired in 1981 while at Swansea, to become physiotherapist at Rangers in Scotland. Phil has now returned to Merseyside to rejoin Liverpool where he is currently first team coach.

BOLDER, Bob. *Sheff W, Liverpool, Sunderland, Charlton (1977-1994)* Joined Sheffield Wednesday in 1977 from non-league Dover Town and retired from the professional game some seventeen years later which had included a spell at Liverpool, in 1994. However, Bob can still be found between the sticks, currently for Dagenham & Redbridge FC in the Vauxhall Conference and occasionally for the ex-Charlton Charity side.

Back : J Bumstead;, T. Hales, M Flanagan, **Bob Bolder,** C Powell, P Hunt, B Bonds, P Reeves, B Kinsey
Front : R Bowman, K Peacock, H. Gritt, S Gritt, J Gritt, D Hales, A Curbishley, L Gaskin *(Pic: Tom Morris)*

BOLLAND, Gordon. *Chelsea, Leyton O, Norwich, Charlton, Millwall. (1961-1974)* Was born in Boston, Lincs, but played his League football for five Southern clubs. Gordon has now returned to his roots, living in Boston and working as a Sales Rep for a tyre company. Also acts as commercial manager at Boston United.

BOLTON, Joe. *Sunderland, Middlesboro, Sheff United. (1971-1985)* Left back who was a Sunderland regular for eight years before moving to North Eastern neighbours, Middlesborough in 1981. Joe is now working as a lorry driver for a haulage firm based in the Sheffield area.

BOND, John. *West Ham, Torquay. (1951-1968)* Colchester born, John, played for West Ham side of the sixties which produced so many future managers. After thirteen years and 381 League appearances for the Hammers, he started his travels, firstly as a player with Torquay, followed by a nomadic coaching trail. His management career started at Gillingham as a coach, subsequently held appointments at Bournemouth, Norwich City, Manchester City, and latterly Shrewsbury Town where he worked from 1991 until May 1993.

(Courtesy: Southampton Evening Echo.)

BOND, Kevin. *Norwich, Man C, Southampton, Bournemouth, Exeter. (1975-1994)* Full bak, son of John (see above) Now living near Southampton and owns a cafe in the area. Currently playing non-league soccer for Dover Athletic FC.

BOND, Len. *Bristol, Exeter, Torquay, Scunthorpe, Colchester, Brentford, Exeter. (1970-1983).* Len ran a newsagency in Exeter, but now works coaching the keepers at Exeter and Torquay.

BONDS, Billy. *Charlton, West Ham. (1964-1987)* An extremely competitive half back and captain. Joined West Ham from Charlton in May 1967 for a bargain £50,000. He collected two F.A, Cup winners medals and was instrumental in helping the Hammers back to the first division, with a runaway title victory in 1980/1. After over 25 years service at Upton Park, as player, coach, then manager, Billy finally resigned in August 1994. Now works for Q.P.R. as their Youth Team manager.

BONE, Jim. *Norwich, Sheff U. (1971-1973)* A bustling forward whose long career was spread over a wide selection of clubs. An electrician by trade, Bone became Player/ Manager at Arbroath before joining St Mirren as their manager.

BONETTI, Peter. *Chelsea, (1959-1978)* **"The Cat", son of a Swiss born restaurateur, Peter was unfortunate to be in the wings of the great Gordon Banks, collecting only seven England caps, but with Chelsea was a great hero of many victories, notably the 1970 Cup Final. He made 600 League appearances, before taking his family off to the Isle of Mull, where he worked as a postman and occasionally turned out for Scottish league sides. Now lives in Birmingham and coaches goalies for several league clubs as well as helping out with the England squad.**

BONNYMAN, Phil. *Carlisle, Chesterfield, Grimsby, Stoke, Darlington. (1975-1988)* Lives in his hometown of Glasgow and works at Hamilton Accidemicals, ironically his first club, as an Officer for the Football in the Community Scheme.

(Courtesy: Manchester Evening News)

BOOK, Tony. *Plymouth, Man C. (1964-1966)* Was plucked from relative obscurity with Bath City when working as a bricklayer at the age of 29. He then became a great success at full back with Plymouth Argyle. Malcolm Allison and Joe Mercer took him to Man City in July 1966. During a glorious period they became league champions in 1968/9; F.A. Cup winners 1968/9; European Cup Winners Cup winners 1969/70; and Football League Cup winners in 1969/70. In 1969, Tony won the "Footballer of the Year" award with Dave Mackay and is still at Maine Road as a Coach.

BOOKER, Bob. *Brentford, Sheff U, Brentford (1978-1994)* Currently youth team manager at Brentford, where he played most of his professional career, a three year spell at Sheffield United between 1988 and 1991 being the only exception.

BOOTH, Dennis. *Charlton, Blackpool, Southend, Lincoln, Watford, Hull. (1966-1984)* Eighteen years as a player preceded Dennis's progression into management. Currently working for Bristol Rovers as their Assistant manager.

Dennis Booth

BOOTH, Tommy. *Man C, Preston. (1968-1984)* Earned four caps at Under 23 level with England during his thirteen years at Manchester City. Left League Soccer in 1986, having spent eighteen months as Manager of Preston North End. Now lives near Manchester and works for locally based television rental firm, Granada TV.

BOROTA, Peter. *Chelsea (1978-1981).* **Joined Chelsea from Partizan Belgrade in 1987. Was their Player of the year in 1980 and 1981. Returned to Yugoslavia where he ran a Duty free shop and was allegedly involved in a stolen picture racket resulting in a major court case.**

BOTHAM, Ian. *Scunthorpe (1979-1984)* **Although now internationally known as a cricketer/television celebrity and charity fund-raiser, Ian was also a talented footballer. He signed for Scunthorpe Unitedas a non-contract player in March 1980, played seven league games and another four as sub, staying until 1984. Also played non-league football for Yeovil. his amiable nature has made him a natural for television and has been a captain on BBCtv's question of sport for many years. Recently signed as one of several big names to work as a commentator on Satellite TV with Sky Sports.**

BOULTON, Colin. *Derby, Soton, Lincoln. (1964-1980)* Colin established himself as Derby's regular keeper for twelve years following his move from Cheltenham Town in 1964. Played for three years in America but a leg injury forced him to quit and he returned home to become a policeman. Still lives in Derby, but now sells boots and balls for Huddersfield based sports firm, Mitre.

BOVINGTON, Edward *West Ham (1959-1967)* **Former West Ham wing half now runs his own woman's clothes store, Jays fashion discount market at Archway, London. He regularly takes part in the London marathon.**

BOWEN, Dave. *Northampton, Arsenal, Northampton. (1947-1959)* Now living in semi-retirement in Northampton. Retired from soccer in 1986 and decided to activate the bookmakers license that he had held since 1966 but could not use due to League regulations, also acted as a football reporter for the Sunday People newspaper.

BOWEN, Keith. *Northampton, Brentford, Colchester. (1976-1985)* Son of Dave (see above) Keith followed in his fathers footsteps by playing for Northampton Town from 1976-1981. Now works as an accountant and still lives in the town. Also acts as Assistant manager for United Counties league side, Northampton Spencer.

BOWKER, Keith. *Birmingham, Exeter, Cambridge, Northampton, Exeter, Torquay. (1970-1981)* Served his apprenticeship with Birmingham City but made his biggest impression in his two spells at Exeter City. The area clearly suited him, as Keith has lived there ever since and now works locally for the Post Office as a postman.

Ian Bowyer

BOWLES, Stan. *Manchester C, Bury, Crewe A, Carlisle U, QPR, Notts For, Leyton O, Brentford. (1967-1980)* **One of the games most colourful characters, who despite winning five England caps, never fully realised his potential. Although a real entertainer and fans favourite, Stan's love of gambling has taken its toll and was unemployed for a long spell before being invited by David Webb to help out with some coaching at former club, Brentford.**

BOWYER, Ian. *Man C, Leyton O, Notts F, Sunderland, Notts F, Hereford (1968-1989)* Born in Ellesmere Port and started his career with Manchester City, Ian played a vital part in Nottingham Forest's flourishing years in the 1970's and 1980's, making over 400 appearances in his two spells at the City Ground. Acted as Assistant Manager to his former team-mate, Peter Shilton at Plymouth Argyle for a short spell in 1994.

BOYCE, Ronnie. *West Ham (1960-1972)* A one club man, who signed professional terms in 1960 having come through the ranks at West Ham. Ronnie then went on to play 275 League games for them over the next twelve years. Appointed Chief Scout at Upton Park in October 1992.

BOYER, Phil. *Derby Co, York C, AFC Bournemouth, Norwich C, Southampton, Man City. (1966-1982)* Formed a deadly partnership with Ted MacDougall firstly at York City, then later at Bournemouth, Norwich City and Southampton. Won one England cap against Wales in 1976. Phil was Assistant Manager/Coach at Grantham FC from December 1985 until February 1987, but now works as a bank courier as well as acting as a scout for a number of football league clubs.

BOYLE, Terry *Tottenham H, C Palace, Wimbledon, Bristol C, Newport Co, Cardiff C, Swansea C. (1975-1989)* Former Spurs junior captained both the Welsh schools and Youth international teams and won two full caps. Moved into non-league soccer in a £5,000 transfer from Swansea City to Merthyr Tydfil, whom he has now rejoined after a spell as player/manager at Barry Town.

BOYLEN, David. *Grimsby, (1966-1977)* Made 370 appearances for Grimsby between 1966 and 1977. Still lives in Grimsby, working as a sales representitive for Caxios E & I Ltd. Still plays with a number of other ex-professionals for the 'Tartan Forties' in the Grimsby Local League.

BRABROOK, Peter. *Chelsea, West Ham, Leyton O. (1954-1970)* Full England international who won three caps during his Chelsea days. Ran a butchers shop, but now lives in Hornchurch and works for paper tycoon, Neville Ovendon.

BRADD, Les. *Rotherham, Notts Co, Stockport, Wigan, Bristol R, (1967-1982)* Les scored 125 goals in his 381 leage games for Notts County. Then after twelve years as Promotions manager at Meadow Lane, has now crossed the Trent to take up a similar role for Nottingham Forest.

BRADY, Liam. *Arsenal, West Ham (1973-1989).* One of the few players to have succeeded abroad, Liam had successful spells with Juventus, Ascoli and Sampadoria in addition to a distinguished career in this country particularly with Arsenal. Joined Brighton as Manager in 1993 having cut his teeth with the mighty Celtic.

BRADFORD, Geoff. *Bristol R (1949-1963).* Bristol Rovers' only full England international, who scored on his one appearance against Denmark in 1955. Played 523 games for Rovers, scoring 260 goals, a club record. Worked for a company at Avonmouth Oil refinery after his playing days but died in December 1994, aged 67.

BRADLEY, Don. *WBA, Mansfield. (1943-1961)* Played 385 games for Mansfield between 1949 and 1961. Now an engineer, but still in the town.

BRADSHAW, Paul. *Blackburn, Wolves, WBA, Bristol R. Newport Co, WBA. Peterboro. (1973-1990).* Goalkeeper who saw action with seven league clubs and won four Under 23 caps with England. Currently working as a Security Supervisor and living back in Wolverhampton.

BRANFOOT, Ian. *Sheff Wed, Doncaster, Lincoln (1965-1977)* Solid right back and veteran of over 300 league games, after joining Sheffield Wednesday in 1965. Was in charge at both Reading (1984-89) and Southampton (199194) before taking on the managers job at Fulham in 1994.

BRANSTON, Terry. *Northampton, Luton, Lincoln (1960-1972)* Centre half who played more than 400 league games for three clubs. Now lives in Rugby where he runs his own Driving School.

BRAY, John. *Blackburn, Bury (1954-1965)* Blackburn's first team regular full back for several years in the early sixties. Lives in the town, but has had to retire from work due to ill health.

BRAZIER, Colin. *Wolves, Birmingham, Lincoln, Walsall (1975-1986)* Lives in Tamworth, Staffs and joined Midland Division side Tamworth in 1995 after three years rest from the game.

BRAZIL, Alan. *Ipswich, Tottenham, Man U, Coventry, QPR. (1977-1986)* Started at Celtic Boys Club in Glasgow before moving South to become an apprentice at Ipswich, turning professional in 1977. Moved to Tottenham for £400,000 in 1983, then on to Manchester United for £700,000 in June 1984. Won a total of 13 Scottish caps. Was Player-manager at Witham Town, and then Dartford. Now mine host at the Black Adder Inn, Ipswich.

BRECKIN, John. *Rotherham, Darlington, Bury, Doncaster. (1971-1983)* Played over 400 games for Rotherham in twelve years from 1971. After spells with three other clubs, John then returned to Millmoor as Assistant Manager.

BREMNER, Des. *Aston V, Birmingham, Fulham, Walsall. (1979-1989.)* Best known as a member of the successful Villa side of the early eighties which won the League and the European Cup. Retired in 1991 after a spell with Stafford Rangers, now a working as a financial advisor with the P.F.A. based in their Birmingham offices.

(Photo courtesy: Shaun Flannery.)

BREMNER, Billy. *Leeds U, Hull C, Doncaster R. (1959-1981)* Bustling midfield dynamo who always gave his all, made his debut for Leeds United as a seventeen year old alongside Don Revie in 1960, eventually becoming a key player in the clubs great successes under his former partner. Billy captained the Elland Road side to two League Championship victories and lifted the F.A. Cup in 1972. In Europe, he won a Fairs Cup winners medal in 1968 and appeared in the 1975 European Cup final.Won 54 Scottish caps, and was voted Football Writers "Player of the year" in 1970. Managed Leeds from October 1985 until October 1988 and had two spells as boss at Doncaster Rovers. Now lives in the Doncaster area and is in regular demand for public appearances.

BRENNAN, Robert. *Luton, Birmingham, Fulham, Norwich. (1947-1959)* Inside forward who played five times for Northern Ireland. Now lives in retirement in Norwich, his adopted home since moving to the City from Fulham in 1953.

BRENNAN, Shay. *Man U (1957-1969).* Republic of Ireland international, who played 19 times for his country. Spent fourteen years at Old Trafford after signing professionally in 1955 at the age of 17. Now lives in Tremore near Waterford, from where he runs his own parcel courier company. Shay has recovered from triple heart by pass surgery, and is the father of five children.

BRIDGES, Barry. *Chelsea, Birmingham, QPR, Millwall, Brighton. (1958-1973)* A sprint champion who joined Chelsea after winning international honours at school. He was the centre of controversy, resulting in him being sold to Birmingham City, when the "Doc" dropped him to allow the young Peter Osgood to play regularly. By then he had already won four England caps. Played in South Africa, then managed St Patricks Athletic and Sligo Rovers in Ireland before returning to Norfolk where he took on a milk round and managed a couple of local non-league sides.

BRIGGS, Max. *Norwich, Oxford (1968-1977)* Lives in Norwich, where he has run his own a conservatory and double glazing firm since 1990, having been employed in the business since 1978.

BRIGGS, Tommy. *Plymouth, Grimsby, Coventry, Birmingham, Blackburn, Grimsby. (1946-1958)* England 'B' international goal scorer who netted 256 times from 392 league appearances. Died on 10th February 1984 at the age of 61.

BRIGNULL, Phil. *West Ham, Bournemouth, Wrexham, Cardiff, Newport Co.* Former West Ham apprentice. Now lives in the Cardiff area and works in the insurance business for Allied Dunbar

BRILEY, Les. *Chelsea, Hereford, Wimbledon, Aldershot, Millwall, Brighton. (1974-1994)* Started at Chelsea, but is remembered for his six years as a bustling midfielder with Millwall. Was player/manager of Slough Town until May 1994

BRINDLEY, John. *Notts For, Notts Co, Gillingham (1965-1976)* Played for both Nottingham clubs. John now combines his job as a sales manager for a Cleaning company with managing Ilkeston Town FC in the West Mids League.

BRISLEY, Terry. *Leyton O, Southend U, Millwall, Charlton Ath, Portsmouth. (1967-1980)* Former Leyton Orient and Millwall midfielder, finished while at Portsmouth in 1980. Terry now lives in Brentwood, Essex, and works in the City of London as a Foreign Exchange Broker.

BROADBENT, Peter. *Brentford, Wolves, Shrewsbury, Aston V, Stockport. (1950-1969)* Was one of Wolves' key players during the fifties and sixties, during which time they were Football League Champions three times and F.A. Cup winners in 1959/60. He also played for the England Under 23 and "B" sides before winning seven full caps. After retiring in 1969, he went on to own a childrens clothes shop in Halesowen, but now works as a publican in Codsall, Staffordshire.

BROADHURST, Kevin. *Birmingham, Walsall. (1976-1983)* Now on the coaching staff at Birmingham City, where he served his apprenticeship and played most of his League football.

BROADBENT, Peter. *Brentford, Wolves, Shrewsbury, Aston V, Stockport (1950-1969)* One of Wolves' all time greats, who played over 450 games in the fifties and sixties during which time they were League champions three times and FA Cup winners in 1959/60. Peter played for the England Under 23 and 'B' sides before winning seven full caps. He has now been a Nursery retailer in the Midlands for the past twenty eight years.

BROADIS, Ivor. *Carlisle, Sunderland, Man C, Newcastle, Carlisle. (1946-1958)* Won 14 England Caps as a goalscoring inside forward. After over 400 League games he became a Journalist, but is now retired, living in Carlisle, Cumbria.

BROCK, Kevin. *Oxford, Q.P.R., Newcastle (1979-1994)* An England Under 21 international who was hailed as a great prospect during his days at Oxford. Big money moves to Q.P.R. (£260,000 in 1987) and Newcastle (£300,000 in 1988) followed before dropping into non-league football, initially with Stevenage but he then moved with team-mate Graham Roberts to Yeovil in 1994

BRODIE, Chic. *Man C, Gillingham, Aldershot, Wolves, Northampton, Brentford (1954-1970)* Former Manchester City apprentice keeper, made over 400 appearances for his six League clubs before retiring in 1970. Now works as a Taxi driver based in the Hampshire town of Aldershot.

BROMLEY, Brian. *Bolton, Portsmouth, Brighton., Reading, Darlington (1962-1974)* Born in Burnley and spent six years with Bolton Wanderers before moving South to play for Portsmouth. Settled in the area and now runs the White Hart public house in nearby Porchester, Hampshire.

BROOKES, Eric. *Barnsley, Northampton, Peterborough. (1960-1972)* Made 324 appearances for Barnsley. Ended his League days at Peterborough, where he now lives and has a job working for the Cummings Diesel factory

BROOKING, Trevor. M.B.E. *West Ham U (1967-1983)* **Trevor spent his sixteen year career in professional football with West Ham United, making a total of over 500 appearances, and scoring nearly 100 goals. Gained FA Cup winners medals in 1975 and 1980. He represented England at all levels, winning his first full international cap in 1974 and making a total of 47 England appearances before retiring after the 1982 World Cup. Trevor is now a regular contributor to BBC television's Match of the day and is part of the commentary team for BBC Radio sport. In 1989 was appointed to the Sports council as the representative of regional Chairmen. He is Chairman of Colbrook Plastics Ltd, a plastic binding company based in the East End of London and was awarded the M.B.E. for services to football in 1981**

BROOME, Frank. *Aston V, Derby, Notts Co, Brentford, Crewe. (1934-1954)* England international forward who won seven caps, Frank was originally turned down by Tottenham and Arsenal, but eventually proved them both wrong by developing into a most effective centre forward initially with Aston Villa then with Derby County and Notts County. Finished playing in 1954 and went on to manage Notts County, Exeter City and Southend United as well as coaching in Ireland, Australia and the Middle East. Died in 1994.

BROWN, Alistair. *Leicester C, WBA, Crystal Palace, Walsall, Port Vale. (1968-1986)* Played over 250 games as a forward for the 'Baggies' before finishing in 1976 while at Port Vale. Alistair became a publican at The Beech Tree Public House, Aldridge, but is now back in West Bromwich as landlord of the Throstles Club

BROWN, Allan. *Blackpool, Luton, Portsmouth (1950-1962)* Joined Blackpool from East Fife where he had won a Scottish Cup winners medal in 1950, and won fourteen full Scottish caps. Went on to manage Wigan, Torquay, Bury, Notts Forest, Southport and had a stint in Qatar before returning to his first club, Blackpool between March 1981 and May 1982. Remained in the area, now living in retirement in nearby Lytham St Anne's.

BROWN, Tony. *WBA, Torquay. (1963-1982)* **A lethal finisher who formed a deadly partnership with Jeff Astle in the 1960's and 1970's. Tony scored 217 goals in close to 600 league apppearances for West Bromwich Albion, before a spell in the USA and finally ending at Torquay United in 1982. Won an F.A. Cup winners medal in 1968, and one full England cap. In a 17 year career he became the proud possessor of both West Brom's appearance and goal scoring records. Returned to the Hawthorns as Coach (1984-6) and held the same post at Birmingham from 1987 to 1989. He has just had one hip replaced and is waiting to have the other done. Still keeps in touch with the game by attending all of West Brom's home games.**

BROWN, David. *Middlesboro, Plymouth, Oxford, Bury, Preston, Scunthorpe, Halifax. (1977-1990)* Well travelled goalkeeper who played almost 300 league games during his seven club career, ending at Halifax in 1990. Now has a job working at Manchester International airport.

BROWN, Eddie. *Preston N.E, Southampton, Coventry C, Birmingham C, Leyton Orient. (1948-1960)* **Brown, one of the great clowns of the game, caused havoc to many opposing defences with roving tactics. He will probably be best remembered for regularly shaking hands with the corner flag after scoring. He netted seven times in Birmingham City's 1955/6 cup run which culminated in losing to Manchester City in the famous Bert Trautmann final. After his playing days, became a schoolteacher and during his ten years as games master at Preston Catholic School "discovered" Mark Lawrenson. Now describes himself as "sublimely" retired and enjoying golf twice a week!**

BROWN, Jim. *Chesterfield, Sheff U, Cardiff, Chesterfield. (1972-1988)* Played four times for the Scotland under 23's, and won one full cap. Enjoyed several spells playing in the North American League, where in 1981 whilst with Washington Diplomats, he became the first keeper to score a goal. Now Commercial manager at Chesterfield and helped the club out when during a goalkeeping crisis, he sat on the bench as substitute for the 1995 play off final win over Bury at Wembley.

BROWN, Laurie. *Darlington, Northampton T, Arsenal, Tottenham H, Norwich C, Bradford P.A. (1958-1969)* Former England Amateur international centre half who played for both Arsenal and Tottenham Hotspur in the 1960's. Became a manager in non-league soccer with Kings Lynn and then at Altrincham, before taking over as licensee of a public house. Laurie now lives in Shildon where he is working in a milk business.

BROWN, Ken. *West Ham, Torquay (1952-1968)* Ken was a first team regular in the Hammers defence for fourteen years folowing his debut in 1952. Won one England cap and went on to manage Plymouth Argyle, but is now director of a Norwich Sports Centre. His son Kenny now plays for his old club, West Ham United and daughter Amanda was a professional tennis player.

BROWN, Roger. *Bournemouth, Norwich, Fulham, Bournemouth. (1977-1986)* Roger started and ended his career at Bournemouth, having played for Norwich and Fulham in the interim. Then returned to live in his home town, Tamworth in Staffordshire. Acted as joint manager of Interlink Express Midland Alliance, Bolehall Swifts with his brother Gary until February 1995.

BROWNLIE, John. *Newcastle, Middlesboro, Hartlepool. (1978-1984)* Defender who won seven Scottish caps during his playing days. Having spent six years in England with Newcastle, Middlesborough and Hertlepool, John is now back in Scotland on the coaching staff at Clyde .

BROWN, Sandy. *Everton, Shrewsbury, Southport. (1963-1972)* After seven years as a first team regular defender with Everton, Sandy ended his professional career at Shrewsbury. This popular Scottish defender went on to run a boarding house in Blackpool and was still enjoying his football with Blackpool Rangers in the West Lancs league after his 40th birthday. Now works in the Peak Frean factory and still lives on the Fylde.

BROWN, Willie. *Burnley, Carlisle, Barrow, Newport, Hereford, Brentford, Torquay. (1968-1977)* Scottish born striker who started with Burnley, then move steadily further south, ending up at Torquay. Willie is now manager of a newsagents business in Minehead, Somerset.

BROWNSWORD, Jack. *Hull, Scunthorpe. (1946-1964)* Played 600 games in 15 seasons for Scunthorpe Utd and was described by Bill Shankly as the best full-back never to play for England. Now retired in the area after many years as a representative for Solaglas, Glass & Glazing.

Dietmar Bruck

BRUCK, Dietmar. *Coventry, Charlton, Northampton (1960-1973).* German full back who made his home in Britain. Still lives in Coventry - where he started as an eighteen year old and played for the greater part of his career. Held non-league management positions at Weymouth and then Redditch, but has been a financial consultant for C.I.S. Insurance for the past seventeen years.

BRUSH, Paul. *West Ham, C Palace, Southend. (1977-1989)* Former West Ham apprentice ended his career at Southend United. Now with Heybridge Swifts, and works as a schoolteacher.

BRYCELAND, Tommy. *Norwich, Oldham . (1962-1971)* Joined Norwich City from St Mirren in 1962 and went on to play over 250 games for the 'Canaries'. Has now returned to Scotland where he runs the Craiglea Hotel in Ayrshire.

BUCHAN, Charles. *Sunderland, Arsenal (1909-1928)* England international who was considered to be one of the best players of his time. Went into journalism upon retirement from the game, and in 1951 was appointed editor of the newly launched 'Football monthly' which still carried his name long after his death in 1960.

BUCHAN, Martin. *Man Utd, Oldham. (1971-1984)* Born and bred in Aberdeen, captained his local side at the age of 20 to victory in the Scottish Cup final of 1970. When he was transferred to Manchester United in March 1972. It cost them a then club record fee of £125,000. He then led United back into Division One in 1974-5 after their dramatic drop into the second, and three F.A. Cup finals in four years, gaining a winners medal in 1977. Moved on to Oldham in August 1983 but was forced to retired through injury in October 1984, briefly becoming manager at Burnley. Now lives in Sale, Cheshire and works as Football promotions manager for Puma U.K.

In 1995, a testimonial committee was formed to help Bobby Stokes, scorer of the winning goal in the 1976 FA Cup final. Among the many firms that they wrote to for assistance was Puma. Their reply apologised for not being to help. But with a footnote explaining that the decision had nothing to do with the fact that the writer happened to be on the losing side that afternoon. It was signed, Martin Buchan, Promotions manager.

BUCHANAN, John. *Northampton, Cardiff, Northampton (1970-1982)* Forward who played almost 400 games in his twelve year league career. Now manger of Ross County in Scotland.

BUCK, Tony. *Oxford, Newport, Rochdale, Bradford C, Northampton. (1962-1973)* Now lives in Northampton where he is a factory worker.

BUCKINGHAM, Vic. *Tottenham. (1935-1948).* Joined Spurs in 1935 and played for them either side of the War, making over 200 league appearances.Managed Bradford Park Avenue, then led W.B.A. to FA Cup and Division One runners up in his first season. Died in February 1995

BUCKLEY, Alan. *Notts F, Walsall, Birmingham, Walsall. (1971-1984)* Became manager of Walsall and took them to promotion to the third division in his first season. Had a spell as the helm of Kettering Town before returning to League management with Grimsby Town. His term office at Blundell Park was voluntarily vacated when he accepted the challenge of taking over at West Bromwich Albion in November 1994

BUCKLEY, Steve. *Luton, Derby, Lincoln. (1974-1986)* Luton Town lifted Steve from non-league football in 1974, but it was during his time at Derby County that he really made his name following a £165,000 move in 1978. Now lives in Long Eaton and scouts for his brother, Alan.

BULLESS, Brian. *Hull (1952-1963)* Lives in Hull close to Boothferry Park, where he starred for thirteen years in the fifties and sixties and now has a job working for a local building firm.

BULLIVANT, Terry. *Fulham, Aston V Charlton, Brentford (1974-1985)* Lambeth born midfielder who played most of his football in the Capital, is now on the coaching staff at Barnet.

BULLOCH, Norman. *Chester (1952-1959).* Was a regular for Chester City in the fifties. Still lives in the area today working as a housebuilder

BUMSTEAD, John. *Chelsea. Charlton (1979-1991)* Finished his career at Charlton after fourteen years at Chelsea, where he played over 300 games. Now turning out for non-league, Bromley

BUNN, Frankie. *Luton, Hull, Oldham (1980-1989).* Frankie set a record when he scored six goals against Scarborough whilst playing for Oldham, Now Community Officer at Wigan. Plays for Radcliffe Borough in the Unibond League.

BURGESS, Ron. *Tottenham, Swansea. (1938-1955)* Signed by Tottenham just before the war, and was an automatic choice for both club and country. Played for Great Britain against the Rest of Europe in 1947. He captained the great Spurs side which won the First and Second division championships in the early 1950's. Ron returned home to Swansea in 1954 becoming player-manager. Now retired, in the Rhondda, his birthplace.

BURKETT, Jack. *West Ham, Charlton. (1961-1969)* Was Assistant Manager at Fulham, now lives in Southend and organises educational programmes for Y.T.S boys clubs in the local area.

BURGIN, Ted. *Sheff U, Doncaster, Leeds, Rochdale. (1949-1965)* England 'B' international goalie who played over 500 league games between 1949 and 1965. Was employed by Rochdale Council but has now retired and lives on the Fylde.

BURKINSHAW, Keith. *Liverpool, Workington, Scunthorpe. (1953-1967).* As a player Keith joined Liverpool from non-league Denaby United in 1953. However after only one game moved to Workington, where he became a first team regular notching up almost 300 appearances. High profile coaching and management roles since, have included six years at Tottenham and more recently at West Brom until October 1994.

BURLEY, George. *Ipswich, Sunderland, Gillingham (1973-1988)* Scottish Under 23 international made a memorable league debut, when at the age of seventeen, he marked George Best at Old Trafford. Joined Sunderland after twelve successful years at Portman Road during which time he had won an F.A. Cup Winners medal in 1978. Appointed manager of Colchester in May 1994, having had spells as manager of Ayr and coach at Motherwell. In January 1995, his career completed a full circle, returning to Ipswich, as manager.

BURNETT, Dennis. *West Ham, Millwall, Hull, Millwall, Brighton (1965-1976).* After spending four successful years with Ilauger in Norway, during which time the club achieved promotion twice, won the Cup and qualified for Europe, Dennis returned home and has run a building/decorating business in Brighton for the past fourteen years.

BURNS, Michael. *Newcastle, Preston, Ipswich (1927-1951)* Had a twenty four year career as a keeper either side of the War. Died in 1982.

BURNS, Micky. *Blackpool, Newcastle, Cardiff, Middlesboro. (1969-1980).* An England amateur international while with Skelmersdale, Mickey signed for Blackpool in 1969 and went on to play professionally eleven years. Now works for the Professional Footballers Association.

BURNS, Francis. *Man Utd, Southampton Preston. (1967-1980)* Spent seven years at Manchester United before a £50,000 move in 1972 took him to Southampton. Now lives in Perth, where he runs his own cleaning business, having emigrated down under to Australia in 1987.

(Photo courtesy of Nottingham Evening Post)

BURNS, Kenny. *Birmingham, Notts F, Leeds, Derby, Notts Co, Barnsley. (1971-1985)* A Scottish international who hails from Glasgow, but came to England to join Birmingham as a youngster. Developed through their apprentice ranks and made 170 league appearances for the St Andrews club before moving to Notts Forest in July 1977. Voted "Footballer of the year" by the Football Writers' Association at the end of the season 1977-8. He won a league championship medal followed by two European Cup winners medals in succession to add to his collection of 20 Scotland caps. Now licensee of a pub in Stoke on Trent.

BURNSIDE, Dave. *WBA, Southampton, C Palace, Wolves, Plymouth, Bristol C, Colchester. (1957-1971)* Now lives in Bristol and works as an F.A. Regional Director to the programme of Excellence. Had two spells as manager of the England Youth team in 1983/4 and from 1989 to 1993.

BURROWS, Adrian. *Mansfield, Northampton, Plymouth (1979-1992)* Central defender who was the mainstay of many a Plymouth defence. Plays for Great Mills Western League side Elmore.

BURTENSHAW, Steve. *Brighton. (1952-1966)* A wing half who spent fourteen years at Brighton as a player, notching up 237 league starts. Now works for Arsenal as their Chief Scout.

BURROWS, Frank. *Scunthorpe, Swindon, Mansfield. (1965-1973).* Scunthorpe brought Frank into the League from Raith in 1965, but he made his name at Swindon. Progressed into management with Cardiff , then achieved promotion in the first of his two spells at Portsmouth. Returned to Wales in 1991 to take over at Swansea.

BURTON, Alwyn (Ollie). *Newport, Norwich, Newcastle. (1958-1971)* Won nine Welsh caps. After retiring in 1972 due to a knee injury, he was employed as a brewery representative, then set up the sandwich bar he now runs in Diss, Norfolk.

BURVILL, Glen. *Aldershot, Reading, Fulham, Aldershot. (1983-1990)* Former West Ham apprentice who had two separate spells at Aldershot, now plays for Newhaven FC in the Sussex League.

BUSBY, Martin. *QPR, Portsmouth, Notts Co, QPR, Burnley (19870-1979).* Brother of Viv, had a spell as manager of Beaconsfield and until recently ran a pub, but is currently between jobs.

BUSBY, Sir Matt. Died on 20th January 1994, just eight months after his beloved Manchester united their first League title in 25 years. Started his career with Manchester City in 1928 before moving on to Liverpool in 1936 for £8,000. Became Manchester United manager in 1945 and over the next 24 years won five league titles, the F.A. Cup twice and the Europeans Champions Cup in 1968, resulting in his knighthood in the same year. Later became a Director and Club President, having survived the Munich air crash which wiped out much of his team that stood on the verge of greatness. Looked upon as a father figure at Old Trafford, and "Sir Matt Busby Way" at the ground will remain as a permanent tribute to his success.

BUSBY, Viv. *Luton, Newcastle, Fulham, Norwich, Stoke, Sheff U, Blackburn, York. (1969-1983)* After thirteen years and numerous clubs including two terms with Tulsa in America, Viv became Assistant Manager at Sunderland, then appointed Manager at Hartlepool in February 1993. Since then has been working for Metro Radio in Newcastle, summarising on Sunderland matches. Also does some scouting for West Bromwich Albion and Southampton, but is keen to get back into soccer in a full time capacity.

BUTCHER, Terry. *Ipswich, Coventry. (1977-1990)* After spells as manager at Coventry and then Sunderland, Former England internatioinal (77 caps) Terry, decided to change direction and now runs an eighteenth century hotel, "The Old Manor Hotel", in Bridge of Allen, near Stirling in Scotland. He still has many football connections including his weekly column in the Scottish Daily Express, and his regular commentaries on Radio Clyde and Sky Television's sports channel.

BUTLER, Ernie. *Portsmouth (1946-1952).* Pompey's goalkeeper during some of their great years in the late forties. Ran a fruit & vegetable shop, then was licensee of the "George & Dragon" pub in the city for 18 years before his retirement.

(Photo courtesy: Salisbury Journal)

BUTLER, Geoff. *Middlesboro, Chelsea, Sunderland, Norwich, Bournemouth, Peterborough. (1965-1981)* Experienced full back, now Manager of both team affairs and the commercial dept at Salisbury City in the Beazer Homes League.

BUTLER, Joe. *Newcastle, Swindon, Aldershot (1963-1977).* Loyal servant to Swindon, for whom he turned out on over 350 occasions. Now runs a taxi firm in the same Wiltshire town.

BUXTON, Mick. *Burnley, Halifax. (1962-1970)* Became player/coach at Halifax town before holding coaching positions at Southend, Sunderland, and Wimbledon. Moved into management with Huddersfield and Scunthorpe United before taking over at at Sunderland in November 1993. He retained this post until March 1995.

BYRNE, Gerry. *Liverpool (1957-1968).* England international left back who played 273 League matches for his only club, Liverpool. Worked as an odd job man at Pontins, Prestatyn, but had to give up work due to bad knees. Lives in Aintree

BYRNE, Johnny. *C Palace, West Ham, C Palace, Fulham (1956-1968)* **"Budgie" was capped by England when playing Third division soccer for Crystal Palace, being transferred soon after to West Ham in March 1962 for £58,000 plus a player, a then record between British clubs. He was part of West Hams FA Cup winning side in 1963-4 and played 11 times for England. Moved over to South Africa to manage Hellenic, where he was named South Africa's manager of the year in 1993 and has lived there ever since. Not bad for someone who only went over for a weekend - twenty years ago!!**

BYRNE, Roger. *Man Utd. (1951-1957)* Byrne joined United at the age of 20, went on to captain the "Busby babes" and win 33 England caps. Three Football League Championship medals were attained, before he and his team mates were struck down in the Munich air disaster of 1958 - Roger losing his life at the peak of his career.

BYRNE, Tony. *Millwall, Southampton, Hereford, Newport (1963-1978).* Republic of Ireland defender who won fourteen caps for his country. Ended at Hereford United, he then went on to become foreman of a golf course in the area.

CALLAGHAN, Fred. *Fulham (1963-1973)* Ex Fulham full back and Brentford manager. Now drives a black taxi cab in and around South London. Also acts as manager of Wealdstone FC.

CALLAGHAN, Ian. *Liverpool, Swansea, Crewe. (1959-1981)* Callaghan featured in the great Liverpool sides of the 1960s and 1970s during which time he won five Championship medals as well as two F.A. Cup, two European Cup, EUFA Cup and Super Cup winners medals. Holder of the clubs appearance record of 640 games, Ian played four times for England and was voted 1974 "Football Writers Player of the Year". Lives in Ormskirk, and runs the "Hesketh" public house in Rufford, that he owns with his friend, and old Liverpool team-mate, Geoff Strong. In between this and his part time role on the Littlewoods Pools Panel, he manages to play the occasional round of golf with Roger Hunt and Ron Yeats.

CALLAGHAN, Nigel. *Watford, Derby, Aston V, Derby, Watford, Huddersfield (1980-1991)* Spent six months running a disco on the island of Corfu after a spell in South Africa as player/manager of Hellenic FC. Now returned to the U.K. and passed his FA preliminary coaching badge.

CAMPBELL, Bobby. *Liverpool, Portsmouth, Aldershot. (1958-1966)* Started as a player with Liverpool, but made his name as a manager at Portsmouth (1982-4) and then Chelsea (1988-1991). Bobby is now coaching in Saudi Arabia.

Ian Callaghan (2nd right) with Fellow Littlewoods Spot the Ball Panellists
Brain Labone (2nd Left) and **David Sadler** (far right)

CAMPBELL, Dave. *Wrexham (1964-1966)* One club man, works as a process worker for a fibre glass company, and lives near Wrexham.

CAMPBELL, Jock *Charlton (1946-1957)* Full back who played 255 games for Charlton Athletic in twelve post war years. Died in 1983

CANNON, Jim. *C Palace (1972-1987).* Went on to manage Dulwich Hamlet in the Diadora League. Now concentrates on running his own roofing business in Hewley in Surrey.

CANOVILLE, Paul *Chelsea, Reading (1981-1987)* Currently playing for Egham Town

CANTELLO, Len. *WBA, Bolton, Hereford, Bury. (1968-1982)* Played in over 360 games for West Brom and retired in 1986. He then became Assistant Manager at Stockport County (1987-9), managed Radcliffe Borough (1989-90), then undertook scouting duties for Peterborough United.

CANTWELL, Noel. *West Ham, Man U, (1952-1966).* Full back who was capped 36 times by the Republic of Ireland. Managed Peterborough Utd and still lives in the area, where he runs a pub.

CARLIN, Willie. *Liverpool, Halifax, Carlisle, Sheff U, Derby, Leicester, Notts Co, Cardiff. (1959-1973)* **Moved to the island of Majorca where he runs a bar/restaurant in Cala Bona.**

CARR, Graham. *Northampton, York, Bradford P.A. (1962-1969)* Took Northampton to the fourth division title 1987 then became manager of Kettering in 1992. Relinquished this role in May 1995 to take over at BHL side Weymouth .

CARR, Willie. *Coventry, Wolves, Millwall (1967-1982)* A Scottish international (six caps) Ended up at Millwall before joining non-league Worcester City. Now lives near Wolverhampton and has been a salesman selling nuts & bolts for the same company for the past eleven years.

CARRODUS, Frank. *Man C, Aston V, Wrexham, Birmingham, Bury (1969-1983)* Despite three knee operations, still managed to win two League Cup winners medals during his time with Aston Villa. Now lives in Altrincham, Cheshire, where he runs his own company organising corporate hospitality and is still involved with the former-Manchester City players charity team.

CARTER, Raich. *Sunderland, Derby, Hull. (1932-1951)* One of England's greatest inside forwards, he played for England for 14 years in the 1930's and 1940's. Captained Sunderland when they won the F.A. Cup in 1937. He became player-manager of Hull in April 1949. Raich also excelled at other sports, playing Cricket for Derbyshire and Durham. He had suffered a stroke in 1987 and died at home aged 80, in October 1994.

CARTWRIGHT, John. *West Ham, C Palace (1959-1962).* Played only a handful of League games, but has become a most accomplished Youth coach, currently working with Charlton Athletic.

CARTWRIGHT, Les. *Coventry, Wrexham, Camb U, Southend. (1973-1983).* Welsh international midfield/winger (seven caps), retired in 1985 to take a sub post office in Wolvey, Leics, but helps at Coventry, running the Under 14 side.

CASPER, Frank. *Rotherham, Burnley (1962-1975)* Manager at his former club, Burnley from January 1989 until his resignation in 1992. Now owns a retail clothing business in the area.

CASSIDY, Tommy. *Newcastle, Burnley (1970-1982)* A Northern Ireland international midfield player who won 24 caps, had a spell managing a side in Cyprus but returned in June 1994 to take over as Manager of Glentoran, in Ireland.

CATON, Tommy. *Man C, Arsenal, Oxford, Charlton. (1979-1990)* Collapsed and died at his home near Oxford in April 1993, aged 30, whilst a Charlton player. Made his league debut for Man City aged 16, later sold to Arsenal for £500,000.

CATTERICK, Harry. *Everton, Crewe. (1946-1952)* Died in the Main Stand at Goodison Park while watching an FA Cup tie in March 1985. As manager, had achieved success leading Everton to League Championship titles in 1963 and 1970.

CATTLIN, Chris. *Huddersfield, Coventry, Brighton (1964-1978).* **Has been out of football since leaving Brighton in 1986 after 2 years as manager. He now owns a hotel, flats and some shops on Brighton seafront. During his managerial days, once signed Dean Saunders for the price of his train ticket, which cost £18!**

CAVENER, Phil. *Burnley, Bradford C, Gillingham, Northampton, Peterboro. (1979-1985)* Now a health centre manager, living in Sandy, Beds.Assistant manager at Arseley Town.

CAWSTON, Mervyn. *Norwich, Southend, Newport, Gillingham, Southend, Stoke, Southend. (1970-1984)* Had three separate spells at Southend playing over 200 games. Mervyn now plays for Southend Manor in the Essex Senior League.

Brian Chambers

CEGIELSKI, Wayne. *Northampton, Wrexham, Port V, Hereford (1973-1986)* Welsh under 21 cap who also played for Stuttgart (Germany), Tacoma Tides (USA), Umes (Sweden). Now lives in the Potteries, works as a sales rep.

CHADWICK, David. *Southampton, Middlesboro, Halifax, Bournemouth, Torquay, Gillingham (1961-1974)* A Southampton junior who went on to play League soccer for six clubs. Now coaching Soccer in the United States.

CHAMBERS, Brian. *Sunderland, Arsenal, Luton, Millwall, Bournemouth, Halifax. (1970-1980)* Well travelled midfielder, is currently Manager of BHL League outfit, Poole Town.

(Photo courtesy: Southampton Evening Echo)

CHANNON, Mick. *Southampton, Man C, Southampton, Newcastle, Bristol R, Norwich, Portsmouth. (1965-1985)* **Made his debut in 1966 and formed a deadly partnership with Ron Davies. Mick played nearly 500 games for the "Saints" during two spells, scoring close to 200 goals. Won an F.A. Cup winners medal in 1976 against Man United and a total of 46 England Caps. Now nationaly known as a very successful racehorse trainer based at his stables in Berkshire. Can also often be heard commentating on both radio and television.**

(Photo courtesy: Yorkshire Evening Post.)

CHARLES, John. *Leeds United, Cardiff City. (1948-1965)* "Gentle giant", John's regular goal scoring earned him 38 Welsh international caps, the first just after his 18th birthday. Had two spells in Italy, joining Juventus for a world record £65,000. Won three championship medals and has the unique distinction of having been voted Italy's Footballer of the year, before finishing up back in his native Wales, at Cardiff. In 1973 became youth coach at Swansea but left three years later to take on a pub in Leeds. He now looks after the toy department of the children's shop which he runs with his wife.

CHARLTON, Bobby C.B.E. *Man Utd, Preston N.E. (1956-1974)* A survivor of the horrific Munich air crash, Bobby went on to win honours galore: 106 England appearances, two league championship medals, an F.A. Cup winners medal, Footballer of the Year in both England and Europe in 1966. Joined Manchester United in 1953. Scored twice on his debut in October 1956, also scored on his international debut two years later. He was awarded the C.B.E for services to football and knighted in 1994. Finished at Preston as Player/manager before retiring to concentrate on matters commercial. He is still involved with soccer as a director of Manchester United and running his own highly successful sports school. This started with football, but now has expanded to offer courses in 35 different sports !

CHAPMAN, Bob (Sammy). *Notts F, Notts Co, Shrewsbury. (1963-1979)* Played almost 350 games while at the City ground ending at Notts County. Now licensee of a pub in East Leake.

CHAPMAN, Les. *Oldham , Huddersfield, Oldham, Stockport, Bradford C, Rochdale, Stockport, Preston.* Played over 700 League games in his pro career, now reserve coach at Man City.

CHAPMAN, Roy. *Aston V, Lincoln, Mansfield, Lincoln, Port V, Chester. (1953-1969)* Played in all four divisions over 20 years, scoring over 200 goals in 400 odd games. Died 1983, father of Lee.

CHAPPELL, Les. *Rotherham, Blackburn, Reading, Doncaster, Swansea. (1965-1977)* Now in industrial cleaning, living in Torquay, Devon.

CHARLES, Jeremy. *Swansea, QPR, Oxford. (1976-1986)* Welsh international winger who played 224 games for Swansea. Son of Mel, Jeremy is now working as an insurance salesman.

CHARLES, John. *West Ham (1962-1969).* Retired aged 26 and set up a fruit and veg business. Suffered from depression and drinking too much when the business folded. Now on the mend, and looking forward to a happier future.

(Photo courtesy: South Wales Evening Post)

CHARLES, Mel. *Swansea, Arsenal, Cardiff, Port V (1952-1966)* Signed for Swansea City in 1952 and ended his playing days at Port Vale fourteen years later, having won 31 Welsh caps along the way. Upon retirement Mel ran a wholesale food business back in Swansea. Then later became involved in the Swansea Council's scheme of sport for the unemployed. Father of Jeremy (q.v.)

CHARLTON, Jack. *Leeds (1952-1972)* **Jack retired at the age of 37 to go into management with Middlesborough, Newcastle and Sheffield Wednesday before becoming the Republic of Ireland's most successful boss in their history. In 1994, in recognition of his success at the World Cup of that year, Jack was honoured with the freedom of the city of Dublin - the first Englishman to do so this century. In between his management duties; advertising Shredded Wheat; and regular television and radio appearances, he still manages to find time to indulge in his other great passion - fishing**

CHARLTON, Stanley. *Leyton O, Arsenal , Leyton O (1952-1964)* Was secretary/manager at Weymouth between 1965 and 1972 but now works as a district manager for a major pools company.

CHARNELY, Ray. *Blackpool, Preston, Wrexham, Bradford P.A. (1957-1969)* Prolific goal scorer, netting 193 times in 363 games for Blackpool. Now in business as a painter and decorator.

CHATHAM, Ray. *Wolves, Notts Co (1946-1958)* Although retired from a career as a mechanical engineer, Ray is now President of Sanderstead Cricket club, having previously held the posts as Captain and then Club Chairman.

Trevor Cherry *(Courtesy: Huddersfield Examiner)*

CHATTERLEY, Lew. *Aston V, Doncaster, Northampton, Grimsby, Southampton, Torquay. (1962-1976)* Assistant manager at Southampton, one of the six clubs that appeared for as a player.

CHERRY, Trevor. *Huddersfield, Leeds, Bradford C. (1966-1984)* Trevor missed less than 40 matches in nine years at Leeds and won 27 England Caps. Became player/manger at Bradford City and guided them to promotion into the second division in 1985. Now runs a sports promotion company, SLP Consultancy, in Huddersfield.

CHIEDOZIE, John. *Leyton O, Notts Co, Tottenham, Derby, Notts Co, Chesterfield. (1976-1989)* Nigerian international, who started as an apprentice with Orient, but big money moves took him to Notts County (£450,000) and Spurs (£375,000). Now runs a company providing bouncy castles, based in the New Forest.

CHILTON, Allenby *Man U, Grimsby (1946-1956).* England international centre half who played 352 league games for Man United before leaving to take over as player/manager of Grimsby Town. Now lives in retirement in Sunderland.

CHILTON, Chris. *Hull, Coventry (1960-1971)* He scored just under 200 league goals from 441 games for Hull City, however this total was prevented from increasing when his career was cut short by injury. Now works as a signwriter in Hull.

Martin Chivers
(Courtesy: Raymonds Press Agency)

CHIVERS, Martin. *Southampton, Tottenham, Norwich, Brighton. (1962-1979)* Martin scored over 200 league goals in his career. His consistent scoring earned him 24 England caps, and would have won more if it had not been for injuries. Now mine host at the Brookmans Park Hotel, in Hertfordshire. Can also be regularly heard on Radio 5 sport and organises the ex-Spurs Charity XI.

CHRISTIE, Derrick. *Northampton, Camb U, Reading, Cardiff, Peterboro. (1973-1986)* Now a government clerk, living in Deeping St James.

CHRISTIE, Trevor. *Leicester, Notts Co, Notts F, Derby, Man C, Walsall, Mansfield. (1977-1990)* Now a salesman in Mansfield and still playing non-league soccer, currently for Arnold Town.

CHUNG, Sammy. *Reading, Norwich, Watford (1953-1964)* Played 220 League games for Watford before developing into a widely respected coach. Had a spell as boss at Wolves and then coach at Stoke, Currently manager at Doncaster Rovers.

CLAESEN, Nico. *Tottenham (1986-1988).* Starred for Spurs between 1986-1988, Belgian international, now playing for Royal Antwerp FC.

CLARK, Brian *Bristol C, Huddersfield, Cardiff, Bournemouth, Millwall, Cardiff, Newport . (1960-1978)* **Scored the first League goal on a Sunday while playing for Millwall. On the way to the match, his car broke down and was given a lift to the ground by Fulham fans, who then had to watch their side lose with Brian scoring the only goal of the game! He now lives in Cardiff working as a sales rep selling protective clothing to industry, but still involved in the game running the Wales Boys Club's Under 14's**

CLARK, Frank. *Newcastle , Notts F. (1963-1978)* Became Assistant Manager at Sunderland, followed by a similar post at Leyton Orient, where he went on to become Manager, then M.D. before leaving for Forest in May 1993 where he took over from Brian Clough and led them to promotion back into the Premiership in his first season.

CLARKE, Allan. *Walsall, Fulham, Leicester, Leeds U, Barnsley (1963-1979)* Allan won a championship medal in 1973/4 and scored the only goal against Arsenal in 1972 when collecting an F.A. Cup winners medal with Leeds. An outstanding forward who played 19 times for England, he went on to manage Barnsley, his old club Leeds and a spell at Lincoln. Now lives in Scunthorpe and works as a travelling salesman for a firm that makes ventilating extractors for industry.

CLARKE, Colin. *Ipswich, Peterboro, Gillingham, Tranmere, Bournemouth, Southampton, QPR, Portsmouth (1980-1992)* Injury forced Irish international goalscorer, Colin, to hang up his boots in 1992 after several big money moves and over 100 league strikes. He decided to carve out a career in catering. He is now running a pub/ restaurant in a village near Newbury in Berkshire.

CLARKE, Colin. *Arsenal, Oxford (1965-1977)* In 12 years at Oxford United Colin made 443 appearances. Then became Youth coach at Aston Villa, a post that he held until January 1995.

CLARKE, Dennis *WBA, Huddersfield, Birmingham C. (1966-1974).* **Made his way into the record books as the first substitute in FA Cup final history when he came on for West Brom when they beat Everton 1-0. Ended at Birmingham, then tried a number of business ventures from Ice Cream to fabrics - before finally becoming a partner in a property company.**

Colin Clarke, relaxing after a hard day at the restaurant ! *(Courtesy Portsmouth News)*

CLARKE, Derek *Walsall, Wolves, Oxford, Leyton O, Carlisle. (1967-1978)* Played for five clubs, but made most of his League appearances for Oxford United in the seventies. Ran his own Builders merchants business in London for five years between 1979 until 1984 before returning to the West Midlands to live in Walsall, where he has worked as a machine operator ever since.

CLARKE, Harry. *Tottenham (1948-1956)* Made 295 appearances for Spurs during which time he played once for England. Managed Romford for many years and still lives in the area.

CLARKE, Jeff. *Man C, Sunderland, Newcastle, Brighton (1974-1984)* Yorkshire born Jeff, is currently Reserve team coach at Newcastle United, for whom he appeared on more than 100 occasions during his ten year playing career.

Ronnie Clayton *(pic: Reed Northern papers)*

CLARKE, John. *Northampton (1966-1974)* Now a factory worker living in Northampton.

CLARKE, Roy. *Cardiff, Man C, Stockport . (1946-1958)* Welsh international winger who found fame with Manchester City in the late forties/early fifties. Went on to run the Social Club at Maine Road until his retirement in 1988.

CLAYTON, Ronnie. *Blackburn (1950-1968)* Made nearly 600 appearances for Blackburn before leaving to become manager at Morecambe in 1969. Took early retirement from tyre company ATS after working for them for twelve years as a representative. Still attends all home games at Ewood Park and most away, plays a lot of squash and golf as well as turning out in charity games.

CLEMENCE, Ray. *Scunthorpe Liverpool, Tottenham (1965-1987)* Played over 1000 league games before finally retiring at the age of 39. Won 61 England caps, but may have reached a far higher taget had he not been around at hte same time as a certain Peter Shilton. Now Manager of Barnet, and his son, Stephen is on the books at one of his former clubs, Tottenham Hotspur.

CLEMENT, Dave *QPR, Bolton, Fulham, Wimbledon (1966-1981).* England international full back who made 402 league appearances for Queens Park Rangers. Died in 1982 aged 34.

CLEMENTS, Dave. *Wolves, Coventry, Sheff Wed, Everton (1963-1975)* Played for Ireland at Schoolboy, youth, and amateur levels before playing 48 times for the full side. After leaving Everton in 1976, was still being capped while playing for New York Cosmos. He is still in the U.S. running an Irish goods store in Georgetown, Colorado.

CLEMENTS, Kenny. *Man C, Oldham, Man C, Bury, Shrewsbury (1975-1990).* Kenny stayed in the game as Commercial Manager at Huddersfield before achieving his life long ambition of driving heavy goods vehicles. Now runs his successful "Kenny Clements School of Motoring" from his home near Oldham. Still plays football for Curzon Ashton FC and at almost 40 is their captain and was their player of the year in 1993. This achievement means that he has captained and won the player of the year award at all his clubs.

CLIFTON, Brian. *Southampton, Grimsby T (1957-1965)* Now lives in Holton-Le-Clay near Grimsby and has taken early retirement from his job as a drawing house manager that he held with a local freezer company, at the age of 61.

CLINTON, Tommy. *Everton, Blackburn, Tranmere (1948-1956)* After five years with Everton, ended at Tranmere, then ran a Confectionery/tobacconists shop. Has since worked in the Insurance business for a number of years. His wife Muriel, is well known to many fans who call into the Souvenir shop at Goodison Park.

CLISH, Colin. *Newcastle, Rotherham, Doncaster. (1961-1971)* Newcastle born left back, is now a British transport police officer in Doncaster.

CLOSE, Brian. *Leeds, Arsenal, Bradford C (1949-1952)* **Never played a league game for his first two clubs, Leeds and Arsenal, signed for Bradford City in 1952 but played only six games scoring two goals. Later went on to make his name in Cricket, captaining Yorkshire, Somerset, and England. Now Chairman of the committee at Yorkshire C.C.C. and occassionally captains their team in the Yorkshire League.**

CLOSE, Shaun. *Tottenham, Bournemouth, Swindon, Barnet (1984-1994)* Now with St Albans City after a previous spell with Bishop Stortford.

CLUMP, Eddie. *Wolves, Arsenal, Stoke, Peterboro. (1953-1964.)* Now a self employed builder, living in Wednesfield, Wolverhampton.

COATES, Ralph. *Burnley, Tottenham, Leyton Orient. (1964-1980)* Played four times for England, made 214 appearances for Burnley before moving on to White Hart Lane, in 1971. Now runs a catering business in Hertfordshire, and still occasionally turns out for charity soccer matches.

COCHRANE, Jim. *Middlesboro, Darlington, Torquay (1973-1980).* Played 222 games for Darlington, now a Solicitor in Stockton-on-Tees.

COCHRANE, Terry. *Burnley, Middlesboro, Gillingham, Millwall, Hartlepool (1976-1986)* Northern Ireland International, is now a fully qualified soccer coach and trains the youngsters at Middlesborough's school of excellence. and lives in nearby Normanby. Can regularly be heard on local radio assisting match commentaries.

COCKBURN, Henry. *Man U, Bury (1946-1955)* Full England international with thirteen caps to his name, played the best years of his career at Manchester United. After working as Coach at Oldham Athletic, then Huddersfield Town, joined "Mitre Sports" , where he worked until retiring to Ashton-Under-Lyne, the town of his birth.

COCKER, Les *Stockport, Accrington S (1946-1957).* A strong centre forward who scored 91 goals during his 295 game career. Les qualified as an FA Coach and became Don Revie's right hand man at Leeds as well as working for many years as trainer with the England squad . Considered to be one of Britain's leading coaches, the whole nation mourned his death in 1979.

COCKERILL, Ron. *Huddersfield, Grimsby. (1955-1967)* Now a lorry driver, living in Cleethorpes, south Humberside. Father of Glenn, who currently plays for Leyton Orient.

COCKRAM, Allan. *Tottenham, Bristol R, Brentford, Reading (1981-1991)* Former Tottenham apprentice, is now player/manager at Diadora League premier division side, St Albans City.

COCKROFT, Joe. *Rotherham, West Ham, Sheff Wed, Sheff U. (1930-1948)* Wing half who played over 250 games for the 'Hammers' and ten appeared for both Sheffield clubs. Joe is now retired and living in the same Yorkshire town.

(Photo courtesy of Nottingham Evening Post)

CLOUGH, Brian. *Middlesboro, Sunderland (1955-1964)* Although best remembered for his brilliant managerial ability, Brian scored an incredible 251 goals in 274 games, a post war ratio that is unlikely to be beaten. After spells in charge of Hartlepool, Derby, Brighton and Leeds, he took over at Notts Forest in 1975. Bowed out of management following the club's relegation from the top flight in 1993. In his 18 years at the City Ground they won the League; two European Cups; Four League Cups and in 1978 was voted Manager of The Year. The F.A. Cup was the only trophy that eluded him.

George Cohen (back row far left,) with Alan Ball; Ray Wilson; Geoff Hurst; Martin Peters; Pat Jennings; Martin Chivers; Alan Birchenall; Mark McGee; and front: Gordon Banks and former referee, Arthur Ellis.

COHEN, George. *Fulham (1956-1968)* A star of the England World cup winning side of 1966. Even though he retired early in 1968-9, played over 400 matches for Fulham, and earned 37 England caps. George won a five year battle with cancer, and is now a wealthy businessman with interests in building and property development. Helps raise necessary funds for Cancer charities.

COLDWELL, Cecil *Sheff U (1951-1966)* Defender, who played over 400 League games for the "Blades", now runs a newsagents in the city.

COLEMAN, Tony. *Tranmere, Doncaster, Man C, Sheff Wed, Blackpool, Southport, Stockport. (1962-1975)* Now lives in Australia and works for the State railways driving a seven ton vehicle.

COLLARD, Ian. *WBA, Ipswich, Portsmouth (1964-1975).* Played more than 300 League games and won an FA Cup winners medal with WBA in 1968. A hip injury forced him to retire from soccer in 1976, but has been involved with sport ever since. From his home near Bristol, Ian has travelled extensively, currently employed in America.

Ian Collard keeping in shape for his travels, which have taken in Australia, and now America!

COLLETT, Ernie *Arsenal (1937-1946).* **Joined the backroom staff at Arsenal as a coach, later becoming Chief Scout. Died in London in 1980 after being knocked down by a fire engine.**

COLLINS, Bobby. *Everton, Leeds, Bury, Oldham. (1958-1972)* Went to Australia in 1971 as player/coach to Ringwood City (Melbourne), followed by a spell coaching to Hakoah FC (Sydney). Returned to England in 1972 and held a number of coaching and management posts, before leaving the game to spend eight years working in the wholesale fashion business. Now retired after two years working at the Leeds University Garage as a Chauffeur. Still plays in the occasion al charity match and keeps fit by playing golf off a very respectable eleven handicap.

COLLINS, Peter. *Tottenham. (1968-1972)* Now a Physical education teacher in the Chelmsford area and works as part time manager of Braintree Town in The Beazer Homes League.

COLQUOUN, Eddie. *Bury, WBA, Sheff U (1963-1977)* Won nine full international caps for Scotland and played a total of 360 League games, most in the red and white of Sheffield United. Now runs a Post Office in South Yorkshire.

COLQUHOUN, John *Oldham, Scunthorpe, Oldham, (1961-1969)* John works as a driver for White Arrow, having previously been a salesman for various companies selling sweets and meat !

COMFORT, Alan. *QPR, Camb U, Leyton O, Middlesboro (1982-1989)* **Injury ended Alan's career at the age of 24 in 1990. Became a Curate to St Chads, Chadwell Heath, in September 1994, and also acts as Chaplain to Orient .**

COMPTON, Denis CBE. *Arsenal (1936-1949)* **As well as winning a Championship medal in 1947-8 with Arsenal, Denis was also a very successful cricketer for Middlesex and England. After his playing days, he became a TV commentator; sports reporter for the Sunday Express; and director of an advertising agency**

COMPTON, Leslie *Arsenal (1931-1951)* Elder brother of Denis, Leslie became coach and scout at Arsenal his only League Club. Later took on a pub in North London, but suffered with arthritis which resulted in him having a foot amputated in 1982. Died in Essex in December 1984 aged 72.

COMPTON, Paul. *Bournemouth, Aldershot, Torquay, Newport, Torquay (1980-1994)* Now Reserve and Youth Team coach at Torquay

CONEY, Dean. *Fulham, QPR, Norwich (1980-1989).* England under 21 international forward, whose league career was cut short by injury, now with Farnborough in the Vauxhall Conference.

CONN, Alfie *Tottenham, Blackpool (1974-1980).* Son of a Scotland international, striker Alfie also won two caps. Was a cult figure during his spell in England with Spurs Now manager of the "Captains Rest" public house in Glasgow.

CONNELLY, John. *Burnley, Man U, Blackburn, Bury. (1956-1972)* John won 20 England caps as and helped Burnley win the League in 1959/60. Won another championship medal in his first season at Man United in 1964. Now the owner of a fish and chip shop near Nelson

CONNOR, Terry *Leeds, Brighton, Portsmouth, Swansea, Bristol C, (1979-1994)* Bustling former England Under 21 forward. Now works as a Football in the Community officer at Bristol Rovers.

CONROY, Terry. *Stoke, Crewe. (1967-1980)* Dublin born striker who won 26 Irish Republic caps. Spent eleven years at Stoke City following his move from Glentoran in 1967. Now runs his own insurance business in Ashton-Under-Lyne.

CONSTANTINE, David. *Bury (1978-1981)* England semi-pro international, is now a part time player with Hyde Utd, and works as a fireman.

CONWAY, James. *Fulham, Man C (1966-1976).* Played over 300 games for Fulham before ending his career at Man City. Won 19 caps for the Republic of Ireland. Jimmy is now coaching at Oregon State University in America and his son, Paul now plays for Carlisle United.

COOK, Michael. *Colchester (1969-1983)* Made an impressive 609 appearances for Colchester, where he now works as a Community Officer.

COOKE, Charlie. *Chelsea, C. Palace, Chelsea. (1966-1977)* **Played in Scotland for Aberdeen and Dundee before moving to Chelsea in 1966 . Enjoyed tow spells at Stamford Bridge before stints with Memphis Rogues and California Surf gave Charlie the taste of American life that tempted him to stay. Now lives in Cincinnati, and runs a successful soccer school.**

COOKE, Robbie. *Mansfield Peterboro, Camb U, Brentford, Millwall (1976-1987)* Works in Peterborough for a well known travel agents and is manager of Warboys Town in the Jewson League.

COOP, Mick. *Coventry, York, Derby (1966-1981)* Played over 400 games for Coventry after signing professional in 1966. Mick's now back at the club on the coaching staff after a spell at Derby.

COOPER, Leigh. *Plymouth, Aldershot (1979-1990).* Reading born full back who joined Plymouth as an apprentice and played for the Pilgrims for the next ten years. Now manager of Truro in the South West Counties League.

COOPER, Paul. *Birmingham, Ipswich, Leicester, Man C, Stockport. (1971-1990)* Long serving goalkeeper who played over 400 League games for Ipswich Town in his thirteen year stay at Portman Road. Now lives in the Liverpool area where he works for a fim selling nuts and bolts.

COOPER, Terry. *Leeds, Middlesboro, Bristol C, Bristol R, Doncaster, Bristol C. (1963-1984)* Battling England international full back with 20 caps to his name.Became the country's first player/director while with Bristol City, who he also managed until early 1988. Most recently had a second term of office at Exeter City, after an interlude at Birmingham City. having previously guided them to the Third Division title in 1990, He returned to St James's Park in January 1994, but resigned due to ill health in June 1995.

COPPELL, Steve. *Tranmere, Man U (1973-1982)* Signed for Tranmere while at Liverpool University. Manchester United spotted his promise and took him to Old Trafford in February 1975 for £60,000. Before injury cruelly took him out of the game, Steve had played for his country 42 times and made over 300 appearances as a "Red Devil". Went into management at Crystal Palace and was tipped to be a future England manager. However, he chose to resign in 1993 and became Chief Executive of the Football League Managers Association, a post that he held until March 1995. Returned to Selhurst Park as manager weeks later.

CORMACK, Peter. *Notts F, Liverpool, Bristol C. (1969-1979)* Retired in 1980 when appointed Partick Thistle manager, a post held until May 1984. Subsequently became Manager of Anartosi FC, Cyprus; Botswana's national coach in 1986; assistant manager at Hibernian. Peter then invested in kareoke equipment and can now be found touring the pubs and clubs of Edinburgh. Also runs a successful painting and decorating company and lives in a luxury house in the city.

CORRIGAN, Joe. *Man C, Brighton., Norwich, Stoke. (1968-1984)* A brilliant 6ft 4in goalkeeper, Joe proved himself outstanding in the losing FA Cup final side of 1981, where he collected the Man of the Match award. Between 1967 and 1982, Joe was consistently Man City's first choice keeper. Now lives in Cheshire and has coached keepers at Celtic, Middlesborough, Tranmere, and Barnsley, before being offered a post at Anfield as Liverpool's first full time goalkeeping coach.

Joe Corrigan *(Courtesy: John Cocks)*

COURT, David. *Arsenal, Luton, Brentford (1962-1972).* Retired in 1975, when he became a retail foodshop owner for ten years. Now employed by D.B.S. Financial Management Plc as a Compliance Official, and is the current captain of the Arsenal ex-professional & celebrity XI.

COX, Freddie *Tottenham, Arsenal, WBA. (1938-1953)* Became Assistant Manager at West Brom, before managing Bournemouth, Portsmouth and Gillingham. Eventually returned to Bournemouth to run his newsagents until his death in 1973.

COX, Geoff. *Birmingham, Torquay (1952-1966)* Played over 250 league games for Torquay, having joined them from Birmingham in 1957. Works for a local Estate Agents and still lives in the town.

COXON, William. *Derby, Norwich, Lincoln, Bournemouth (1950-1965)* Now lives in Bournemouth, the home of his last club, where he now runs a taxi firm and owns a guest house.

COYLE, Tony. *Stockport, Chesterfield, Stockport, Exeter (1979-1989)* Still lives within a mile of Edgeley Park, and works as a civil servant for the Benefits Agency within the DSS.

COZENS, John. *Notts Co, Peterboro, Camb U, (1970-1979)* Londoner, who joined Notts County from Hillingdon Borough. Works in Peterborough for Peterborough Automatics.

CRAGGS, John. *Newcastle, Middlesboro, Newcastle, Darlington (1966-1984)* Former Newcastle United defender. Runs a sports shop in Teeside Park (which was once owned by Willie Maddren).

John Craggs (left) with former Newcastle team-mates Bobby Moncur and 'Pop' Robson.

CRAIG, David. *Newcastle, (1963-1977)* Played 347 games during his fourteen years at St James Park. Then became player/assistant-manager at Carlisle in July 1983; player/coach at Hibernian in October 1984. Ran a newsagents in Dunston but now owns a milk business back in Newcastle

CRAIG, Tommy. *Sheff Wed, Newcastle, Aston V, Swansea, Carlisle. (1968-1984).* Was chief scout at Celtic until October 1994. Tommy was appointed Aberdeen's Assistant manager in May 1995 and is coach to the Scotland Under 21side.

CRAVEN, John. *Blackpool, C Palace, Coventry, Plymouth. (1965-1977).* Moved to Canada to play for Vancouver Whitecaps and still lives there.

CRAWFORD, Ray. *Portsmouth, Ipswich, Wolves, WBA, Ipswich, Charlton, Colchester. (1957-1970).* Great goalscorer (2 England caps), now lives in the Portsmouth area and works as a representative and merchandiser in large stores.

CRERAND, Pat. *Man Utd (1962-1970)* Joined the coaching staff at Manchester United when he hung up his boots in August 1981, later becoming their Assistant Manager until 1975. Went on to become Manager at Northampton Town from July 1976 until January 1977. On leaving football be became a Public Relations Officer to a Manchester engineering company. Now Pub landlord at the Park Hotel, Altrincham, and TV pundit.

CRIBLEY, Alex. *Liverpool, Wigan (1978-1987).* Physio and Coach at Wigan Athletic, where he had played over 250 league games in the 1980's.

CRICKMORE, Charlie. *Hull, Bournemouth, Gillingham, Rotherham, Norwich, Notts Co. (1959-1971).* A speedy winger and accomplished penalty taker, Charlie has now retired from his job as a fireman, and lives in Hull, Humberside.

CRIPPS, Harry. *West Ham, Millwall, Charlton. (1958-1975)* Played over 400 games for Millwall. Now works as an Insurance broker for the Royal London Assurance company and lives in Upminster, Essex. Harry also coaches East Ham United in the Essex Senior League

CROKER, Ted. *Charlton (1950)* Became the first professional footballer to become Secretary of the Football Association when he succeeded Denis Fellows in 1973, a position that he held until his retirement in 1989. Outside football, he owned a successful concrete business that made him his fortune. Passed away at his Cheltenham home surrounded by his family on Christmas day in 1992, after a long battle against cancer.

Ray Crawford.

CROMBIE, Dean. *Lincoln, Grimsby, Reading, Bolton, Lincoln. (1976-1990)* Was assistant manager at Lincoln, but now Youth Coach at Bolton.

CROOKS, Garth. *Stoke, Tottenham, Man U, WBA, Charlton (1975-1990).* Former England Under 21 international, who joined Tottenham from Stoke City in 1980 for £600,000. Garth is carving out a career in the media, appearing on BBcTV and co-hosting GLR Radio 'Saturday sport' .As well as being Chairman of the Institute of Professional Sport, he is Chairman and founder of SCAR charity for Sickle Cell Anaemia Relief.

CROPLEY, Alex. *Arsenal, Aston V, Newcastle, Portsmouth. (1974-1981).* Scottish international (3 caps) was lured to London by Arsenal in a £150,000 transfer from Hibernian in 1974. Retired in 1983, now runs a pub in Edinburgh.

Malcolm Crosby

CROSBY, Malcolm. *Aldershot, York, Wrexham (1979-1991)* Played most of his League soccer for Aldershot but moved into coaching at his last club,York City. He struck up a partnership with Dennis Smith, which continued at Sunderland and now at Oxford, where he is assistant Manager.

CROSS, David. *Rochdale, Norwich, Coventry, WBA, West Ham, Man C, Oldham, WBA, Bolton, Bury. (1969-1985)* Has worked as a financial advisor for Allied Dunbar in Manchester since 1988. Scouts for Oldham and runs their Under 15 side

CROSS, Graham. *Leicester, Chesterfield, Brighton., Preston, Lincoln (1960-1978)* Played in two losing F.A. Cup finals, Graham was also an all-rounder at cricket with Leicestershire. Now runs a post office in the Leicester area.

CROSS, Roger. *West Ham, Leyton O, Brentford, Fulham, Brentford, Millwall (1968-1978)* Former West Ham striker, left Q.P.R. in November 1994, to follow Gerry Francis to White Hart Lane, where he is now reserve team manager.

CROSS, Steve. *Shrewsbury, Derby, Bristol R. (1976-1994)* Enjoyed nine years at Shrewsbury Town, playing 240 league games, before going on to play for Derby. Now works as reserve team manager at his last club, Bristol Rovers.

CROWE, Matt. *Bradford P.A., Norwich, Brentford (1952-1963)* Had two spells in the league, playing for Partick Thistle in the interim. Matt now lives and works in South Africa.

CROWE, Vic. *Aston V, Peterboro (1954-1966)* Served Aston Villa as player, coach and manager. Vic played over 300 league games and skippered both his club and country (Wales). As a manager he took Villa to the 1971 League Cup final promotion into the Second Division in 1972. Left in 1974, and had a second spell in the NASL with Portland Timbers (he had earlier coached Atlanta Chiefs), before returning to England. Now acts as an advisor to BHL side Bilston Town.

CROWN, David. *Brentford, Portsmouth, Exeter, Reading, Camb U, Southend, Gillingham, (1980-1992)* After scoring 165 league goals for his seven League clubs, David moved into non-league soccer, joining Dagenham & Redbridge. Now combines running his own accountancy practice with knocking in the goals and coaching for Purfleet FC in the Diadora Premier League.

CRUDGINGTON, Geoff. *Aston V, Bradford C, Crewe, Swansea, Plymouth (1970-1987).* Works for former Plymouth Argyle sponsors, Beacon Electrical, but is still involved with soccer, regularly coaching in the Plymouth area.

CUFF, Pat. *Middlesboro, Grimsby, Millwall, Darlington (1973-1982).* Middlesborough born former England schoolboy international keeper now runs a chain of betting shops on Teeside.

CULLIS, Stan. *Wolves. (1934-1946)* Became Wolves' manager two years after he had stopped playing due to bouts of concussion, and went on to lead them to three League titles. They missed the League and cup double in 1960 by one point, but he was sensationally sacked in 1964. Joined an advertising agency and was appointed to the Midlands Sports Council in 1972, before retiring.

CULPIN, Paul. *Leicester, Coventry, Northampton, Peterborough, Hereford (1981-1991)* Former England semi-professional striker, moved to New Zealand in April 1995 to join Christchurch Utd.

CUMBES, Jim. *Tranmere, WBA, Aston V, Southport (1966-1977)* During his West Bromwich Albion days, teamed up with John Osborne his fellow goalkeeper and opened a sports shop in Bilston. He also played cricket for four counties. Now working as Commercial manager at Lancashire CCC and lives in nearby Altrincham.

CUMMING, Bobby. *Grimsby, Lincoln (1974-1989)* Full back who played 338 league games for Grimsby. Emigrated to the United States in 1989.

CUMMINGS, George. *Aston V (1935-1948)* A Scottish international full back who was a regular for Aston Villa either side of the War. Retired in 1949 and had brief spells as Coach at Villa Park and then as Manager of Hednesford Town. Became a scout for Wolves while working for the Dunlop Rubber Company. Died in April 1987.

CUMMINGS, Tommy. *Burnley, Mansfield. (1948-1963).* After appearing in 432 first division games for Burnley as a solid centre-half, Tommy steered Mansfield to promotion from Division four in 1963. Tommy then had 16 months at Aston Villa. Following a spell out of football, he went on to coach abroad and has since scouted for several clubs including Burnley and Sunderland.

CUNNINGHAM, Laurie. *Leyton O, WBA, Man U, Leicester, Wimbledon (1974-1987)* Sadly died in 1989 aged only 33, while playing in Spain with Rayo Vallencano. He won six England caps and in 1979 moved from West Brom to Real Madrid, for the then staggering sum of one million pounds. He stayed at Real for five years, then played for five more clubs before moving to Rayo. While with Wimbledon in 1988, he realised his dream of a winning Cup Winners medal by coming on as substitute in the final against Liverpool.

Jim Cumbes, at the other "Old Trafford", home of Lancashire County Cricket Club.

CURBISHLEY, Alan. *West Ham, Birmingham, Aston V, Charlton, Brighton, Charlton (1974-1993).* England Under 21 cap who started at West Ham. Was appointed joint manager at Charlton in July 1991 taking full control in 1995.

CURRAN, Hugh. *Millwall, Norwich, Wolves, Oxford, Bolton, Oxford (1963-1978)* Former Manchester United apprentice, who went on to win five Scottish caps whilst with Wolves. Retired through injury in March 1979 and returned to his native Scotland, where he is now a publican.

CURRAN, Terry. *Doncaster, Notts F, Bury, Derby, Soton, Sheff Wed, Sheff U, Everton, Huddersfield, Hull, Sunderland, Grimsby, Chesterfield (1973-1987)* Have boots - will travel! Terry played for thirteen clubs over fourteen years before retiring in 1987. Now works as a salesman in Yorkshire. Managed Goole Town for a brief spell.

CURRIE, Tony. *Watford, Sheff U, Leeds, QPR, Torquay (1967-1984)* One of the classiest players of his time, Tony won only 17 caps but widely acclaimed as a true star. Now an officer for "Football in the Community" based at Sheffield United.

CURTIS, Alan. *Swansea, Leeds, Swansea, Southampton, Stoke, Cardiff, Swansea. (1971-1989).* Played in the First Division with both Leeds United and Southampton. Alan won a total of thirty five full Welsh international caps during a career which started and ended at Swansea City, the club where he currently works as "Football in the Community" Development Officer.

CURTIS, George. *Coventry, Aston V (1955-1971)* Known as "Iron man", George played almost 500 games before finishing his career at Aston Villa. He appeared in five divisions during his time at Coventry, starting in the old Third division South, winning medals in the Third and Second en route to the First division for the first time in the "Sky Blues" history. Retired in 1994, having previously been M.D. at Highfield Road but still helps with Pools & Lotteries.

CUSACK, Dave. *Sheff Wed, Southend, Millwall, Doncaster, Rotherham. (1975-1989).* Central defender who graduated from the junior ranks at Sheffield Wednesday to make a career total of almost 500 league appearances. Appointed manager of Dagenham & Redbridge FC in 1994

CUTBUSH, John. *Tottenham, Fulham, Sheffield U. (1966-1980).* Born in Malta, John was an apprentice at Tottenham before playing over 250 games for his next two clubs. Has since worked in the insurance industry and the car trade.

Tony Currie.

Photo courtesy: Lancashire Evening Telegraph)

DALGLISH, Kenny. *Liverpool (1977-1989)* When Kevin Keegan left Liverpool in the Summer of 1977 bound for S.V. Hamburg, Kenny was purchased from Celtic. With him he brought a magnificent record of almost a goal a game from over 200 matches. Went on to win almost every honour possible in Scotland, England and Europe as well as winning 102 caps. His move into management at Anfield was equally as successful, picking up three championship titles and two F.A. Cup wins before deciding to quit the game for a less stressful existence. However, it was not long before he was tempted back, to take the helm at Blackburn Rovers, whom he has now shaped into a Championship winning side. Relinquished team duties in June 1995 to take on the new role of General Manager.

Gerry Daly

DAINES, Barry. *Tottenham, Mansfield. (1971-1983)* Ex Spurs keeper is now running a shop in Chelmsford, Essex, which specialises in the sale of a variety of continental ice creams.

DALEY, Steve. *Wolves, Man C, Burnley, Walsall. (1971-1985)* England 'B' international who was valued at over £1 million in 1979 when he moved from Wolverhampton Wanderers to Manchester City. After a couple of spells in America, Steve returned to play non-league football with Kettering but now turns out in the Birmingham Amateur Football Alliance.

DALTON, George. *Newcastle, Brighton. (1960-1967)* After a league career as a full back, George studied to become a physiotherapist and currently works as Club Physio at Coventry City.

DALY, Gerry. *Man U, Derby, Coventry, Leicester, Birmingham, Shrewsbury, Stoke, Doncaster (1973-1988)* Dublin born, Gerry won 46 caps for his country, Eire during his playing days which saw him play for eight League Clubs. Unfortunately is now unable to work because of a back problem His last job was as Manager of Telford United, a post that he held from 1989 until 1994.

DANIEL, Peter. *Hull, Wolves, Sunderland, Lincoln , Burnley (1974-1988).* Manager of North Ferriby town in the North East Counties league for four years until the end of 1994. Now holds the same post at nearby Winterton Rangers FC.

DANIEL, Ray. *Arsenal, Sunderland, Cardiff, Swansea. (1948-1959)* 21 Welsh caps. Became a publican, then area manager for Courvoisier Brandy. Now postmaster at Cockett Post office.

DARE, Billy. *Brentford, West Ham, (1948-1958)* **The first soccer player to be transferred on television signing for West Ham in front of the cameras in 1955. Died May 1994 aged 67.**

DARKE, Peter. *Plymouth, Exeter, Torquay. (1971-1978)* Exeter born defender, still lives in the city, where he now works as a salesman.

DARRACOTT, Terry. *Everton, Wrexham (1967-1979)* Following a twelve year league career Terry had a stint in America with Tulsa Roughnecks before progressing into coaching. Was Assistant manager at Everton, now on the Coaching Staff at Blackburn Rovers.

(Photo courtesy: News & Star, Carlisle)

A reunion of **Carlisle United** players in 1995, twenty years after topping the First Dvision (L to R) Ross, Balderstone, Winstanley, McIlmoyle, Ashman, Dent, Parker, Martin.

DAVEY, Steve. *Plymouth, Hereford, Portsmouth, Exeter. (1966-1981)* A former England Youth international who played 214 games for Argyle and 415 in his career total, now owns a residential rest home for the elderly in Plymouth.

DAVIDSON, Andy. *Hull C, (1952-1967)* A consistently reliable defender who played over 500 games for Hull despite suffering three broken legs. Now has a fish round in his adopted home.

DAVIES, Alan. *Man U, Newcastle, Swansea, Bradford C. Swansea (1981-1991).* An unknown when he played for Manchester United in the 1983 Cup final. in 1992, he was found dead in his car near his home on the Gower Coast, thought to have been suffering from depression.

DAVIES, Cyril. *Swansea, Carlisle, Charlton (1966-1972).* A promising inside forward who although capped once by Wales never fulfilled his early promise and was forced to retire at the age of 25 due to a knee injury. Now works for the school playing fields dept of a London Council.

DAVIES, Dai. *Swansea, Everton, Swansea, Wrexham, Swansea, Tranmere. (1969-1983)* **Was involved in a Welsh book & craft shop in Mold, and football commentating on Welsh TV. Although a qualified teacher he now runs a natural healing centre in Llangollen, North Wales.**

DAVIES, E. Reginald. *Southend, Newcastle, Swansea, Carlisle. (1949-1963)* **Emigrated to Australia in 1971 after a spell in non-league. Down under, he achieved great success as a coach, winning the Cup with Bayswater. Then the League Title with Ascot. He also represented Western Australia against New Zealand at the age of 47, and finally hung up his boots at the age of 50!! Now retired, living in Perth.**

DAVIES, Fred. *Wolves, Cardiff, Bournemouth (1961-1973)* Liverpool born keeper, Fred moved into coaching after 12 of years minding the posts and has been manager at Shrewsbury since 1993.

DAVIES, Gordon. *Fulham, Chelsea, Man C, Fulham, Wrexham (1977- 1993)* Welsh international striker, who made his biggest impact during two spells at Fulham, where he scored over 150 goals from his 350 plus league appearances. Gordon now lives in Leighton Buzzard, Bedfordshire and is currently employed as a pest control officer for theRentokil group of companies.

DAVIES, Roger. *Derby, Preston, Leicester, Derby, Darlington (1971-1983)* Goal-scoring England Under 21 international who was plucked from non-league soccer by Derby County in 1971. The following twelve years included spells in Belgium and America. Roger now works as a manager for Rolls Royce and is still an active member of Derby County's Ex-Rams team.

DAVIES, Ron. *Chester, Luton, Norwich, Southampton, Portsmouth, Man Utd, Millwall (1959-1975).* **One of the all time great goalscorers, netting 277 goals during his sixteen years as a pro, which also saw him win 29 full Welsh caps. Became a demolition worker for a while after retiring in 1975 and also proved that he had talent with his hands as well as his feet by selling art sketches - including portraits of players. Moved over to the States in 1988, where he still lives, in a luxury house within an acre of secluded woodland outside Orlando. Also coaching local semi-pro side - Orlando Lions.**

DAVIES, Wyn. *Wrexham, Bolton, Newcastle, Man C, Man U, Blackpool, C Palace, Stockport, Crewe. (1960-1977)* Know affectionately as "Wyn the Leap" because of his ball winning skills in the air, played for nine league clubs and won 32 full Welsh Caps. After a career spanning 14 years, he became a baker in Bolton. Although happy in the area, he still holds on to the dream to own a smallholding in his native Caernarfon.

DAVIS, Gareth. *Wrexham (1967-1983).* Played for Wrexham for over 16 years during which time he made three appearances for the full Welsh side. On retirement Gareth moved into hotel management and now owns a hotel in Wrexham.

D'AVRAY, Mich. *Ipswich, Leicester (1979-1986).* Although born in Johannesburg, Mich won two England Under 21 caps during his ten years at Portman Road. Ended at Leicester and is now Manager of South Africa's Olympic Soccer team.

DAWKINS, Derek. *Leicester, Mansfield, Bournemouth, Torquay. (1977-1988)* Started at Leicester but played most of his league soccer for Torquay, where he now works as Youth Officer.

DAWTRY, Kevin. *Soton, Bournmth, Reading (1976-1982).* Lives near Southampton and works as a Distribution Supervisor for Exxon Chemicals. Manager of Hampshire League, Esso Fawley.

DAY Billy. *Middlesboro, Newcastle, Peterboro (1955-1963).* Nippy winger, who ended his days at Peterborough. Bill has now returned to Teeside, where he currnetly works as a bookmaker.

DAY, Eric. *Southampton (1946-1956).* Goalscoring outside right who played 398 games for Southampton. Worked as a handyman on a Country Estate in Wiltshire until his retirement.

DAY, Mervyn. *West Ham, Leyton O, Aston Villa, Leeds, Luton, Sheff U, Carlisle (1973-1994).* Former England Under 23 keeper. Mervyn played over 600 games for the Hammers, Leeds and Villa, before joining Carlisle, where he now combines coaching with his playing duties.

DEACY, Eamonn. *Aston Villa, Derby Co (1979-1983)* Republic of Ireland international (4 caps) had a four year stay in England before returning to his home town of Galway where he now works in the family's fruit and veg business.

DEACY, Nick. *Hereford, Workington, Hull City, Bury (1974-1983)* A player with a colourful career behind him. Born in Cardiff and won full Welsh caps during spells in Holland with PSV Eindhoven and Beringen. Now works as a computer analyst with British Aerospace in Bristol

DEAKIN, Alan. *Aston Villa, Walsall. (1959-1971).* An England Under 23 international who won a League Cup Winners tankard with Aston Villa in 1961-2. Now works as a fitter/welder for an engineering firm in Aldridge, West Midlands.

DEAN, Dixie. Died at Goodison Park, Everton in 1980 aged 73. Famed for creating a scoring record when in 1927-28 season he scored 60 league goals, another 19 in representative matches and three in the FA Cup, making an incredible haul of 82 in one season. Took a pub, "The Dublin Packet", in 1946, which he gave up 15 years later. Went onto work for John Moores's pools empire as a security man. Finally retiring to Babington in 1971.

DEANS, Dixie. *Luton, Carlisle. (1976)* A great character and very popular in Scotland, Dixie spent three years in Australia, playing for Adelaide City, then returned to Scotland via Shelbourne in Ireland and soccer in the States.

DEAR, Brian. *West Ham, Brighton, Fulham, Millwall, West Ham. (1962-1970)* Had few opportunities during his time at West Ham due to the Peters/Hurst duet, but still managed to score a goal every other game during his six year stay at Upton Park. Now works as assistant club steward at the Freemasons hall in Southend.

DEARDEN, Bill. *Oldham, Crewe, Chester, Sheff U, Chester, Chesterfield (1964-1978)* Played for five clubs, but made almost half of his 400 odd League appearances for Sheffield United. Now works as Assistant manager at Port Vale.

DEEHAN, John. *Aston Villa W.B.A, Norwich, Ipswich, Man C, Barnsley. (1975-1990)* Became player/coach at Man City in July 1988 and switched to Barnsley in the same role in 1990. Returned to his old club Norwich to succeed Mike Walker in January 1994, however he left the following year after a string of poor results.

DELAPENHA, Lloyd *Portsmouth, Middlesboro, Mansfield (1948-1960).* **After 380 league games for his three clubs, Lloyd returned to his Jamaica and became a popular face on local television as a sports reporter.**

DEMPSEY, John. *Fulham, Chelsea, (1964-1975).* Republic of Ireland international (19 caps), played 310 games in his career. John joined Chelsea from Fulham in 1969 for £70,000 and won FA Cup and Cup Winners Cup medals before leaving Stamford Bridge, for Philadelphia Furies six years later. Now works at a special school for handicapped children in North London.

DENNIS, Mark. *Birmingham, Soton, QPR, C. Palace, (1978-1990).* A stormy career was wrecked by brushes with authority, he was cautioned 60 times and appeared before the FA on disrepute charges more than once. Undoubtedly a talented player who should have achieved more, Mark now works as a sign writer in Spain.

DENNISON, Bob. *Newcastle, Notts F, Fulham, Northampton. (1932-1947)* Centre half, whose four club career spanned fifteen years either side of the war, now retired living in Kent.

DENYER, Peter. *Portsmouth, Northampton. (1975-1982)* Played over 250 league games before moving to Australia to Coach Blacktown FC.

DEPLIDGE, Bill. *Bradford P.A. (1946-1955)* Inside forward who scored 62 goals from 274 league games. Went on to manage in Non-league football. Now retired, living in South Australia.

DERRETT, Steve. *Cardiff, Carlisle, Aldershot, Rotherham, Newport. (1966-1977)* Welsh international full back (4 caps). Now a representative for a protective clothing firm in Cardiff.

DEVINE, John. *Arsenal, Norwich, Stoke. (1977-1985)* **A badly broken leg terminated his career whilst playing for Stoke. He recovered sufficiently to play in non-league soccer and had a spell at Chelmsford before venturing east to play for East Bengal in India !! Now closer to home as manager of Shelbourne in Ireland.**

DeVRIES, Roger *Hull, Blackburn, Scunthorpe, (1970-1981).* Left back who played 314 games for the Tigers before spells with Blackburn and Scunthorpe. Still works in the Hull area today, as a teacher in a local primary school.

DICKENS, Alan. *West Ham, Chelsea, Brentford, Colchester (1982-1994)* Former West Ham apprentice who won one England Under 21 cap. Now at Hayes, previously with Chesham United.

DICKINSON, Jimmy M.B.E. *Portsmouth (1946-1964)* Pompey's all time great, won 48 England caps as a dependable wing half. Jimmy continued to serve at Fratton Park as Scout; P.R.O.; and briefly manager, having set a record of 764 appearances for one club, which stood until 1980 when John Trollope played six games more for Swindon Town. Suffered three heart attacks, and sadly died in 1982 at the age of 57.

DICKSON, Will. *Notts Co, Chelsea, Arsenal, Mansfield T (1946-1956).* In his playing days, won 12 caps for his country, Northern Ireland. He returned there to live and work as scout for Arsenal. Now works in the joinery trade.

DILLON, Kevin. *Birmingham, Portsmouth, Newcastle, Reading (1977-1994)* Joined Stevenage after being released by Reading in September 1994, then followed team-mate Graham Roberts to Yeovil Town, as his assistant manager.

DITCHBURN, Ted. *Tottenham (1946-1958)* He played well over 400 games for his only club, Tottenham, including a spell of 247 consecutive appearances. Played six times for England, now lives in retirement in Romford, Essex.

DIXON, Johnny. *Aston Villa (1946-1960)* An Inside forward who scored 131 goals in 292 appearances for Aston Villa. was captain of the Villa side that triumphed in the 1957 F.A. Cup final. Coached the youngsters at Villa park for six years before running an ironmongery business in Erdington. Now retired, in Sutton Coldfield.

DIXON, Will. *Arsenal, Reading, Colchester, Swindon, Aldershot (1968-1977)* After serving his apprenticeship at Highbury, despite never establishing himself in the Arsenal first team, Will went on to make over 400 League appearances. Now on the coaching staff at Watford.

DOBING, Peter *Blackburn, Man C, Stoke. (1955-1972)* Peter's seventeen year career took in 564 league starts and saw him win England Under 23 and Football League honours. Ended his career at Stoke City. He still lives in the Potteries area running a company which sells cups and saucers to local hotels and restaurants.

DOBSON, Martin. *Bolton, Burnley, Everton, (1966-1985)* Midfielder who played five times for England. Became manager at Bury (1984-1989) and Bristol Rovers (1991-2) before taking up a post in Malta. Coached youngsters back in Lancashire prior to his appointment as Manager of Unibond League side, Chorley in 1995.

DOCHERTY, John. *Brentford, Sheff U, Brentford, Reading, Brentford (1960-1973)* Had three playing stints with Brentford and went on to manage Millwall, now in charge at Slough Town.

DOCHERTY, Mick. *Burnley, Man C, Sunderland (1968-1978)* Coached at Preston NE, then became Assistant Manager at Rochdale in September 1991 and promoted to manager in January 1995. Son of Tommy 'The Doc' Docherty.

DOCHERTY, Tommy. *Preston., Arsenal, Chelsea (1949-1961)* As a player 'The Doc' won 25 Scottish caps and played over 400 league games following his £4,000 move to Preston from Celtic in 1949. Became Player/coach at Chelsea in 1961, and their manager in 1962. A full and colourful management career then took in stops at: Rotherham ; QPR (twice); Aston Villa; FC Oporto (Portugal); Hull; Scotland national side; Man Utd; Derby; Sydney Olympic (Australia) (twice); Preston ; South Melbourne FC (Australia); Wolves. Now uses all this experience to entertain as an after dinner speaker.

DODSON, David. *Arsenal, Swansea, Portsmouth, Aldershot (1957-1966)* England Youth winger, ended his career at the age of 26 in 1966. Now owns his own plumbing business in Fleet.

DOHERTY, John. *Fulham, Aldershot (1956-1965)* Centre forward set off to Australia in 1965 to play for South Coast United FC. John is now employed as an insurance consultant.

DOHERTY, Peter. *Blackpool, Man C, Derby, Huddersfield, Doncaster. (1933-1952)* Northern Ireland international with 16 caps. Won a League championship medal with Man City before the war, and a cup winners medal in 1946 with Derby. In 1949 at the age of 36 became player-manager to Doncaster Rovers, winning promotion that season from the Third Division North. Now retired but doing the occasional scouting. Lives at Poulton-le-Fylde, outside Blackpool.

DOLAN, Terry. *Bradford P.A., Huddersfield, Bradford, Rochdale (1968-1981)* Bradford born Terry played for both of his home town clubs and a total of over 350 league games before moving into management. Now Manager at Hull City.

DONACHIE, Willie. *Man C, Norwich, Burnley, Oldham. (1969-1990)* Glasgow born Scottish international (35 caps) started at Celtic before moving South to join Manchester City in December 1968. Had two spells in America with Portland Timbers before ending his playing days at Burnley, then Oldham where he became assistant Manager/Coach. Moved to Everton in the same capacity with boss, Joe Royle in early 1995.

DONOVAN, Donal. *Everton, Grimsby. (1951-1963)* After five years with Grimsby Town, went on to manage Boston United, before taking a job with a shipping company on the East coast. Now working for the Volvo import terminal at Grimsby.

DONOVAN, Terry. *Grimsby, Aston Villa, Oxford, Burnley, Rotherham, Blackpool (1976-1984)* Former Republic of Ireland international forward is now working as an insurance broker living in picturesque Tetney, Gloucestershire.

(Photo courtesy: Sheffield Newspapers Ltd)

DOOLEY, Derek. *Lincoln, Sheff Wed (1946-1952).* Scored 62 goals in 61 games for the Owls before injury forced him to quit at the age of 23. Now a director at neighbours, Sheffield United.

DORNEY, Alan *Millwall (1968-1976)* A central defender who progressed through Millwall's junior ranks to become a first team regular, making almost 250 League appearances. Now lives in Bexleyheath and works as a general builder.

DOUGAN, Derek. *Portsmouth, Blackburn, Aston Villa, Peterborough, Leicester, Wolves.* Retired from playing in 1975 after winning a League Cup winners tankard at Wembley in 1974 and a UEFA Cup runners up medal in 1972, whilst playing for Wolveerhampton Wanderers. At International level he made 43 appearances for Northern Ireland. Dougan was Chairman of the PFA and later returned to Molineux in August 1982 as Chairman and Chief Executive. He still lives in the Wolverhampton area where he now works as a marketing and P.R. consultant.

Derek Doogan

(Photo: Express & Star, Wolverhampton.)

DOUGLAS, Bryan. *Blackburn (1954-1968)* A one club man who was a loyal servant to his local side, Blackburn Rovers. He made over 400 League appearances in their colours and won 36 caps. Finished playing after 19 years at Ewood Park and became Northern area sales representative for a paper manufacturing company, until the firm was taken over in 1992. Bryan then accepted the opportunity of voluntary redundancy.

DOWD, Henry W (Harry) *Man City, Oldham Stoke (1961-1973)* Guarded the goal for Manchester City for eight years before finally ending his playing days at Stoke City. Harry has worked in the brewery trade since retiring from soccer, currently employed as an Area Manager by the J.W. Lees Brewery, which is based in Middleton.

DOWMAN, Steve. *Colchester U, Wrexham, Charlton, Newport, Camb U, (1976-1986).* Experienced defender who played over 350 league games, Steve is now manager at Wivenhoe Town

DOWNES, Bobbie. *WBA, Peterborough, Rochdale, Watford, Barnsley, Blackpool. (1966-1983).* Tricky winger is now using experience gained in over 450 league games to Assist Graham Taylor at Wolverhampton Wanderers.

DOWNES, Wally. *Wimbledon, Newport Co, Sheff U (1978-1994).* Wally played almost 200 league games for theWimbledon before following his boss, Dave Bassett, to Sheffield United where he now works on the coaching staff.

DOWNS, Greg. *Norwich. Torquay, Coventry, Birmingham, Hereford (1977-1994).* Left back, joined Hereford United in June 1991 as player/ manager, a post held until his dismissal in November 1994. Then played for a succession of non-league sides including Merthyr Tydfil and Forest Green Rovers, all in the following season !

DOWNSBOROUGH, Peter. *Halifax, Swindon, Brighton, Bradford C (1959-1978)* Veteran goalie who played in Swindon Town's historic League Cup victory of 1968/9. Lives in Elland near Huddersfield and works at a power station.

DOYLE, Bobby. *Barnsley, Peterboro, Blackpool, Portsmouth, Hull, (1972-1986).* Injuries forced Bobbie to quit after only 43 games for his last club, Hull City. However he remained in the area and set up a successful haulage business.

DOYLE, Mike. *Man C, Stoke, Bolton, Rochdale (1964-1983)* Former Manchestre City defender who won five full England caps. Mike now lives in Ashton-under-Lyne, has now been a Sales manager for Slazenger for ten years. Commentates regularly for local radio.

DRAKE, Ray. *Stockport Co. (1956-1957).* **There aren't many footballers who have had to endure what Ray Drake did as a youngster. However, his courage and determination saw him play for the side he supported as a boy, after meningitis suffered at the age of three left him totally deaf in one ear and with only 30% hearing in the other. Although predominantly a reserve team player, Ray had an incredible goal scoring record, when he left Edgeley Park he had scored a 234 goals from 201 games, including 19 in 23 first team appearances. After many years working for bookmaking firm, he retired in February 1992, but still lives a stones throw away from the club, and remains a season ticket holder.**

Bryan Douglas (far left) with former team-mates at a Ewood Park reunion.
(Photo courtesy: Lancashire Evening Telegraph.)

DRAKE, Ted. Scored seven goals in one game for Arsenal against Aston Villa on December 14th 1935, the first six goals coming from his first six shots ! That feat still stands as a record for goals scored by one player in an away match. Died in South London the age of 82 in June 1995.

DRINKELL, Kevin. *Grimsby, Norwich, Coventry, Rangers, Birmingham (1976-1993)* Grimsby born striker, who caught he eye whilst playing for his hometown club. Moves to Norwich City and then to Rangers north of the border followed before Coventry paid £800,000 for his services in 1989. Kevin is currently back in Scotland, where he is manager at Stirling Albion.

DROY, Mickey. *Chelsea, Luton, C Palace, Brentford (1970-1986)* Tower of strength upon which many a Chelsea defence was structured. Lives in South London and is a Director of an Electrical Wholesalers. For many years was involved with Kingstonian FC, as player, coach, then briefly their manager until 1994.

DUGDALE, Jimmy. *WBA, Aston Villa, QPR. (1952-1962).* For 25 years was a licensee, working in Perry Barr, Aston (at the Villa Lions Club), Hall Green, Moseley Rugby Club and the Hasbury Conservative club. He sadly had to have a leg amputated in 1990, forcing him to retire. Jimmy is the uncle of Alan Dugdale, the former Coventry, Charlton and Barnsley defender.

DUNCAN, John. *Tottenham, Derby, Scunthorpe (1974-1982)* Scottish forward who scored 53 goals in just over 100 games for Spurs Managed at Ipswich, but now in his second spell as boss at Chesterfield, the first being 1983-1987.

DUNGWORTH, John. *Huddersfield, Barnsley, Oldham, Rochdale, Aldershot, Shrewsbury, Hereford, Mansfield, Rotherham. (1972-1987)* Now Youth Coach at Sheffield United.

DUNN, Jimmy *Leeds, Darlington (1947-1959)* Still lives in Leeds, Jimmy's adopted home since he signed pro terms at Elland Road in 1947. Appeared in 443 first team games before working for the post office until his retirement in 1987.

DUNNE, Jimmy *Millwall, Torquay, Fulham, Torquay. (1966-1978)* **Coaching "Combined 89" in the South Devon League and works as a maintenance man for the Churchill Hotel in Torquay which is owned by Gerald Rowell, whose wife was killed by Michael Rose, one of the inmates who caused a major alert by escaping from Parkhurst jail on the Isle of Wight.**

DUNNE, Tony. *Man Utd, Bolton (1960-1978)* Republic of Ireland full back who earned 32 full caps. Played over 400 League gamese for the Reds before moving to Bolton in 1973. Now runs a golf driving range in Altrincham, which he opened upon leaving the game. Lives in Sale.

DUNPHY, Eammon. *Man U, York, Millwall, Charlton, Reading (1962-1976)* **Back in Dublin working as a writer and broadcaster. He writes a regular column for an Irish Sunday newspaper, the Sunday Independent and frequently appears on Irish television. Played in England for 17 years (5 with Manchester United). He is the author of the classic soccer book "Only a game" and also wrote the international best seller "Unforgettable fire - the story of U2"**

DUQUEMAN, Len. *Tottenham, (1947-1956)* Guernsey born forward, who scored 114 goals in 274 games for his only club. Now mine host at The "Haunch of Venison" pub in Cheshunt.

DWIGHT, Roy. *Fulham, Notts F, Coventry, Millwall (1954-1964)* **Broke his leg in the 1959 Cup final. Uncle of Elton John, became a teacher. Now Racing manager of the Crayford Greyhound stadium. Living in Bexleyheath.**

DWYER, Alan. *Wrexham, Stockport Co (1974-1981)* Played 169 games for Wrexham, where he still lives and now works as a lorry driver.

DWYER, Phil. *Cardiff, Rochdale (1972-1984).* After making 466 games for Cardiff, Dwyer ended his playing days at Rochdale before joining the South Wales Police Force, based at Barry.

DYSON, Barry. *Tranmere, C Palace, Watford, Leyton O, Colchester. (1960-1974)* Scored 99 goals in 174 games for Tranmere, lives in Colchester and runs his own Road Haulage business.

DYSON, Paul. *Coventry, Stoke, WBA, Darlington, Crewe (1977-1989)* England Under 21 international defender. Joined Telford, but since 1993 Paul has been with Solihull Borough.

EARLE, Steve. *Fulham, Leicester, Peterboro, (1963-1977).* Steve made his mark at Fulham and Leicester before jetting off to America. Now lives in Tulsa, where he is an insurance salesman.

EARLES, Pat. *Southampton, Reading (1974-1982)* Started at Southampton, but moved to Reading after only a few games and went on to play for the Royals for six years . Lives near Portsmouth and works as a probation officer.

EARLS Mick. *Southampton, Aldershot (1973-1978).* Republic of Ireland international central defender, is now a social worker managing a home for children in care in Gosport, Hampshire.

EASTHAM, George O.B.E.. *Newcastle, Arsenal, Stoke. (1956-1973)* **Created history when he took his club, Newcastle United, to court in 1961 when they refused to let him leave - thus the freedom of contract clause was introduced. Became manager at Stoke City. and George was awarded the O.B.E. in 1975. Now lives in Johannesburg, runs his own sportswear business and acts as Vice President of the Arsenal Supporters Club in South Africa !**

ECCLES, Terry. *Blackburn, Mansfield, Huddersfield, York (1969-1980)* Went over to Greece to play for Ethnikos as well as knocking in the goals for four English clubs. Now a publican at the "White Horse", Upper Poppleton, York.

EDDY, Keith. *Barrow, Watford, Sheff Utd (1962-1975).* Midfielder remembered by fans of Watford and Sheffield United, ended his career in 1975 and now coaches Soccer in Tulsa, USA.

EDWARDS, Bryan. *Bolton W. (1950-1964).* Wing half who played over 500 games and won an FA Cup medal in 1958. Now retired in Lancs.

EDWARDS, Duncan. *Manchester U. (1952-1957).* **Duncan was potentially one of the best players that the world may have ever seen, Before he was killed in the Munich air disaster, dying in his sleep in February 1958. He was only aged 21 but had already won three FA Youth Cup winners medals, two League Championship medals, FA Cup runners up medal, two charity shield trophies and had played eighteen times for England. Two stained glass windows are dedicated in his memory at St Francis Church in his home town of Dudley.**

EDWARDS, Ian. *WBA, Chester, Wrexham, C Palace (1973-1982)* Retired injured in 1983 aged 28. Owned two milk rounds in Wrexham for five years. Selling these made it possible to purchase an old country house in Criccieth Gwnedd, which he has converted into a hotel and runs today.

EDWARDS, Keith. *Sheff U, Hull, Leeds, Hull, Stockport, Huddersfield Plymouth, (1975-1990)* Slightly built goalscoring forward, whose consistent strike rate made him popular at all his clubs. Now works as a lorry driver in Sheffield.

EGLINGTON, Tommy. *Everton, Tranmere R. (1946-1960)* Earned 24 caps for his native Eire, to where he returned after playing over 500 games for Everton and Tranmere. Returned to Dublin in 1961 to become a successful butcher, but was forced to retire due to a serious illness in 1992.

ELLAM, Roy. *Bradford C, Huddersfield, Leeds, Huddersfield, (1961-1974)* Played all of his league football for Yorkshire sides, including two spells at Huddersfield Town which were separated by a brief stay at Leeds United. Now Landlord of the Nelson Inn, Thornton Lees.

ELLIOTT, Billy. *Bradford P.A., Burnley, Sunderland (1946-1958)* Capped by England five times , went on to become a much travelled coach and manager. As well as posts in Norway, Belgium, and Germany (where he trained an American side !), he also Coached the Libyan National Team! At home he managed Darlington until his retirement, and was on the staff at Sunderland, when they reached the F.A. Cup final in 1973.

ELLIOTT, Paul. *Charlton, Luton, Aston Villa, Chelsea. (1981-1992)* In 1992, aged 28, Paul was Chelsea's Player of the Year when his career was ended as a result of a tackle which has since been the subject of media publicity, a court case and much discussion. Now works as a T.V. pundit and helps with the sponsorship office at Chelsea.

ELLIOTT, Shaun. *Sunderland, Norwich, Blackpool (1976-1989)* Former England 'B' International defender is currently playing for Whitley Bay FC in the Unibond League.

ELLIS, Benjamin. Died in 1966, but his memory lives on, as he is probably one of very few footballers to have a road named after him, Ellis Way in Motherwell, Scotland.

ELLIS, Sam. *Sheff Wed, Mansfield, Lincoln, Watford (1965-1978)* Former 'Owls' defender, managed Blackpool and was number two at Man City, before becoming Lincoln City's eighth managerial appointment in nine years when he took on a two year contract at Sincil Bank in 1994.

ELSTRUP, Lars. *Luton T. (1989-1990).* **Danish International forward who joined Luton Town from Odense for a 50 game stay in 1990. Returned to Denmark, where he was most recently reported to have joined a religious cult.**

ELWISS, Mike. *Doncaster, Preston, C Palace, Preston (1971-1979).* Married the daughter of the Preston Chairman ! Mike played a total of 201 league games for the Lancashire club in two spells. Now runs a dairy just outside the town.

ENDERSBY, Scott. *Tranmere R, Swindon T, Carlisle U, York C, Cardiff C. (1979-1987).* Became the youngest goalkeeper ever to play in the FA Cup proper whilst on the books with non-league Kettering Town. This led to an eight year league career with five clubs in the 1980's. Now working as a chef for a bistro/restaurant in York.

ENGLAND, Mike. *Blackburn, Tottenham, Cardiff. (1959-1975).* After a long successful career which saw him win 44 Welsh caps and star as a dominant feature in the Spurs side, England became manager of the Welsh national side in 1980. He held this post for eight years, during which time he was awarded the M.B.E. for services to Soccer. He is now a businessman and owns residential homes in Rhyl and Colwyn Bay.

EUSTACE, Peter. *Sheff Wed, West Ham, Rotherham, Sheff Wed, Peterborough (1962-1975)* Manager of Sheffield Wednesday in 1989, but has been out of the game since being sacked as Leyton Orient boss in April 1993. Now back in his native Yorkshire, running a pub in Sheffield.

EVANS, Allan. *Aston Villa, Leicester, Darlington. (1977-1990)* Enjoyed a successful career at Villa Park, earning European and Super cup medals as well as four full England Caps. Evans was eventually released by Aston Villa in 1990, and after a spell in Australia he returned to England in May 1991 to become Assistant manager-coach of Leicester City. Then in 1994, followed his manager, Brian Little to Aston Villa.

EVANS, Alun. *Wolves, Liverpool, Aston Villa, Walsall. (1967-1977)* Son of the former West Brom left-half of the same name, Alun became Britain's first £100,000 teenage footballer when he was sold by Wolves to Liverpool in 1968. Also played for Aston Villa and Walsall before trying his luck in the America and then Australia, quitting soccer in 1980. Now lives near Melbourne in Australia where he has worked as a used car salesman and a delivery driver at a fish market, but is currently a painter and decorator.

EVANS, Brian. *Swansea, Hereford (1963-1974).* Welsh international winger (7 caps) played over 350 games for Swansea after joining them from Abergavenny in 1963. Now runs a successful painting and decorating business in Swansea.

EVANS, David A professional with Aston Villa who also played County Cricket for Gloucestershire and Warwickshire, he founded Office Cleaning Ltd in 1980 and became a Director of Luton Town in 1977. Took over as Chairman seven years later and was behind the controversial idea to ban away fans from Kenilworth road in 1987 to save on Policing costs. David remained in charge until 1989, two years after being elected as Conservative Member of Parliament M.P. for Welwyn Hatfield.

EVANS, Dennis. *Arsenal (1951-1959).* Became assistant manager at Arsenal in 1963, where he had played for eight years.Was coach at Luton Town before becoming a private hire chauffeur.

EVANS, George. *Wrexham, Chester (1957-1968)* Wing half with over 275 games of League experience. Now lives in Hightown, Wrexham and works at the nearby Bersham Colliery.

EVANS, Ian. *QPR, Crystal Palace, Barnsley, Exeter C, Cambridge Utd. (1970-1983)* Welsh international defender who won thirteen fullcaps for his country. Ian ended his league career at Cambridge United in 1983. Now works as first team coach at the Den, with Millwall.

EVANS, Maurice. *Reading (1955-1966)* Played over 400 matches for Reading and later became their Manager. Took over at Oxford until March 1988, when he was appointed General Manager.

EVANS, Mickey. *Wolves, Wrexham (1964-1978)* Served Wrexham for 16 years, leaving in 1982 as Assistant manager. He then returned to his home village of Caersws and took up work as a sales manager for a petroleum company.

EVANS, Ray. *Tottenham, Millwall, Fulham, Stoke, (1968-1981).* Former England Youth player who ended a fourteen year career at Stoke in 1981 Now living near Seattle in America.

EVANS, Roy. *Liverpool (1969-1973).* Joined Liverpool straight from school and made his debut in 1970, however, he only made a total of eleven appearances in nine seasons. In 1974 at the age of 25, Roy became reserve team coach - a post at which he excelled, earning him promotion to Assistant Manager at the end of the 1992/3 season. Took over as Manager in January 1994, following the departure of Graham Souness.

EVANSON, John. *Oxford, Blackpool, Fulham, Bournemouth (1966-1980).* Went into catering after 19 years as a pro, becoming a partner in the Key Eating House, Southampton. Can now be found at the Owl & Pussycat Pub in London EC2.

John Evanson (right)

EVES, Mel. *Wolves, Huddersfield, Sheff U, Gillingham, Mansfield. (1977-1987)* Has been in the financial services industry since 1989, and is now a Director of Premier Promotions Financial Advisors - specialising in help for pro sportsmen.

EYRE, Fred. *Man C, Lincoln, Bradford P.A. (1961-1969)* **Although Fred only appeared in very few league games, his football career has provided him with an abundance of memories which he now uses to very amusing effect, in his successful books and as a popular after dinner speaker. He is also a wealthy businessman running his own chain of stationery shops.**

FACEY, Ken. *Leyton O (1952-1960).* Played over 300 games for his only club. Retired from the Post Office in 1991 and lives in Hackney.

FAGAN, Joe. *Man C. Bradford P.A. (1946-1953).* Quit in tears as Liverpool boss in the wake of the Hysel riot in May 1985, less than two years after taking over from Bob Paisley. Was a former member of the famous Liverpool "boot room" before taking over as boss, played as a centre half with Manchester City and Bradford P.A. During his relatively brief Anfield reign, they won the European Cup, Milk Cup and a League title.

FAIRBROTHER, Barrie *Orient, Millwall (1969-1976).* An Orient regular for 5 years in the early seventies before ending his career at nearby Millwall. Now lives and works in South Africa.

FAIRCLOUGH, David. *Liverpool, Norwich, Oldham, Tranmere, Wigan. (1975-1990)* "Supersub" now lives in Formby, Liverpool and works as a freelance journalist, having successfully completed a course for the National Council Training Journalists during his playing days.

FAIRFAX, Ray. *WBA, Northampton. (1962-1970)* Retired 1979 Worked at West Brom, as a Commercial Assistant and then as Assistant Secretary. In 1985 became Club Secretary at Port Vale. before joining the ticket office at Aston Villa.

(Photo courtesy: Worthing Herald)

FALCO, Mark. *Tottenham, Chelsea, Watford, QPR, Millwall (1978-1991)* Striker who played most of his soccer for London clubs, had a spell at Rangers in Scotland before Q.P.R. paid £350,000 to bring him back to the capital in 1988. Joined Worthing of the Isthmian League in 1994.

FALLON, Steve. *Camb U (1974-1986)* Now works in the commercial department at Cambridge United, the club for whom he made over 400 appearances as a player. Also currently player/manager of neighbours Cambridge City.

FANTHAM, John. *Sheff Wed, Rotherham (1957-1969)* Sturdy forward won one England cap and scored 147 goals in 380 games for the 'Owls'. Now a successful businessman in Sheffield.

FARM, George. *Blackpool (1948-1959)* Goalie who played 462 games for Blackpool, and ten games for Scotland. Now living near Edinburgh and is involved in a woollen and textile business.

FARMER, Ted. *Wolves, (1960-1963)* **England Under 23 international who may well have been in the 1966 World Cup Squad, but for an injury sustained in 1964. Ted scored an incredible 28 goals in 27 matches in his first season. Also during that season (1960/1), he achieved another remarkable unique feat by scoring his 21st League Goal in his 21st League match on his 21st Birthday on the 21st of January !! A serious knee injury forced Ted to prematurely pack in the game and to become a sports outfitter. Then after working for fifteen years in the computer industry, Ted had to retire due to an accident that left him with osteo-arthritis. Now lives in Wombourne, Wolverhampton.**

FARMER, Terry. *Rotherham, York. (1952-1959)* Goalscoring forward of the fifties is now working as a steel erector in Rotherham.

FARRELL, Peter. *Everton, Tranmere. (1946-1959)* Eire 28 caps. After playing 421 games for Everton moved to Tranmere, where he became Player/manager. Followed by spells with Hollyhead and Shamrock Rovers. Later had a job in Insurance and went into broadcasting with RTE in Dublin. Now in hospital in Dublin, aged 73

FARRIMOND, Syd. *Bolton. Tranmere, (1958-1973).* Spent twelve years at Burnden Park as a reliable full back, clocking up almost 400 league appearances. Now owns a newsagents in Leigh.

FASHANU, Justin. *Norwich C, Notts For, Southampton, Notts Co, Brighton & H.A., Man C, West Ham U, Leyton O, Torquay U. (1978-1991)* **Justin was a former A.B.A. heavyweight boxer and is elder brother of Aston Villa's John. He started his professional career with Norwich City and after shooting to fame with some spectacular goals, Brian Clough took him to Nottingham Forest in a one million pound deal. However his stay was brief and despite repeated comebacks from injury with a variety of clubs both here and abroad, he never recaptured the form that brought him to prominence. He has since had spells in Canada and Scotland and media interest in his colourful private life means that he is probably better known for his off the field activities which allegedly have included a rather unlikely liaison with famous TV actress, Julie Goodyear - Coronation Street's barmaid Bet Lynch.**

FAULKENER, John. *Leeds, Luton (1969-1977)* Caught the eye of Leeds United while starring in Sutton United's famous FA Cup run of 1969. Now on the coaching staff at Norwich City

FAZACKERLEY, Derek. *Blackburn, Chester, York, Bury. (1970-1988)* Played almost 600 games in central defence for Blackburn Rovers. Now First team coach at Newcastle United.

FEELEY, Andy. *Hereford, Leicester, Brentford, Bury (1978-1990)* Psychiatric nurse at Prestwich hospital, and currently playing for Bamber Bridge

Terry Fenwick

FELL, Jimmy. *Grimsby, Everton, Newcastle, Walsall, Lincoln. (1956-1965)* Former Grimsby winger, Still lives in the town and works as a Recreation Officer at Grimsby Leisure Centre.

FELTON, Graham. *Northampton, Barnsley (1966-1976)* Now working as a painter & decorator, from his home in Billing, Northants.

FENTON, Ron. *Burnley, WBA, Birmingham C, Brentford (1960-1969)* Became Coach at his last club, Notts County, then Assistant Manager at Notts Forest with Brian Clough for 16 seasons.

FENWICK, Terry. *C. Palace, QPR, Tottenham, Swindon, (1977-1995).* A £550,000 transfer in 1987 took Terry, who won one England cap, across London to Spurs from QPR. Finished playing at Swindon to take up the vacant manager's seat at Portsmouth in February 1995

FERGUSON, Bobby. *West Ham, Sheff Wed, (1967-1973).* **Emigrated to Australia in 1981 to take over as player/coach for Adelaide City FC. In 1982, became the owner/operator of a scuba diving business which he successfully ran for six years. However, Bobby sold his share after the enduring the horror of an employee being taken away by a shark. Has been company director of a flooring business ever since.**

FERGUSON, Mike. *Accrington S, Blackburn, Aston V, QPR, Cambridge, Rochdale, Halifax. (1960-1976)* Took over as Manager of Evagoras in Cyprus, September 1991, but now lives in Burnley from where he covers games for Terry Venables. Also has acted as a players agent.

FERN, Rod. *Leicester, Luton, Chesterfield, Rotherham U. (1967-1982)* Now Publican at the "Ferriers Arms", in Lount, Leicestershire

FERNS, Phil. *Bournemouth, Charlton, Wimbledon, Blackpool, Aldershot (1978-1985)* Lives in Poole, is F.A. Coaching rep for Dorset and an F.A. Fun week director. Playing for Trowbridge.

FERRIER, Ron. *Grimsby, Man U, Oldham, Lincoln (1933-1947)* Became a Schoolteacher, and lived in Cleethorpes until his death in 1991.

FIDLER, Dennis. *Man C, Port V, Grimsby, Halifax, Darlington (1957-1967)* Winger, who started at Manchester United as an amateur, then played professionally for rivals, City. Dennis set up his own business working as a fishmonger.

(Photo courtesy: Evening Sentinel, Stoke.)

FINNEY, Tom O.B.E. *Preston N.E. (1946-1959)* Undoubtedly one of the finest players to have played in the League, Tom scored 187 goals for his only club, Preston in 433 League games. In 1954 he became the first player to be chosen "Footballer of the Year", an honour he received again three years later. Tom played 76 times for England, retired from the game at the age of 38 in 1960 and was awarded the O.B.E. the following year. Had set up Tom Finney Ltd, plumbing, heating and electrical contractors in 1946, and held the role of managing director until 1992. Worked as a part time writer for the News of the World, and was Chairman of the Preston Health Authority from 1983 until 1987.

FIELDING, Wally. *Everton, Southport (1946-1959)* Played 381 games for Everton, went on to become manager at Southport, Coach at Luton, Youth Coach at Watford. Later Scouted for Luton.

FILLERY, Mike. *Chelsea, QPR, Portsmouth, Oldham, (1978-1992).* Strong former Chelsea midfielder, was Assistant Manager of BHL League side Crawley Town until August 1994.

FINNEY, Tom. *Luton, Sunderland, Camb U, Brentford, Camb U. (1973-1985)* Made 15 Appearances for Northern Ireland, but a back injury ended his career. Tom now works with Securicor.

FIRM, Neil *Leeds, Oldham, Peterboro(1979-1984)* Now a policeman working for the Norfolk Constabulary, currently based in Thetford.

FISHENDEN, Paul. *Wimbledon, Crewe (1981-1989)* Now plays for BHL side, Crawley Town.

FISHER, Bobby. *Leyton O, Camb U, Brentford (1973-1984)* **Former Orient full back, Bobby is now working as an Actor in television commercials and has recently appeared as a baddie in Sky TV's "Space Precinct".**

FISHER, Hugh. *Blackpool, Southampton, Southport (1963-1977)* Played almost 300 games for the Saints and still lives in the area, where he works as a representative for Courage brewery.

FLANAGAN, Mike. *Charlton, C Palace, QPR, Charlton, Camb U. (1971-1986)* Manager of Gillingham until early 1995, Mike then joined Diadora League side Hornchurch as a player!

FLETCHER, Paul. *Bolton, Burnley, Blackpool, (1968-1981).* Now risen to the heady heights of Chief Executive at Huddersfield Town FC. Also an accomplished after dinner speaker

FLOWERS, Ron. *Wolves, Northampton. (1952-1968)* Wing half who played 469 games for Wolves between 1952 and 1966 and won 49 England caps. Now lives near Stafford and runs his own Sports Shop in Wolverhampton. Father of Tim, the Blackburn and England keeper.

(Photo courtesy: Aberdeen Journals Ltd)

FITZPATRICK, John. *Man U, (1964-1972).* After eight successful years at Old Trafford at Wing half, injury forced John to quit at the age of 26. After a year off, he joined an Aberdeen wine company before setting up on his own in the same trade. Now works as a self employed agent selling quality French and German wine. Can also be regularly heard on local radio sports programmes.

FLINT, Kenny. *Tottenham, Aldershot, Leyton O. (1947-1958)* Outside left, who played over 300 games for Aldershot, Kenny now works for a firm of bookmakers in Enfield, Middlesex.

FLYNN, Brian. *Burnley, Leeds, Burnley, Cardiff, Doncaster, Bury, Wrexham (1972-1991)* Won 66 caps in a playing career which took him to Burnley in 1972 and then to Leeds United (1977-1982) before returning to Turf Moor. Spells at several other League Clubs and a time in Ireland led him to Wrexham, where in 1989 he was appointed Manager in succession to Dixie McNeill.

FOGG, David. *Wrexham, Oxford, (1970-1984).* Spent fifteen years at Oxford as player, coach and Assistant Manager. Then returned to his native Liverpool, joining the coaching staff at Everton.

FOGGO, Ken. *WBA, Norwich, Portsmouth, Southend. (1962-1975)* Retired from soccer in 1982 and began working on a London Market stall. Now believed to be running a dry cleaning business in the East End of the Capital.

FOGGON, Alan. *Newcastle, Cardiff, Middlesboro, Man U, Sunderland, Southend, Hartlepool, (1967-1977).* Winger, whose 45 goals in 105 games for Middlesborough prompted a move to Manchester United in 1976. Alan now lives in Jarrow, where he currently works as a Security manager for a North Eastern company.

FOLEY, Peter. *Oxford, Gillingham, Aldershot, Exeter. (1974-1986).* After a spell in Hong Kong, became Manager of Marlow FC until February 1995. Now on the management team at Hendon.

FOLEY, Theo. *Exeter, Northampton, Charlton. (1955-1967)* Was Coach at Arsenal and Manager of Northampton Town, before joining Southend United as assistant manager. Became part of their three man management team in early 1995.

FORBES, Duncan. *Colchester, Norwich, Torquay. (1961-1976)* Took his tally of league appearance to over 500 while at Norwich, following his move from Colchester in 1961. Now works for the 'Canaries' as their Chief scout.

FORD, David. *Sheff Wed, Newcastle, Sheffield, Halifax. (1963-1975)* Former England Under 21 inside forward, David is now running a Plumbing and Heating business in Sheffield.

FORD, Tony *Grimsby, Sunderland, Stoke, WBA., Grimsby, (1975-1992).* Speedy winger who won England 'B' honours and played in over 500 league games is now a Coach at Scunthorpe Utd.

FORD, Trevor. *Swansea, Aston V, Sunderland, Cardiff, Newport. (1946-1960)* **Centre forward who played 38 matches for his national team, Wales, Trevor now runs a Garage business. He was also a capable cricketer and was playing as a substitute fielder for Glamorgan in the match that Sir Garfield Sobers set a new world record by scoring six sixes in one over.**

FORGAN, Tommy. *Hull, York. (1953-1965)* Played 388 games for Hull. Also played for York in their 1954-5 FA Cup semi final, while in the Third Division North. Now lives in New Zealand.

FOREMAN, Dennis. *Brighton. (1952-1960)* Played 212 games for Brighton, scoring 62 goals. Also played Cricket for Sussex. Now a teacher at Shoreham Grammar school in the same county.

FORREST, Gerry. *Rotherham, Southampton, Rotherham. (1977-1990)* A serious knee injury suffered while at Southampton ended Gerry's career prematurely. Breifly coached at Darlington

FOSTER, Barry. *Mansfield, (1971-1981)* Played 282 games for Mansfield in the 70's, now runs a market stall selling shoes and slippers.

FOSTER, Colin. *Mansfield, Peterborough. (1971-1980)* Managed non-league sides: Corby Town, Peterborough City and Stamford, but now works as a painter in the Peterborough area.

FOULKES, Bill. *Man Utd (1952-1969)* Sadly, was forced to sell his collection of medals accrued during his very successful career with Manchester United, raising him £37,000 at Christies in October 1992. His last managerial post was over in Japan, in charge of the Mazda Club.

FOULKES, Reg. *Walsall, Norwich. (1946-1955)* Now a retired Accountant in Shrewsbury

FOWLER, Tom. *Northampton, Aldershot (1946-1962)* Played over 500 games for Northampton. Lives in the town working in a factory.

FOX, Peter. *Sheff Wed, Barnsley, Stoke, (1972-1990).* Took over as manager of Exeter City in June 1995 following Terry Cooper's resignation due to ill health. Peter had been voted the club's "Player of the Year" the season before.

FOX, Steve. *Birmingham, Wrexham, Port V, Chester. (1976-1985).* Skilful winger, ended at Chester in 1985 to become a lorry driver. Lives in Tamworth, currently working as a debt collector and helping out with old peoples gardens.

FRANCIS, Gerry. *QPR, C Palace, QPR, Coventry, Exeter, Cardiff, Swansea, Portsmouth, Bristol R. (1969-1987).* Captained club and country and would have won more than his twelve caps but for a series of niggling injuries. Cut his managerial teeth at Bristol Rovers (1987-1991) and Q.P.R.(1991-1994) before taking over at Tottenham Hotspur in November 1994. Also runs a successful antiques shop in Chertsey, Surrey.

FRANCIS, Trevor. *Birmingham, Notts F, Man C, QPR, Sheff Wed. (1970-1991)* Became Britain's first million-pound footballer (£1,150,000) when he joined Forest from Birmingham City in February 1979. moved into management with QPR before taking over at Sheffield Wednesday in 1991. A difficult 1994/5 season resulted in his departure from Hillsborough in May 1995.

(Courtesy: Evening Sentinel, Stoke)

FRANKLIN, Neil. *Stoke, Hull, Crewe, Stockport (1946-1957)* One of Stoke city's post war stars, Neil won 27 caps for England as a full back. Managed Colchester United and had a spell in Cyprus before becoming a publican in Oswaldthistle. Now retired living in the Potteries.

FRASER, Doug. *WBA, Notts F, Walsall. (1963-1973)* Wing half who played for West Brom in the League Cup finals of 1966, 1967 and 1970, and was a member of their F.A. Cup winning side against Everton. A Scottish international, who won two caps in the mid sixties, he ended his playing days at Walsall, where he was appointed Manager in 1975. Retired from football in 1977 to become a prison warder at Nottingham.

FRASER, John. *Fulham, Brentford (1971-1979).* Former full back, now lives in Chertsey, Surrey and works as a London Cabbie.

FRIZZELL, Jimmy. *Oldham (1960-1969)* Wing Half who played over 300 games for Oldham Athletic, and still lives close to Boundary Park despite having been employed by Manchester City for the past seven years.

FROGGATT, Jack. *Portsmouth, Leicester, (1946-1957).* Capped by England 13 times, won successive league championship medals in 1949 and 1950, during his time with Pompey, for whom he played 300 League games. Died in 1993, aged 71, having been in the licensed trade for 22 years.

FROGGATT, John. *Notts Co, Colchester, Port V, Northampton. (1963-1978).* Self employed Painter and decorator living in Mansfield.

FROGGATT, Redfern. *Sheff Wed, (1946-1959).* On the books at Hillsborough for seventeen years, and capped four times by England, Redfern followed in his fathers footsteps by playing for the Owls. Now retired from his job as a salesman for an oil fuel firm, living in Sheffield.

FRY, Barry *Man Utd, Bolton, Luton, Orient. (1962-1967)* Now known for his larger than life character as manager at Birmingham City, Barry was a Schoolboy International with enough promise to encourage the great Sir Matt Busby to sign him for Manchester United. However his league career was brief, in part due to injury. His passion for the game earned him the Managers job at non-league Dunstable and then Barnet. Although constantly in the news, more often than not, due to disagreements with equally colourful Chairmen, he has proved his pedigree by gaining Barnet entry into the League; bringing life (and Stan Collymore) to Southend; and then promotion to the Blues in his first full year in office.

FRY, Roger. *Southampton, Walsall (1970-1976)* Lives near Southampton and has worked as a production planner for Aerostructures since 1990

FRYATT, Jim. *Charlton, Southend, Bradford P.A., Southport, Torquay, Stockport, Blackburn, Oldham, Southport, Stockport, Torquay. (1959-1974)* **A traditional goalscoring centre forward who was well travelled during his playing days. He continued this trend by moving over to America when he retired from the game, becoming a croupier in a Las Vegas Casino**

FUCCILLO, Lil. *Luton, Southend, Peterboro, Camb U. (1974-1987).* Now lives near Bedford and was a Groundsman/coach at a local Private School, before returning to the game to become a member of the coaching staff at Birmingham City.

FUDGE, Micky *WBA, Exeter. (1963-1967)* Former Exeter inside forward is now landlord of the Lord Hill Public house in Dawley, Telford.

FUNNELL, Tony. *Southampton, Gillingham, Brentford, Bournemouth, (1972-1982).* Former Southampton winger, Tony is currently Manager of Wimborne Town FC in the Wessex League.

FURNELL, Jim. *Burnley, Liverpool, Arsenal, Rotherham, Plymouth. (1959-1975)* Best remembered as a keeper for Arsenal in the sixties and Plymouth Argyle in the seventies, Jim is now youth team manager at Blackburn Rovers.

FUTCHER, Paul *Chester, Luton, Man C, Oldham, Derby, Barnsley, Halifax, Grimsby T, (1972-1995).* Left Grimsby in January 1995 to become manager of Darlington, but relinquished the role after only ten games in April 1995

FUTCHER, Ron. *Chester, Luton, Man C, Barnsley, Oldham, Bradford C, Port V, Burnley, Crewe. (1973-1993).* Lives in Holmfirth a quarter of a mile away from his brother Paul. Runs a business from home selling sportswear to retail outlets throughout the North of England.

(Photo: Courtesy, Liverpool Echo)

GABRIEL, Jimmy. *Everton, Southampton, Bournemouth, Swindon, Brentford. (1959-1973)* One of the best strong tackling wing halfs of his day. Spent ten years in the America after ending his league career at Bournemouth, firstly as a player then coach for Seattle Sounders Returned to Bournemouth to become their Assistant Manager before accepting the same post at Everton. Now reserve team coach at Goodison Park.

GALLAGHER, Joe. *Birmingham, Wolves, West Ham, Burnley, (1973-1985).* England 'B' defender, managed Midland Combination club Kings Heath from July 1994 until February 1995.

GALLEY, John. *Wolves, Rotherham, Bristol C, Notts F, Peterboro, Hereford. (1961-1976).* Best remembered for his goal scoring at Bristol City where he netted 82 times in 174 games. Now a rep for the Berwick Paper Group in Leicester.

GALLOGLY, Charlie. *Huddersfield, Watford, Bournemouth (1949-1954)* **Northern Ireland international full back, moved over to America to run a public house in a suburb of New York.**

GALVIN, Tony. *Tottenham, Sheff Wed, Swindon, (1976-1989).* Former Spurs and Republic of Ireland international winger (29 caps) now works as a college lecturer, and is manager of Royston Town in the South Midlands League.

GARLAND, Chris. *Bristol C, Chelsea, Leicester, Bristol C. (1966-1982)* Popular blond haired forward who won one England Under 23 cap, started and ended his career scoring goals for his home club Bristol City. Still lives in the area but unfortunately suffers from Parkinsons disease.

GARNER, Alan. *Millwall, Luton, Watford, Portsmouth, (1969-1981).* Former Luton defender who is still a regular at Kenilworth Road, where he has an executive box for home games.

GARRETT, Tommy. *Blackpool, Millwall. (1946-1961)* England international defender who played over 300 games for Blackpool. Now believed to have emigrated and living in Australia.

GARWOOD, Colin. *Peterboro, Oldham, Huddersfield, Colchester, Portsmouth, Aldershot. (1967-1981)* Lives in Newark, Notts and works for an engineering company in Wisbech. Holds an FA Coaching badge and is keen to become involved with semi-professional soccer again.

GASKELL, Dave. *Man U, Wrexham. (1957-1971)* Lives in Wrexham and retired from his sales managers job due to achilles tendon trouble

GATES, Bill. *Middlesboro (1961-1973).* **Defender who starred for the "Boro" for 12 years. Made his fortune from sports shops, which he sold and moved to live in the Cayman Islands.**

GATES, Eric. *Ipswich, Sunderland, Carlisle, (1973-1980).* Member of Bobby Robson's successful Ipswich Team. Now lives in Barnard Castle and is player/coach with West Auckland Town, a team managed by his brother, Alan !

GATTING, Steve. *Arsenal, Brighton, Charlton, (1977-1993)* Brother of England cricketer, Mike. Played for Brighton in their 1983 FA Cup final side, now turning out for Stamco FC.

GEDDIS, David. *Ipswich, Luton, Aston V, Luton, Barnsley, Birmingham, Brentford, Shrewsbury, Swindon, Darlington. (1976-1990)* Well travelled goalscoring striker, David is now working as youth team coach at Middlesborough.

GEMMILL, Archie. *Preston, Derby, Notts F, Birmingham, Wigan, Derby. (1967-1983)* Archie collected two Championship medals in a magical period with Derby, and another at Notts Forest, again under Brian Clough. Was reserve coach at Forest until May 94. Became manager at Rotherham in October 1994, linking up again with John McGovern, who is now his assistant.

GENNOE, Terry. *Bury, Halifax, Southampton, C Palace, Blackburn (1972-1993)* Now lives in Preston and is an Education Officer (coach) with the Learning Through Football Scheme.

GEORGE, Charlie. *Arsenal, Derby, Southampton, Notts F, Bournemouth, Derby. (1969-1981)* One of the games most colourful characters. Best remembered for his time at Arsenal, when his goalscoring was a major factor in the club's League and Cup double win in 1971. Won one full cap and five at Under 23 level, and retired in 1983. After a spell in Hong Kong and then running a pub in Hampshire, Charlie returned to London to become a partner in a garage firm. Now helps out back at Highbury as a Match day host and running the club museum. Also can be seen on SKY Sports soccer shows.

GIBBINS, Roger. *Tottenham, Oxford, Norwich, Cambridge, Cardiff, Swansea, Newport, Torquay, Cardiff (1972-1994).* Eight club man Roger, coached at the last of them, Cardiff City until cost cutting resulted in his dismissal in June 1994

GIBSON, Dave. *Leicester, Aston Villa, Exeter C. (1961-1972)* Opened a pet food and garden shop in Exmouth before moving back to Leicestershire. He has been a postman for the past twelve years and is also co-owner of a residential rest home. **Dave is ribbed by his children about an incident in the 1963 FA Cup final while he was playing for Leicester against Man Utd. Gordon Banks threw the ball out to him, but Dave failed to control it, allowing Paddy Crerand to pinch the ball and cross for Denis Law to score This is now regularly shown on television, and his kids say "You have been trying to trap that ball for twenty years and still miss it !!"**

(Photo courtesy: Chris Floyd.)

Charlie George flanked by two more great characters, **Ron Harris** and **Stan Bowles**

GIBSON, Mike. *Shrewsbury, Bristol C, Gillingham. (1960-1973)* Mike helps coach the Bristol City youth side and works as a postman.

GIBSON, Terry. *Tottenham, Coventry, Man U, Wimbledon, Swindon, Barnet, (1979-1995).* Won 11 England Under 21 caps as a bustling forward. Terry is now Player/youth team coach at Barnet.

GIDMAN, John. *Aston V, Everton, Man U, Man C, Stoke, Darlington (1972-1988).* Everton broke their club record to acquire England international (1 cap) John from Aston Villa in 1979. Was manager of Kings Lynn until early 1995.

Billy Gilbert *(Courtesy Portsmouth News)*

GILBERT, Billy. *Crystal Palace, Portsmouth, Colchester U, Maidstone. (1977-1990).* A member of the Crystal Palace 'Team of the Eighties' and a regular England Under 23international. Now buys and sells second hand cars and is manages Waterlooville in the Beazer Homes League.

GILBERT, Tim. *Sunderland, Cardiff, Darlington (1976-1983).* Suddenly died in 1995 aged only 36, whilst coaching a local junior team.

GILCHRIST, Paul. *Charlton, Doncaster, Southampton, Portsmouth, Swindon, Hereford (1969-1979)* Ran a health and fitness club in Swindon, but now works for B.M.W. in Sussex.

GILES, David. *Cardiff, Wrexham, Swansea, Leyton O, C Palace, BirminghamC, Newport , Cardiff . (1974-1986)* Became a double glazing salesman after AFC Cardiff's sponsor pulled out of supporting, the club. Now manages Ebbw Vale.

(Photo courtesy: Daily Express.)

GILES, Johnny. *Man U, Leeds, WBA. (1959-1976).* Won trophies galore, in all he played in 11 FA Cup semi finals and shares the record for FA Cup final appearances. He was the first Eire player to win 50 full caps for his country, his final tally was 60 including a spell as player/manager. In total he made 863 league appearances in a magnificent career, before progressing into management with WBA (1975-77), Philadelphia Fury (NASL), Vancouver Whitecaps (NASL), West Brom (February 1984 to September 1985). Now writes a regular column for the Daily Express.

GILES, Jim. *Swindon, Aldershot, Exeter, Charlton, Exeter. (1965-1980)* Central defender Jim, is now a Builder in Ottery St Mary, Devon.

GILL, Eric. *Charlton, Brighton. (1951-1959)* Goalkeeper, who played 280 games for Brighton, now runs a hotel in the Sussex seaside resort.

GILLARD, Ian. *QPR, Aldershot. (1968-1985)* Made over 400 appearances for Q.P.R. Helped run Aldershot's School of Excellence, then became manager. Now Chief scout at Loftus Road

GILLIGAN, Jimmy. *Watford, Lincoln, Grimsby, Swindon, Lincoln, Cardiff, Portsmouth, Swansea, (1981-1993).* Wore the colours of eight league clubs and is now playing for Stamco FC.

GILLIVER, Alan. *Huddersfield, Blackburn, Rotherham, Brighton., Lincoln, Bradford C, Stockport, Bradford C (1962-1978).* A well travelled centre forward, Alan is now working as Stadium manager at Bradford City's Valley Parade.

GILZEAN, Alan. *Tottenham, (1964-1973)* After his ten years at Spurs, Alan had a spell in South Africa, before returning to Manage Stevenage from May 1975 to August 1976. Now a transport manager for a Lorry firm in Enfield. His son Ian is now on the books at Northampton

GLAZIER, Bill. *C Palace, Coventry, Brentford (1961-1975)* Moved to Spain in 1986, having made his money through property. He once owned a hotel on Brighton seafront, but now can be seen around the seafront of Benidorm in Spain, where he now lives. He earns his beer money by cleaning and maintaining swimming pools.

(Photo courtesy: Raymonds Press Agency)

GLOVER, Len. *Charlton, Leicester (1962-1975)* Great former Leicester City winger, now a publican in Kibworth, Leicestershire and was manager of Harlow Town FC until January 1995.

GODDARD, Paul. *QPR, West Ham, Newcastle, Derby, Millwall, Ipswich, (1977-1995).* 'Sarge' (nicknamed as a result of his connection with the Boys Brigade) won one England cap and broke the West Ham transfer record when he moved across London to Upton Park for £800,000 in 1980. Now First team coach at Ipswich

GODDARD, Ray. *Leyton O, Millwall, Wimbledon. (1966-1980)* **Kept goal in over 300 league games for his three London based clubs. Ray now owns and runs a Bar in sunny Spain.**

GODDEN, Tony. *WBA, Luton, Walsall, Chelsea, Birmingham, Bury, Peterboro. (1976-1989).* Played 267 League games for West Bromwich Albion, Tony is now Manager of Kings Lynn FC

GODFREY, Brian. *Everton, Scunthorpe, Preston, Aston V, Bristol R, Newport. (1959-1975)* Brian appeared in 557 matches and netted 128 goals. He played for Portland Timbers in 1975-6 and then took over as Manager of Gloucester City in January 1992 and works as a site agent for a building company owned by the Club's Chairman.

GODFREY, Kevin. *Orient, Plymouth, Brentford, (1977-1993).* Played 255 games on the wing for Orient now a taxi driver in West London.

GODFREY, Tony. *Southampton, Aldershot, Rochdale, Aldershot. (1958-1975)* Now runs his own Building business in Basingstoke, Hants.

GODWIN, Tommy. *Leicester, Bournemouth (1949-1961)* **Bournemouth goalie for nine years, playing 350 League games. Spent 20 years as a paint sprayer followed by 8 years as a parks patrolman before retiring. His one regret from his playing days was that he left his teeth in the dressing room during one of his 13 appearances for the Republic of Ireland: they were 2-0 up with ten minutes to go when the Danish supporters, accusing them of time-wasting, decided to pelt his penalty area with apples !!**

(Photo courtesy: Southampton Evening Echo.)

GOLAC, Ivan. *Southampton, Bournemouth, Man C, Southampton, Portsmouth. (1978-1984)* Succeeded Jim McLean as manager of Dundee United in 1993 and held the post until March 1995. Born in Croatia, Ivan signed for the 'Saints' in 1978 after 16 years with Partizan Belgrade. Returned home to coach Partizan and then them National team manager and as manager at Torquay before moving north of the border.

GOODFELLOW, Jim. *Port V, Workington, Rotherham, Stockport. (1966-1978).* Now working as Club Physiotherapist at Cardiff City.

GOODING, Mick. *Rotherham, Chesterfield, Rotherham, Peterboro, Wolves, Reading, (1979-1995).* In January 1995, appointed joint manager of Reading with team-mate Jimmy Quinn.

GOODWIN, Freddie *Wolves, Stockport, Blackburn, Southport, Port V, Stockport (1961-1974).* **At 28 years old Goodwin passed his full coaching badge and after retiring as a pro embarked on a thirteen year period coaching in New Zealand. He won two championships with his first club Stop Out before coaching Papatoetoe, Hut Valley Utd and Columbus Waterside. He also spent two years as assistant coach to the New Zealand national team and was coaching director for the School of Excellence. Fred moved back to Stockport to live in November 1993 to the family home right opposite the Railway End of Edgeley Park.**

GOODYEAR, Clive. *Luton, Plymouth, Wimbledon, Brentford, (1979-1990).* Won a cup winners medal with Wimbledon in 1988, he was adjudged to have fouled John Aldridge which led to Dave Beasant becoming the first goalkeeper to save a penalty in an FA Cup final. Has now returned to Luton where he is Club Physiotherapist

GORDON, Colin *Swindon, Wimbledon, Gillingham, Reading, Bristol C, Fulham, Birmingham, Hereford, Walsall, Bristol R, Leicester (1984-1993)* Well travelled striker who played for eleven clubs. Colin is now player/manager at Stourbridge FC in the Beazer Homes League.

GORDON, Dennis. *WBA, Brighton. (1947-1960).* Now retired and living in Hove, Sussex.

GORDON, John. *Portsmouth, Birmingham, Portsmouth (1951-1966).* Johnny played over 500 games Now co-owner of Littles Wine Bar in Southsea, still attends all Pompey home matches.

GORING, Peter. *Arsenal (1949-1958)* Played 220 games for the "Gunners". Became a butcher in Cheltenham, but died in December 1994.

GORMAN, John. *Carlisle, Tottenham, (1970-1978).* Managed Swindon until November 1994. Then joined Bristol City as assistant manager.

GOULD, Bobby. *Coventry, Arsenal, Wolves, WBA, Bristol C, West Ham, Wolves, Bristol R, Hereford. (1963-1979)* Managed Wimbledon to the FA Cup final success of 1988, and was later in charge of WBA and Coventry. Now presents "Talk Back" on Sky Television's Sports Channel.

Trevor Gould

GOULD, Trevor. *Coventry, Northampton. (1969-1972).* Has been Youth Team Manager at Coventry City FC for the past three years, having previously managed Bedford and Aylesbury

GOWLING, Alan. *Man U, Huddersfield, Newcastle, Bolton, Preston. (1967-1982).* A graduate of Manchester University, Alan won England Under 23 honours during his four yeas at old Trafford. Is now General Manager of a Chemicals company based in Buxton, Derbyshire.

GRAHAM, Arthur. *Leeds, Man U, Bradford C. (1977-1986)* Coaches children with the Eddie Gray coaching schools. Arthur has been out of football since leaving Halifax Town, but still turns out for the ex-Leeds United charity side.

GRAHAM, George. *Aston V, Chelsea, Arsenal, Man U, Portsmouth, C Palace. (1962-1977)* Retired from playing in 1980, joining the staff at Q.P.R. Became Manager at Millwall in December 1982, then Arsenal boss for nine years until early 1995. Despite becoming the most successful manager in their history and insisting that he was innocent, Arsenal terminated his employment after a well publicised scandal which accused him of taking transfer related inducements.

GRAHAM, Jackie. *Brentford (1970-1979)* Although born in Scotland, Jackie played 371 League games for his only League club, Brentford. He is now employed as a Security Guard for American Airways based at Heathrow Airport. Coached at Cranleigh until October 1994.

GRAHAM, Tommy. *Barnsley, Halifax T, Doncaster R, Scunthorpe U, Scarborough, Halifax T, (1978-1992).* Lives in Barnsley and works as a Surgical Chiropodist. Still plays non-league soccer, currently for Grimethorpe M.W.

GRANT, Jackie. *Everton, Rochdale, Southport. (1946-1959).* Retired in Liverpool opposite Goodison Park where he played for eight years.

GRAVER, Andy. *Newcastle, Lincoln, Leicester, Lincoln, Stoke, Lincoln. (1947-1960)* Prolific goalscorer with Lincoln in three spells , netted 144 times in 276 league games. Found the net six times during their 11-1 record victory in 1951, the year that they won the Third Division North title. Now retired living near Lincoln after spending 15 years working for the Bank of Scotland.

(Photo courtesy: Sky Sports)

GRAY, Andy. *Aston V, Wolves, Everton, Aston V, Notts Co, WBA. (1975-1988).* Scottish international striker Andy Gray joined Aston Villa in 1975 for £110,000. his stay at Villa park lasted four years before Wolves broke the British transfer record fee to sign Gray for £1,469,000 in September 1989. He won 20 caps for Scotland, was voted PFA 'Player of the Year' and 'Young Player of the Year' in 1977. He returned to Villa Park in the summer of 1991 as assistant manger to Ron Atkinson following a period as a player for Cheltenham Town. Gray's direct attitude is now being utilised as a leading pundit on SKY Sports, and hosts his own show, 'The Boot Room'.

GRAY, Eddie. *Leeds (1965-1983).*Eddie won all the individual honours that Scotland could offer, as did his brother, Frank. He turned professional for Leeds in 1965 and went on to gain two championship medals in 1968/9 and 1973/4, as well as being a member of the team that were first division runners up on four different occasions. Other honours included FA Cup; League Cup; and Fairs Cup winners medals. Had a spell in Management at Leeds, then Rochdale. Now runs soccer camps for youngsters in Yorkshire.

GRAY, Frank. *Notts F, Leeds, Sunderland, Darlington. (1972-1991).* Won 32 caps for Scotland as a player, and went on to Manage Darlington then scout for Blackburn and Sheffield Wednesday. Frank resigned after a brief stay as manager of Harrogate FC in June 1994 to take up a post in the sunshine of Bahrain.

GRAY, Stuart *Notts F, Bolton, Barnsley, Aston V, Southampton. (1980-1994)* When his playing career was prematurely ended by injury, Stuart joined his old boss, Graham Taylor at Wolves, in the role of Reserve Team Manager. However, his family could not settle in the Midlands, so returned South to the house that they had not been able to sell, and now plays for Bognor Regis.

GRAY, Terry. *Huddersfield, Southend, Bradford C, Preston. (1973-1985).* Now working as a financial consultant and lives in Liversedge.

GRAY, William P. *Leyton O, Chelsea, Burnley, Notts F, Millwall. (1947-1964).* Now retired from his role as groundsman at Nottingham Forest .

GRAYDON, Ray. *Bristol R, Aston V, Coventry, Oxford. (1965-1980).* **Scorer of the winning goal in the 1975 League Cup final for Aston Villa at Wembley, Ray had plenty of practice as a young lad, pretending to take part in a victory lap around Wembley. However, when the real moment arrived he was pulled into the crowd and then suffered cramp for the first time in his career - and had to just watch as the rest of his team-mates enjoyed their moment of glory. Later served Coventry City and Washington Diplomats in the United States before joining Oxford United in November 1978 first as a player (retiring in 1981), and thereafter as senior coach. Moved down to the South Coast and Southampton, where he is currently working as the club's youth team manager.**

GREALISH, Tony. *Leyton O, Luton, Brighton, WBA, Man C, Rotherham, Walsall. (1974-1991)* Player/coach for Bromsgrove Rovers until Bobby Hope's resignation in January 1995, when he briefly took over the managerial reins. Now registered as a player with Sandwell Borough.

GREAVES, Danny. *Southend, Camb U, (1981-1984).* Scored 14 goals in 30 games for Southend, where he is now part of a three man management team appointed in 1995. Son of Jimmy.

GREAVES, Ian. *Man U, Lincoln, Oldham. (1954-1962)* Manager at Mansfield Town. Now retired but still can be seen watching matches, acting as a scout for a number of clubs.

GREAVES, Jimmy *Chelsea, Tottenham, West Ham. (1957-1970).* Capped 57 times by England, started his career at Chelsea scoring an incredible 124 goals in 157 league games. After a spell in Italy, returned to the capital to continue rattling in the goals for Tottenham (220 goals in 330 league games) and then finally for West Ham. His bright cheery face and witty view of life have livened up many a television sports programme . His successful double act with Ian St John has now been reinstated on Independent television in a variation of their old "Saint & Greavsie" show.

GREAVES, Roy. *Bolton, Rochdale. (1965-1982).* Played almost 500 games in the Bolton Wanderers midfield. Now runs the Monteraze Public House in the town, close to Boundary Park.

GREEN, Billy *Hartlepool, Carlisle, West Ham, Peterborough, Chesterfield, Doncaster. (1969-1983).* Central defender who played for six league clubs including a brief stint at West Ham. Now manager of Buxton in the H.F.S. Loans League.

GREEN, Colin. *Everton, Birmingham, Wrexham (1960-1970).* Full back who won 15 Welsh caps now lives in Wrexham and works as a sales representative for a veterinary company.

GREEN, Les. *Hull, Hartlepool, Rochdale, Derby. (1961-1970).* Ex-Derby County goalkeeper who had gained experience at Hull, Hartlepool and Rochdale. Appointed manager of Bedworth in March 1995 having previously been in charge at Nuneaton Borough, Hinckley and Tamworth.

GREEN, Tony. *Blackpool, Newcastle. (1966-1972).* Had to retire at the age of only 27 due to knee trouble, but still managed to win six Scottish caps. Now a schoolteacher in Blackpool.Also a member of Littlewoods Pools panel.

GREENER, Ron. *Newcastle, Darlington (1953-1966)* Now a car salesman in Darlington, where he had appeared over 400 times for he local side in his thirteen year playing career.

GREENHALGH, Brian. *Preston, Aston V, Leicester, Huddersfield, Camb U, Bournemouth, Torquay, Watford, (1965-1975).* Played for eight league clubs in ten years before finishing in 1975. Now works at Everton as their Chief Scout.

GREENHOFF, Brian. *Man U, Leeds, Rochdale. (1973-1983).* England international defender (18 caps) who moved from Manchester United to Leeds United for £350,000 in 1979. Now lives in Rochdale and works as a sales representative for a sports goods wholesalers, William Lindop Sports. Also helps coach Chadderton FC in the Carling North West Counties League, the side that his son Paul plays for !

GREENHOFF, Jimmy *Leeds, Birmingham, Stoke, Man U, Crewe, Port V, Rochdale. (1963-1983).* Greenhoff spent most of his career in the first division. After making his name with Stoke City, he was sold to Man United in 1976 for £100,000, and was a major contributor to their FA Cup winning side of the following year. Now runs his own insurance business, Greenhoff Peutz & Co, in Audley, on the outskirts of Stoke.

GREGG, Harry. *Doncaster, Man U, Stoke. (1952-1966).* One of Manchester United's survivors of the Munich air disaster, goalkeeper Harry now owns a hotel in Port Stewart, Ulster.

GREGORY, David. *Peterborough, Stoke, Blackburn, Bury, Portsmouth. Wrexham, Peterboro (1973-1986).* Lives in Holbeach and plays for the local team in the United Counties League. Works as a self employed ceramic tiler and turns out for the ex-Peterborough XI

(Courtesy: West Ham "Who's Who")

GREGORY, Ernie. *West Ham (1946-1959)* England 'B' international who was West ham's first choice keeper for many years after the war. Now retired but caught up with old pals at the launch of the West Ham Who's Who book in 1995.

GREGORY, John. *Northampton, Aston V, Brighton., QPR, Derby, Portsmouth, Plymouth, Bolton. (1972-1989).* Assistant Manager at Leicester City until November 1994, when he followed his manager, Brian Little to Aston Villa.

GREGORY, Tony. *Shrewsbury (1964-1975).* **Served his only club, Shrewsbury for 11 years and was pleasantly surprised to be recognised several years later, by a man the next bed to a relative that he was visiting in hospital - only to be bought back down to earth when the patient said " I used to watch you play - and, by Christ, you had some bad games!" Now lives in Bridgenorth, Shropshire and has worked as an Executive officer for the M.O.D. since 1980.**

GRIFFIN, Colin. *Derby, Shrewsbury. (1974-1988).* Had a time as Coach at Shrewsbury Town before leaving to play for Worcester City. Now working as a postman in the Shrewsbury area.

GRIFFITHS, Arfon. *Wrexham, Arsenal, Wrexham. (1959-1978)* Played almost 600 games for Wrexham and had a spell at Arsenal. Gained international recognition for Wales on 17 occasions and awarded the M.B.E. in 1976. Now runs his own newsagents in Gresford near Wrexham.

GRIFFITHS, Harold. *Swansea (1949-1963).*Died in 1978 at the age of only 47 while working in the treatment room at Swansea City. He had previously served the Vetch Field Club as player (424 appearances), coach, chief scout, assistant manager, and then finally as manager.

GRIMES, Ashley. *Man U, Coventry, Luton, Stoke, (1977-1991).* Back at Old Trafford on the coaching staff of his old club, Manchester United

Steve Gritt

GRITT, Steve. *Bournemouth, Charlton, Walsall, Charlton. (1976-1993).* Until June 1995 held the post of Joint manager at Charlton, where he made over 300 league appearances as a player.

GROVES, Alan. *Southport, Chester C, Shrewsbury T, AFC Bournemouth, Oldham Ath, Blackpool. (1968-1977).* Former Oldham Athletic wingman, sadly died in 1978, aged only 30.

GROVES, Perry. *Colchester, Arsenal, Soton, (1981-1994).* Forced to retire through injury in 1994, but played in the Vauxhall Conference for Dagenham & Redbridge, until February 1995.

GROVES, Victor. *Tottenham, Leyton O, Arsenal. (1952-1963)* Retired from playing in 1965 and became a publican in Edmonton.. Later took a job as a salesman, and then worked his way up to Branch manager with Hambro Insurance.

GRUMMITT, Peter. *Notts F, Sheff Wed, Brighton. (1960-1976).* England Under 23 who was first choice keeper at Nottingham Forest for almost a decade, clocking up over 500 appearances in his three club playing career.. Now the owner of a, newsagents in Bourne, Lincolnshire.

GUDMUNDSSON, Albert. *Arsenal (1946-1947).* **After a playing career which saw him play for a selection of clubs in Scotland, Italy, France, and Arsenal in England, Albert returned to his native Iceland to become a successful businessman. He was President of the Icelandic FA and later was appointed French Consul in Iceland, then FINANCE MINISTER in Reykjavik. Died in May 1994 aged 70.**

GUNTER, Philip. *Portsmouth, Aldershot, (1951-1965).* England 'B' international played over 300 games for Pompey before emigrating to Australia where he now lives in retirement.

GURR, Gerry. *Southampton, Aldershot (1966-1971)* **Former Southampton and Aldershot goalkieQuit football in 1971 to become a musician. Now lives in Stow on the Wold, strums his guitar for a living, as well as acting as musical director for his wife, the singer Lee Ann.**

GUTHRIE, Jimmy *Portsmouth, C Palace, (1937-1946).* Scottish wing half who played for Pompey and Crystal Palace became a leading sports writer with the Sunday People. Died in a London hospital aged 68 in September 1981.

GUY, Dickie *Wimbledon (1977)* The Don's keeper when they joined the league and hero of their famous mid 70's FA Cup run as a Southern League side. Dickie is now a builder in Mitcham.

GWYTHER, David. *Swansea, Halifax, Rotherham, Newport, (1965-1984).* Welsh under 23 midfielder, is now a partner in Jones & Gwyther Painting & Decorating in Swansea.

HABBIN, Dick *Reading, Rotherham, Doncaster. (1969-1978)* Dick is now running his own Building business in Maltby, near Rotherham.

HAGAN, James. *Derby, Sheff U (1935-1957)* England international, who scored 116 goals in his 361 league games for Sheffield United. Now retired, living in Walsall, West Midlands.

HAGUE, Neil. *Rotherham, Plymouth, Bournemouth, Huddersfield, Darlington. (1967-1978).* Now in Property development in Plymouth.

(Courtesy: Kent Messenger Group)

HALES, Derek. *Luton, Charlton, Derby, West Ham, Charlton, Gillingham, (1972-1985).* Great goalscorer who netted 148 goals from his 312 league games. Ran a pub for eight years, but now lives in Sittingbourne and describes his current occupation as "constructional enterprises".

HAIR, Grenville. *Leeds (1950-1963).* Made 443 league appearances for Leeds United. Grenville died in March 1968, aged only 36, when as manager of Bradford City he had a heart attack while supervising a training session.

HALL, Brian. *Liverpool, Plymouth, Burnley. (1968-1979).* Now works as an Public relations executive and head of the community project at Liverpool FC, the club he originally joined as a player from Manchester University in 1968.

HALL, Brian. *Mansfield, Colchester (1958-1972).* A left sided player who made over 300 league appearances for Colchester. He now works in the town for a local heating company.

HALL, Ian. *Derby, Mansfield (1959-1968).* **Ex-Derby County forward who also played cricket for Derbyshire, has certainly made the most of life since retiring from sport. An honours degree was gained at Birmingham University, followed by a Certificate of Education at Loughborough College. He pursued a career in teaching after a spell at Coventry working as a co-ordinator of "Enterprise Sky Blue" However, since 1990 Ian has been a freelance journalist and broadcaster for Radio Derby.**

HALL, James. *Northampton, Peterborough, Cambridge. (1963-1976)* James is now working as a Schoolteacher in a Northampton school.

HALL, John. *Bradford C (1962-1973)* Spent eleven years running down the wing for Bradford . Now a postman, living in Yeadon, Guiseley.

HALOM, Vic. *Charlton, Leyton O, Fulham, Luton, Sunderland, Oldham, Rotherham (1965-1980)* An FA Cup winner with Sunderland, Vic managed Burton, but now works as a P.R. man with Oldham based firm, New Earth Plumbing.

HAM, Bobby. *Bradford P.A., Grimsby, Bradford P.A., Bradford C, Preston, Rotherham, Bradford. (1961-1974)* Bradford born striker who had two spells with each of his home town clubs. Formed the Ham Group in the town. (Ham Plant Hire; Challoner Lighting; Wall Electrical)

HAMILTON, Billy. *QPR, Burnley, Oxford. (1978-1986)* Northern Ireland international who won 41 caps now combines his role as Manager of Distillery in Ireland, with earning his living by selling sporting goods and equipment.

HAMILTON, Bryan. *Ipswich, Everton, Millwall, Swindon, Tranmere, (1971-1984).* Experience gained managing Tranmere; Wigan; and Leicester City, made Bryan the right man for the job when the Northern Ireland team needed a new team manager in 1994. Had previously won 50 full caps and Under 23 honours as a player.

HAMILTON, Ian (Chico). *Chelsea, Southend, Aston V, Sheff U. (1966-1977).* Ian was 18 when he joined Aston Villa from Southend for £40,000 and helped them win the Third Division championship in 1972. In July 1976 he signed for Sheffield United, then spent two years in America. Now works for the Nike organisation coaching soccer, and as a play scheme organiser at Sheffield University. He also finds time to coach and organise soccer at the local "Ritz Super Soccer" complex, mainly working with 5 to 16 year old's.

Eoin Hand

HANCOCKS, Johnny. *Walsall, Wolves (1938-1955)* Scored 158 goals from 343 appearances and won three England caps. known as the "Mighty Atom", because of his 5ft 4in frame and size two boots. Joined Wolves in 1946 from Walsall for £4,000. Went on to work in a local iron foundry in his home town, Oakengates before retiring in 1979. Died in 1994 aged 75.

HAND, Eoin. *Swindon, Portsmouth (1964-1978).* The former Eire international defender, clocked up 300 appearances for Portsmouth. His playing days also took him to South Africa and Limerick. Eoin later had spells as manager of the Republic Of Ireland national side and Huddersfield Town. Now coaching in South Africa.

HANDYSIDES, Ian. *Birmingham, Walsall, Birmingham C, Wolverhampton W. (1980-1986)* Former England youth international winger, died in 1990 after a two year illness, aged only 27.

HANKIN, Ray. *Burnley, Leeds, Middlesboro, Peterborough, Wolves. (1972-1984)* Ray had spells as manager of Northallerton Town, then Darlington. Now working as a football in the community officer based at Newcastle United.

HANSEN, Allan. *Liverpool, (1977-1989).* Joined Liverpool in the Summer of 1977 as a £110,000 signing from Partick Thistle and went on to win every domestic honour possible. He played over 400 League games, captained the Reds to their 1986 League and Cup double success, three European Cups, one FA Cup win, seven League Championships, four League Cups and was capped 26 times by Scotland. Can now be seen working on BBCtv as an analyst on "Match of the Day" and "Sportsnight" as well as writing a column for the Today newspaper.

HANSON, Stanley. *Bolton (1936-1955)* Bolton Wanderers' first choice goalkeeper for many years, making over 350 League appearances either side of the Second World War. Died in 1987.

HANVEY, Keith. *Swansea, Rochdale, Grimsby, Huddersfield, Rochdale. (1971-1984)* Now Commercial Executive with Huddersfield Town, where he played over 200 league games.

HARBURN, Peter. *Brighton, Everton, Scunthorpe, Workington. (1954-1960)* Former Brighton centre forward, Peter is now manager of a public house in Chelmsford, Essex.

HARDWICK, George. *Middlesboro, Charlton. (1937-1955).* Became player/manager at Oldham, followed by Managerial appointments with P.S.V. Eindhoven, Sunderland and the Dutch National team. Lives in Stokesley near Middlesborough and recently retired as M.D. of a quality assurance company. Regularly seen at Ayresome Park, where he acts as a V.I.P. host.

HARFORD, Ray. *Charlton, Exeter, Lincoln Mansfield, Port V, Colchester. (1965-1974)* Ended at Colchester where he became coach before moving to Fulham as Youth Coach in 1981. Promoted to manager at Craven Cottage in May 1984 following Malcolm MacDonald's resignation. Became Assistant Manager at Blackburn Rovers, then team manager in June 1995 following Kenny Dalglish's elevation to General Manager.

HARLAND, Stan. *Everton, Bradford C, Carlisle, Swindon, Birmingham (1959-1972)* Captained Swindon to League Cup success in 1968/9 and coached at Portsmouth before taking over the delicatessen that he now runs near Yeovil.

HARRIS, Alan. *Chelsea, Coventry, Chelsea, QPR, Plymouth, Camb U, (1960-1973).* Brother of Ron, went to do a spell of coaching in the Middle East and has also acted as a players agent.

HARRIS, Bill *Hull, Middlesboro, Bradford C (1949-1965)* Voted the best wing half during the 1958 World Cup finals, although only capped six times in total. Ended as player/manager at Bradford City. Died in 1989 on Tyneside aged 61.

HARRIS, Brian. *Everton, Cardiff, Newport. (1955-1973)* Wing half who turned out in the Blue of Everton on more than 300 occasions in the 50's and 60's. After a period as Manager at Newport, went on to manage a pub in Chepstow, but now runs his own promotions business in the area.

HARRIS, Carl. *Leeds, Charlton, Bury, Rochdale, Exeter C. (1974-1988)* Returned to South Wales in 1989 to play for Briton Ferry in the Welsh League. Later appointed player/manager with the extra duties of general manager.

(Courtesy: Portsmouth News)

HARRIS, Peter. *Portsmouth (1946-1959).* England international winger (2 caps), who scored 194 goals in his 480 matches for Portsmouth in their glory years of the late 40's and early 50's. Now retired, living in Hayling Island, Hampshire.

HARRIS, Harry. *Newport, Portsmouth, Newport, (1954-1970).* Inside forward who clocked up over 500 league appearances for Portsmouth and Newport County in his sixteen year career, now runs a Double Glazing business in Leeds.

HARRIS, Ron. *Chelsea, Brentford. (1961-1983)* **'Chopper' was undoubtedly one of the sternest tests for any forward during the sixties and seventies, when he marshalled the Chelsea defence on more than 600 occasions. After a spell as Manager of Brentford, Ron brought Bramhill golf course in Wiltshire for £400,000 and is reputed to have sold it in 1989 for £2 million to Golf pro Roger Mace and ex-Doncaster Rovers and Aldershot Goalkeeper - Glen Johnson !! Now owns a holiday chalet and fishing complex in a picturesque setting in a village near Warminster, Wiltshire.**

HARRIS, William. *Hull, Middlesboro, Bradford C. (1949-1965).* Welsh international who played almost 500 League matches, died in 1989.

HARRISON, Chris. *Plymouth, Swansea (1975-1987)* Played over 500 league games for his two clubs. Now returned to his roots, running a successful Driving School back in South East Cornwall. Recently resigned as manager of Saltash FC in the Great Mills Western League.

HARRISON, Mark. *Soton, Port V, Stoke (1978-1982)* Manager of Stafford Rangers in the GM Vauxhall Conference until June 1995 when he joined the coaching staff at Oxford United.

HARRISON, Steve. *Blackpool, Watford, Charlton (1971-1981)* Assistant manager at Wolverhampton Wanderers, continuing his successful partnership with manager, Graham Taylor.

HARRISON, Wayne. *Oldham, Liverpool, Crewe. (1984-1991)* Became the most expensive 17 year old in 1985 following a move to Liverpool. However, a succession of injuries led to his release in May 1991. Lives in Stockport in the house purchased with proceeds from the move. Now considering a career in sports management.

HART, Paul. *Stockport, Blackpool, Leeds, Nottingham, Sheffield W Birmingham, Notts Co. (1970-1987).* Director of Youth Coaching at Elland Road, where he played 191 league games for Leeds himself between 1978 and 1983.

HARTFORD, Asa. *WBA, Man C, Notts F, Everton, Man C, Norwich, Bolton, Stockport, Oldham, Shrewsbury. (1967-1990)* A midfield dynamo who hit the headlines when dramatically turned down by Leeds after virtually signing from West Brom, when it was discovered that he had a heart ailment However all this was forgotten when big money moves took him to Man City (£225,000), Notts Forest (£400,000) and Everton (£450,000). Won 50 Scottish caps and has since coached at Stockport, Oldham, Shrewsbury, Blackburn and Stoke. Asa was appointed Assistant manager at Manchester City in July 1995.

HARTLEY, Trevor. *West Ham, Bournemouth (1966-1970)* Former Bournemouth winger, was first team coach at Sunderland until June 1995.

HARVEY, Bryan. *Newcastle, Blackpool, Northampton. (1958-1967)* London born goalkeeper, Bryan is now living in Wotton, Northants and working as a manager of a chemical firm.

HARVEY, Colin. *Everton, Sheff Wed. (1963-1975)* England cap Colin was appointed Assistant manager of Oldham in November 1994. He had previously managed Everton, the club who for whom he had made 317 League appearances.

HARVEY, David. *Leeds, Bradford C. (1965-1984)* **After leaving the game, Harvey firstly ran a pub, then worked delivering fruit and veg to the hotels of Harrogate. Became player/manager at Whitby in 1985 and worked as a postman in Knaresborough, Yorkshire. However, he has now started a new life in the Orkney Islands, where he has purchased a large old farmhouse and several animals and intends to enjoy his retirement - at the age of 46 !!**

HARVEY, James. *Arsenal, Hereford, Bristol C, Wrexham, Tranmere (1977-1993)* Lives in Bromborough, Wirral and is currently manager of Morecombe in the Northern Premier League.

(Courtesy: Orkney Photographic)

David Harvey, enjoying the quiet life (?) in the Orkney Isles.

HARVEY, Martin. *Sunderland (1959-1971)* A great all round player, Harvey worked his way through the junior ranks at Sunderland. Eventually took over from the great Danny Blanchflower in the Northern Ireland side, going on to play 33 times in all. Later coached at Plymouth Argyle?

HARVEY, Joe. *Bradford P.A., Wolves, Bournemouth, Newcastle. (1936-1952)* Captained Newcastle to FA Cup wins in 1951 and 1952 and served the club for a total of 35 years as player; assistant manager; manager; and chief scout. Died of a heart attack at his Tynecastle home in 1989.

HATCH, Peter. *Oxford, Exeter (1967-1981).* After fourteen years as a player at Exeter, remained in the area and works as a postman.

HATELEY, Tony. *Notts C, Aston V, Chelsea, Liverpool, Coventry, Birmingham, Notts C, Oldham. (1958-1973).* A goalscoring centre-forward who played for seven clubs in twenty years. Upon retiring from the game, set up his own business until 1978 when he became Lottery Manager at Goodison Park. Three years later became a drinks rep, firstly with Thwaites brewery, and now with a soft drinks firm. Father of Mark, the England international, currently with Rangers.

HATTON, Bob. *Wolves, Bolton W, Northampton T, Carlisle U, Birmingham C, Blackpool, Luton T, Sheff U, Cardiff C. (1966-1982).* Scored a hatful of goals for each of his nine league clubs. After sixteen years as a player, Bob joined the P.F.A., where he now works as Director of Sales, based in the organisation's Birmingham office.

HATTON, Dave. *Bolton, Blackpool, Bury. (1961-1978)* Played over 500 league games. Dave now works in Blackpool as an Estate Agent.

(Courtesy: Hull Daily Mail)

HAWLEY, John. *Hull, Leeds, Sunderland, Arsenal, Leyton O, Hull, Bradford C, Scunthorpe. (1972-1985.)* After coming through the junior ranks at Hull City, John established himself with spells at Leeds, Sunderland and Arsenal before eventually returning to Humberside with Scunthorpe. Now owns an Antiques shop on the other side of the River Humber - at Beverley.

HAY, David. *Chelsea, (1974-1978).* Retired through injury in September 1979, and was appointed Assistant manager at Motherwell in the November and then Manager in September 1981. Managed his old club, Celtic for a spell, and is now back with them working as Chief Scout.

HAYDOCK, Bill. *Man C, Crewe, Grimsby, Stockport Co, Southport. (1959-1971)* Full back Bill, had a spell in South Africa after twelve years and over 400 games as a player. Became Assistant Manager of Cork City in Eire before joining Blackburn Rovers as their physiotherapist.

HAYES, Austin. *Southampton, Millwall, Northampton. (1976-1984)* Won one full Eire cap Died of lung cancer in December 1986, aged 28.

(Courtesy: Mike Jones)

HAYNES, Johnny. *Fulham, (1952-1969).* In 1961, Johnny became Britain's first ever £100 a week footballer, when the £20 per week maximum wage was abolished. During his career with Fulham, Haynes appeared in nearly 600 league games, scoring 146 goals. He played 56 times for England and was also capped at 'B' and Under 23 Levels. Moved to South Africa in 1970 to join his old mate 'Budgie' Byrne. For the next fifteen years he played for, then coached Durban City, before returning to the U.K. He now lives in Edinburgh where he runs a dry cleaning business, but still manages to fit regular visits to Johannesburg and gets to watch his old club Fulham play five or six times a year.

HEASLEGRAVE, Sammy. *WBA, Northampton T (1936-1947).* **A hard working inside forward who played for West Bromwich Albion before the war and Northampton from 1946. Became a Solicitor in Bearwood. Sammy went on to become All-England Bowls champion in 1963. Died in April 1975 at the age of 59.**

HEATH, Don. *Middlesboro, Norwich, Swindon, Oldham, Peterborough, Hartlepool. (1962-1974).* Played on the wing for five clubs in ten years from 1964 having been released by local club, Middlesborough. Now living back in the North Eastern town where he works as a buyer for I.C.I.

HEATON, Mike *Sheff U, Blackburn (1966-1975)* Sheffield born defender who went on to play 168 games for Everton in the 1970's. Became a coach at Blackburn and then returned to Goodison Park in the same capacity. Sadly died in a car accident in April 1995 at the age of 48.

HEATON, Paul. *Oldham, Rochdale (1977-1985)* Former England Under 21 midfielder who played over 200 league games for Oldham and Rochdale before leaving in 1985 to play in Finland where he married a local girl and stayed!

(Courtesy: Derby Evening Telegraph)

HECTOR, Kevin. *Bradford P.A., Derby. (1962-1981).* Started at Bradford P.A. and broke their scoring record with 44 goals in a season before being snapped up by Derby for £40,000. Gained two Championship medals and was capped twice by England. Now a postman in the East Midlands.

HEFFER, Paul. *West Ham (1966-1971).* Former West Ham defender, coached at Southend, but now teaches P.E. at a School in Essex.

(Photo courtesy: John Cocks)

HEIGHWAY, Steve. *Liverpool (1970-1980)* Signed for Liverpool from Non-league Skelmersdale in May 1970 and spent the next ten years rampaging down the wings of the First Division providing crosses for Keegan and Toshack. In total he played just over 300 times for 'Pool, and appeared in three cup finals, five Championship winning sides and was capped 34 times by Eire. Steve is still employed at Anfield where he is now Director Of Youth Development.

HEMSLEY, Ted. *Shrewsbury, Sheff U, Doncaster, (1960-1978).* Probably as well known as an accomplished Cricketer (Worcs) Ted was a solid defender who played 500 league games in his eighteen years as a pro. Now retired, although still only 52, after ten years as a turf accountant.

HENDERSON, John. *Rotherham, Leeds. (1953-1955).* Now a distribution fitter for the SouthWest Gas Board, Trowbridge, Wiltshire.

HENDERSON, John (Jackie) *Portsmouth, Wolves, Arsenal, Fulham (1951-1963).* Scottish international striker (7 Caps) ended his professional playing days at Fulham before joining Poole Town in 1964. More recently worked for a builders merchants in Poole, until his retirement.

HENDERSON, Stewart. *Chelsea, Brighton, Reading (1964-1982).* Former full back who clocked up a total in excess of 350 League appearances for Brighton and Reading. Stewart is now a Youth development officer at Reading.

HENDERSON, Willie. *Sheff Wed, (1972-1973).* **A real crowd entertainer who briefly played for Sheffield Wednesday after a very successful career with Rangers where he won silverware galore. In addition to his collection of 29 Scottish caps, he also had the distinction of Captaining the Hong Kong national side !!**

HENDRIE, Paul. *Birmingham, Bristol R, Halifax, Stockport (1972-1988)* Played in America with Portland Timbers before returning to England to play for a number of Midlands non-league sides. Was manager at Redditch United before taking over at Tamworth in February 1995.

HENNESSEY, Terry. *Birmingham C, Notts Forest, Derby Co. (1960-1972).* Terry played over 400 league games for his three English clubs and won thirty nine full caps with Wales. Emigrated to Australia following a spell as assistant manager to his former Derby team-mate, Alan Hinton at Vancouver Whitecaps in Canada. Now lives in a village near Melbourne and works as a sales manager for a firm selling cling film products.

HENRY, Tony *Man C, Bolton, Oldham, Stoke, Shrewsbury (1976-1992)* Now lives in Bicton near Shrewsbury and is working as a financial advisor for the Prudential Insurance Company.

Phil Henson

HENSON, Phil. *Man City, Swansea C, Sheff Wed, Stockport Co, Rotherham Utd. (1971-1983).* Phil was Manager at his last playing club, Rotherham United until September 1995, when he took on the senior role of General Manager.

HERD, David. *Stockport, Arsenal, Man U, Stoke (1950-1969).* Started his career at Stockport County, playing alongside his father, Alex. Arsenal signed him in August 1954 for £8,000 while he was still doing his National Service. Became a prolific scorer, scoring over 200 league goals for Arsenal and Manchester United. Spent eighteen months as manager of Lincoln City before being replaced by a young Graham Taylor in 1964. He had bought a garage in Urmston, and after Lincoln, left football for good to concentrate on his business, which he still runs today.

HERD, George. *Sunderland, Hartlepool (1960-1970).* 275 matches for Sunderland caught the eye of the Scottish selectors, earning him five caps. Now working as youth team coach at Roker Park.

HERRIOT, Jim *Birmingham, Mansfield (1965-1970)* **Capped eight times by Scotland, this ex-Birmingham City goalkeeper's name has been made even more famous by a previously unknown Scottish author who decided that James Herriot was a more appropriate pen-name than Alf Wight. Under this adopted pseudonym, he went on to write the now world famous books about the adventures of a country vet, which led to the film and television series "All Creatures Great and Small" The original Jim returned to Scotland after playing 181 games for the "Blues", having joined the Midlands club from Dunfermline in 1965. Once home he became a bricklayer in Strathclyde.**

HESLOP, George. *Newcastle, Everton, Man C, Bury. (1959-1972).* Was on the coaching Staff at Manchester City, then became a licensee in Manchester. Firstly at the Hyde Road Hotel, and later took over the 'City Gates' public house.

HEWIE, John. *Charlton, (1951-1965).* **Played 495 games for Charlton in nearly every position including four games in goal. Won 19 Scottish caps, but also played against them for South Africa in 1956. To cap this remarkable career, John played baseball for England! Lives in the Midlands, now back from South Africa.**

HIBBITT, Kenny. *Bradford P.A., Wolves, Coventry, Bristol R. (1967-1988).* Ended his playing days at Bristol Rovers, where he then became assistant to Gerry Francis for three years. Joined Cardiff City in the Summer of 1995, having previously spent three years coaching at Walsall.

HIBBITT, Terry. *Leeds, Newcastle Birmingham, Newcastle. (1965-1980).* Brother of Kenny, died from stomach cancer at the age of 46.

HICKMAN, Mike. *Brighton, Grimsby, Blackburn, Torquay. (1965-1975)* Youth development manager at Reading, before following Mark McGee to Leicester City in December 1994.

HICKS, Keith. *Oldham, Hereford, Rochdale. (1971-1986).* Now working as a Community scheme organiser based at Rochdale FC

HICKS, Martin. *Charlton, Reading, Birmingham (1977-1992)* Was coaching at Newbury, close to Reading, where he made almost 500 appearances, before joining Worcester in February 1995

HICKSON, Dave. *Everton, Aston V, Huddersfield , Everton, Liverpool, Bury, Tranmere. (1951-1963).* After three years in the reserves at Everton, Hickson made his debut in 1951/2 season, knocking in fourteen goals. His courageous style played a large part in helping get the "Toffees" back into Division One in 1953/4. Leaving Everton in 1955, he became a traveller and was always among the goals. He scored over 170 league goals in a career which stretched over twelve playing seasons. Went to Ireland as Player/manager of Ballymena, then took a job as a bricklayer and later worked in a Public House. Now lives in Ellesmere Port where he works for the Local Authority.

(Courtesy: Liverpool Post & Herald)

Dave Hickson (left) with fellow Merseyside **legend Peter Thompson.**

HICKTON, John. *Sheff Wed, Middlesboro, Hull. (1963-1977).* Now living and working in Chesterfield. Scored 159 league goals in 395 matches during his 11 years at Middlesborough.

HILDITCH, Mark *Rochdale, Tranmere, Wigan, Rochdale.(1977-1991).* Assistant Manager at Northern Premier League Mossley. Lives near Rochdale and works in the prison service.

HILAIRE, Vince. *Crystal P, Luton, Portsmouth, Leeds, Stoke, Exeter. (1976-1993)* Exciting former England Under 23 wingman, was joint manager of Waterlooville FC with his old Palace and Pompey colleague, Billy Gilbert. Resigned in 1994 but is still registered as a player.

HILL, Alan. *Barnsley, Rotherham, Notts F. (1960-1969).* Former Notts Forest keeper, is now Assistant manager and chief scout at the Club.

HILL, Fred. *Bolton, Halifax, Man C, Peterborough. (1957-1974.)* England international inside forward, Fred lives in Peterborough, home of his last club, where he is now running a pub.

HILL, Gordon. *Millwall, Man U, Derby, QPR. (1972-1980).* Former Manchester United winger Gordon, went to North America in the early eightiess to play for Montreal, then Chicago Sting before a brief return to England to coach Northwich. Gordon now lives in Tampa, Florida, where he works as a tennis and football coach.

HILL, Jimmy. *Brentford, Fulham. (1949-1960).* A professional with Brentford and then Fulham, Jimmy was Chairman of the P.F.A. between 1957 and 1961 during which time he was behind the end of the maximum wage rule. In 1961, was appointed General Manager of Coventry City, staying at Highfield Road for six years before taking over as Head of Sport at London Weekend Television. His television career has since flourished, with his strong views often the cause of much heated discussion. He has successfully managed to combine this with his role as Chairman of Fulham, a post that he has held since 1987.

(Photo courtesy: Portsmouth News)

Two members of the Palace "Team of the Eighties" **Billy Gilbert** (left) and **Vince Hilaire**

HILL, Ken. *Gillingham, Lincoln. (1971-1976).* Former England semi pro defender, lives in Maidstone and works as a manager at Britelite Ltd.

HILL, Richard. *Leicester, Northampton, Watford, Oxford. (1981-1988)* Was Community officer at Reading until the Summer of 1994.

HILL, Ricky. *Luton, Leicester, (1975-1990).* Won three England caps and played over 400 games in the League for Luton Town. Now turning out for Chertsey Town after spells with Tampa Bay Rowdies in America, and Hitchin Town.

HILLEY, Dave. *Newcastle, Notts F. (1962-1970).* Former Scotland Under 23 striker, is now a schoolteacher and also writes regularly for the Sunday Post newspaper in the North East.

HINCE, Paul. *Man C, Charlton, Bury, Crewe. (1966-1970).* **Now covers Manchester City's games as a journalist with the Manchester Evening News, having taken up journalism in the afternoons whilst a player with Charlton.**

HINDMARSH, Rob. *Sunderland, Portsmouth, Derby, Wolves, (1977-1994).* Returned to his home in the Stafford area after a spell in Hong Kong. Helps out on a part time basis at his last club, Wolves' in their school of excellence.

HINNIGAN, Joe *Wigan, Sunderland, Preston, Gillingham, Wrexham, Chester. (1978-1989)* Lives in Ashton and is Chester City's physio.

HINSHELWOOD, Martin. *Crystal P (1972-1977)* Former seventies midfielder, now holds the post of Reserve team coach at Portsmouth.

HINSHELWOOD, Paul. *Crystal P, Oxford, Millwall, Colchester. (1973-1987).* Son of Wally, the former Fulham winger and brother of Martin, who also played for Crystal Palace. Now lives in Kent and works as an insurance salesman.

HINTON, Alan. *Wolves, Notts, Derby. (1961-1975).* **Goalscoring winger, who won three England caps to add to his seven at Under 23 level. Moved to America to coach Tulsa Roughnecks, Seattle Sounders, Tacoma Stars and in 1980 was named 'Coach of the Year'. Now lives in Seattle and works as an Estate agent.**

HINTON, Marvin. *Charlton, Chelsea (1957-1974).* England Under 23 defender who proudly wore the blue and white Chelsea colours in over 250 League games. Was running his own Office removals business. But has been unable to work since a head on car smash that he was involved in near his home in Crawley, West Sussex.

HIRON, Ray. *Portsmouth, Reading. (1964-1977).* Lanky striker joined Portsmouth in 1964 and netted 110 goals in 324 appearances, regularly the South Coast Club's top scorer. After three seasons with Reading, returned to Fareham Town in the Southern League. Now a manager at the Mountbatten Sports Centre in Portsmouth.

Ray Hiron *(Courtesy: Portsmouth News)*

HOADLEY, Phil. *C Palace, Leyton O, Norwich. (1967-1981).* Phil now works as a Self employed window fitter in the Norwich area and also helps coach the youngsters at Carrow Road.

(Courtesy: Salisbury Journal)

HOBSON, Gordon. *Lincoln, Grimsby, Southampton, Lincoln, Exeter, Walsall. (1977-1992)* Played 260 games for Lincoln before setting off on his travels. Now a player and Assistant Manager at Salisbury City in the Beazer Homes League. Away from soccer, Gordon also runs a successful sailing business in Southampton.

HOCKEY, Trevor. *Bradford C, Notts F, Newcastle, Birmingham, Sheff U, Norwich, Aston V, Bradford C. (1959-1975).* **Played for seven clubs in 16 years, during which time he played in over 600 matches. Trevor was taking part in a 5-a-side tournament in Keighley in April 1987 when he collapsed and died, aged 43.**

HODDLE, Glen. *Tottenham, Swindon, Chelsea, (1975-1995)* Made his name with Spurs in the mid seventies and early eighties for his creative midfield skills and knack of scoring spectacular goals. Won 53 England caps and successive FA Cup winners medals in 1981 and 1982. In 1987 moved to Monaco in France for £800,000 but was dogged by injuries, returning home in 1990 as Manager of Swindon. Glenn guided them to the Premiership in 1993 via the Play Offs, but left for Chelsea just weeks later. They reached the FA Cup final in his first full season at Stamford Bridge and then in his second, the Semi-finals of the European Cup Winners Cup.

HODGETTS, Frank. *WBA, Millwall (1946-1952).* Became the youngest ever West Bromwich Albion player, when he made his debut in 1940 aged only 16 years and 26 days, a record that still stands today. Now lives in retirement in Kidderminster, but has been active as Chairman of the Herefordshire and Worcestershire County Tennis Association and organiser of Coaching.

HODGKINSON, Alan. *Sheff U, (1954-1970).* Joined Sheffield United from Worksop Town and went on to play 576 league games in goal for the Blades, and win five England Caps. Now coaches goalkeepers for a number of League Clubs.

HODGSON, Dave. *Middlesboro, Liverpool, Sunderland, Norwich, Middlesboro, Sheff Wed, Swansea. (1978-1991)* Went over to Japan to play for Mazda of Hiroshima and then traded as a football players agent before being appointed Director of Coaching at Hartlepool in May 1995.

HODGSON, Roy. One of the few former British footballers to make their mark as a successful coach and manager in Europe. Currently manager of Switzerland's national side.

HOLD, John. *Bournemouth, Crewe, Northampton. (1965-1972).* Former Bournemouth forward is now working as an area Manager for Prestos.

HOLDEN, Bill *Burnley, Sunderland, Stockport, Bury, Halifax, (1950-1962).* Life after football proved extremely varied for this ex-England "B" international centre forward. Jobs included running a driving school; owning a coffee bar; a restaurant; a newsagency; and running the recreation centre at Lancaster University. He then rented out flats and worked for the D.S.S. before buying the guest house he now runs in Morecombe!

HOLDER, Phil. *Tottenham, C Palace, Bournemouth. (1971-1979).* Phil had a spell as Manager at Brentford, but is now Youth team coach at Reading - a post that he has held since late 1994.

HOLE, Barry. *Cardiff, Blackburn, Aston V, Swansea. (1959-1971)* **After retiring in 1972, followed in his fathers footsteps by becoming a shopkeeper. His two brothers, Alan and Colin also played for Swansea. He has now run a newsagency in the area for the past 25 years and is a member of the same golf course as Ivor Allchurch. Ironically, they were room mates while at Cardiff City over 35 years ago!**

HOLLAND, Pat. *West Ham, Bournemouth (1968-1980).* Seen above (left) with Bobby Gould. Now lives in Upminster. Went into catering with "Hollands" wine bar, and "The Red Lion" in Barking. Pat joined Tottenham in 1988 as youth Team Coach and took over the reserves before accepting Barry Hearn's offer to become manager at Orient at the end of the 1994/5 season.

HOLLETT, Ivan. *Mansfield, Chesterfield, Crewe, Camb U, Hereford. (1958-1972).* Now Area Rep for a metals company in Northampton

HOLLINS, David. *Brighton., Newcastle, Mansfield, Notts F, Aldershot (1957-1970.)* The goalkeeping brother of John. Now runs his own painting and decorating business in London.

HOLLINS, John MBE. *Chelsea, QPR, Arsenal, Chelsea. (1963-1983).* John gained an England cap against Spain in 1967, which was unusual because his brother, Dave was already a Welsh international goalie. With Chelsea, he won an FA Cup winners medal in 1969/70. Returned to Stamford Bridge as their Player/Coach and took over as Manager until March 1988. Was awarded the M.B.E. in 1982 and after a spell as a financial adviser, he returned to the game as Reserve Team Coach at old club Q.P.R. in February 1995.

HOLLOWBREAD, John. *Tottenham, Southampton. (1958-1965).* **Became a publican running pubs in Southampton, then Romsey, before taking over the bar at Bramshaw Golf Club in the New Forest. In September 1994, after five years of watching the golfers, retired to Spain to enable him to enjoy playing the game, and to let someone else do the watching!**

HOLLYWOOD, Dennis. *Southampton (1962-1971).* Works in Southampton docks and lives outside the city, where he played for nine years.

HOLMES, Jimmy. *Coventry, Tottenham, Leicester, Brentford, Torquay, Peterborough. (1971-1985)* Republic of Ireland full back (30 caps), after ending at Peterborough Jimmy joined Nuneaton and briefly Managed Hitchin Town.

HOLMES, Nick. *Southampton (1973-1986).* After 18 years at Southampton which included winning the 1976 FA Cup final, Nick has taken on the role of a village shopkeeper in Wiltshire.

HOLSGROVE, John. *C. Palace, Wolves, Sheff Wed, Stockport Co, (1964-1975).* Played almost 300 league games, more than half of which were in the gold and black of Wolves. Now works as a financial advisor in the West Midlands.

HOLTON, Cliff. *Arsenal, Watford, Northampton, C Palace, Watford, Charlton, Leyton O. (1950-1967).* Former Arsenal centre forward who had one of the hottest shots of any post war player. Cliff broke both Watford and Northampton Town's club goalscoring records. Ran his own Precision engineering business in Stonebridge until 1989. Then spent five years organising golf tournaments prior to his retirement in April 1994.

HOLTON, Jim. *WBA, Shrewsbury, Man U, Sunderland, Coventry, Sheff Wed. (1968-1981).* **Manchester United's "Player of the year" in 1973/4. Retired in 1982, and ran the "Old Stag" pub in Coventry until his sudden death in 1993.**

HOOPER, Harry. *West Ham U, Wolves, Birmingham C, Sunderland (1950-1962).* Former England Under 23 and 'B' winger, seen here with current Hammers boss Harry Redknapp at the "West Ham Who's Who" book launch in 1995.

HOOKS, Paul. *Notts Co, Derby. (1976-1984).* **Former Notts county winger , now works as a coal miner in Ollerton, Nottinghamshire.**

HOOLICKIN, Steve. *Oldham, Bury, Carlisle, Hull. (1969-1981).* Former Bury and Carlisle Full back. Now lives in Carlisle, where he was a publican, but is now a self employed contractor.

HOPE, Bobby. *WBA, Birmingham, Sheff Wed. (1959-1977).* Capped by Scotland at Schoolboy, Under 23 and full levels, Bobby appeared in over 400 senior games for West Bromwich Albion and ranks as one of their all time greats. Now owns a sandwich bar in Birmingham, having previously run a Sub post office in the City. Was Manager of Bromsgrove Rovers until September 1994.

HOPKINS, Mel. *Tottenham, Brighton, Bradford P.A.. (1952-1969).* First choice full back for Wales for a number of years, winning 34 caps in total, including a run of 23 consecutive appearances. He then became a sports teacher and football coach, Mel was also secretary to Sussex Coach's Association. Currently works as a sports centre manager, and lives in Horsham, Sussex.

HOPKINS, Robert. *Aston V, Birmingham, Man City, WBA, Birmingham, Shrewsbury (1979-1991)* Played in Hong Kong for Instant Dict but now home and turning out for Solihull Borough.

HOPKINSON, Edward. *Oldham, Bolton (1951-1969).* Consistently reliable goalkeeper who was Bolton's first choice for many years (519 appearances), earning him 14 full England caps. Still lives in the area and works as a Customer Relations officer for Warburton Bakeries.

HORE, John. *Plymouth, Exeter. (1964-1979).* Played almost 600 league games. John now lives in Exeter and is the owner of a own fitness club.

HORSTEAD, Barry. *Scunthorpe (1956-1967).* Worked for British Sugar for 22 years before taking early retirement. Lives in Brigg, Humberside.

HORSWILL, Mick. *Sunderland, Man C, Plymouth, Hull, Carlisle. (1971-1983).* Now manages a public house in Boldon, Tyne and Wear.

HORTON, Brian. *Port V, Brighton, Luton, Hull. (1970-1986).* After a 16 year playing career Brian became manager at Hull, achieving promotion to the Second Division in his first season in 1984. Four years later, succeeded Mark Lawrenson at Oxford and stayed until his appointment as Manager of Man City in August 1993. Persistent speculation about his future meant that it was no surprise when he was sacked two years later. However, he only had to wait five weeks before being re-employed, at Huddersfield Town.

HOSKIN, Ashley. *Burnley (1965-1988).* **A left winger who progressed through the junior ranks at Burnley, signing a pro in 1985. After playing 70 league games drifted into non-league soccer. Now playing for Accrington Stanley, and was rumoured to sponsored by Phil Collins - because of their similarity in looks!!**

HOUCHEN, Keith. *Hartlepool, Orient, York, Scunthorpe, Coventry, Port V, Hartlepool. (1978-1995)* After a gap of over 15 years, returned to his first club, Hartlepool, as player/coach and was promoted to the Manager's post in April 1995

HOUGHTON, Billy. *Barnsley, Watford, Ipswich, Leicester, Rotherham. (1957-1973).* Played over 500 league games in his 16 year career. Now works for British Coal Building dept in Barnsley.

HOUGHTON, Eric. *Aston V, Notts Co. (1926-1948).* **Life president of Aston Villa, Eric had three spells at Villa Park, the third to pioneer a new fund raising lottery for the club. He was later on the board at Walsall, then Villa. Also a successful businessman away from soccer, Eric is now retired living in Sutton Coldfield.**

HOUGHTON, Ken. *Rotherham, Hull, Scunthorpe. (1960-1973).* Manager of a freight forwarding firm in Immingham, Humberside.

HOUSEMAN, Peter. *Chelsea, Oxford. (1963-1976)* **Winger who played 252 League games for Chelsea, picking up an FA Cup Winners medal along the way, before moving to Oxford United. Killed in a car crash in 1977 aged 32.**

HOUSTON, Stewart. *Chelsea, Brentford, Man U, Sheff U, Colchester. (1967-1985).* Player/coach at Colchester United from August 1983 until April 1986. Joined the Coaching staff at Arsenal in 1986: temporarily took over the managerial reins in 1995 following George Graham's departure. Stewart agreed to stay on at Highbury, to work with newly appointed boss, Bruce Rioch.

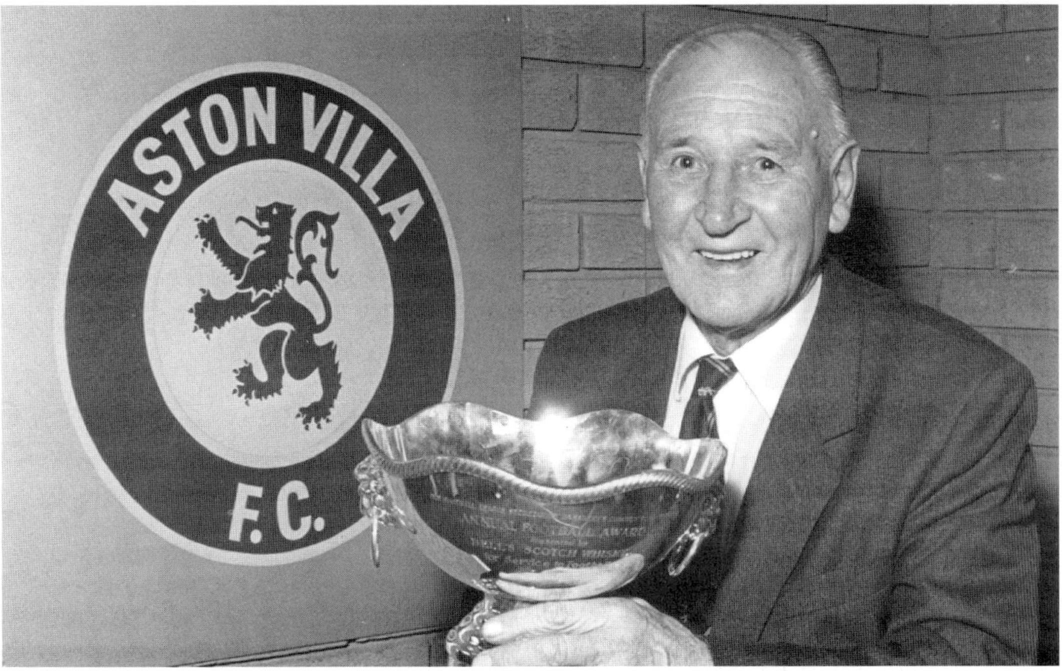

Eric Houghton, one of Aston Villa's all time greats.

HOW, Trevor. *Watford (1974-1979).* Now Publican at "The Crown", Little Missenden, Bucks.

HOWE, Don. *WBA, Arsenal (1952-1966).* Played 375 appearances for West Brom before joining Arsenal, where a leg fracture in 1966 ended his playing career. He made 23 consecutive appearances for England, and won six Under 23 caps. He then coached the 'Gunners' when they lifted the League and Cup double in 1971. Howe returned to the Hawthorns to manage West Brom in 1971 a post that he held until 1975. he has since made stops at: Galatasaray (Coach), Leeds United (Coach), Arsenal (Coach, then Manager), England 'B' team Coach, then Chief Scout, Saudi Arabia (Coach 1986-7), Bristol Rovers (Coach 1987), Wimbledon (Coach, then Assistant Manager), Q.P.R (Assistant Manager November 1989, Manager 1989-91). Wimbledon (Chief Scout), Barnet (Coach), Coventry (Manager 1991-2), Chelsea (Assistant Manager/Coach.) and Don is still very much involved with Terry Venables and the current England set-up.

HOWE, Ernie. *Fulham, QPR, Portsmouth. (1973-1983).* Commanding former West Ham defender, is now Manager of Basingstoke Town.

HOWE, George. *Huddersfield, York. (1946-1960).* York City stalwart (307 apps), died in 1991

HUBBARD, Terry. *Swindon, (1970-1975).* Welsh under 23 international midfielder is now working as shift supervisor of Cwmbran Stadium.

HUCKER, Peter. *QPR, Oxford, W.B.A., Millwall, Aldershot. (1980-1990)* Former Queens Park Rangers keeper who won two Under 23 caps with England, Peter gave up the milk round franchise that he had owned since 1994 to try and make use of his FA Coaching qualifications.

(Courtesy: Evening Sentinel, Stoke)

HUDSON, Alan. *Chelsea, Stoke, Arsenal, Chelsea, Stoke C. (1968-1985)* Started as an Apprentice with his local club, Chelsea before signing as a professional in June 1968. Played in their Cup Winners Cup success in 1971 and stayed at Stamford Bridge until January 1974, when along with Peter Osgood, was placed on the transfer list after a training ground row. Nine days later was transferred to Stoke for £240,000, although he returned to the Capital less than two years later with Arsenal, then had spells in America and a brief return to Chelsea. Alan has now settled in the Potteries where he has business interests and writes for the local paper, the Evening Sentinel.

HUGHES, Emlyn. *Blackpool, Liverpool, Wolves, Rotherham, Hull, Swansea. (1965-1983)* Son of a former Rugby League star, Emlyn started his career with Blackpool and in 1967 Liverpool paid a then club record £65,000 for his services. Nicknamed "Crazy Horse", Emlyn captained Liverpool for a number of years lifting a host of trophies, and was named Footballer of the Year in 1976-7. He played a total of 474 League games for the 'Pool' an managed Rotherham for two years before becoming a nationally recognised celebrity - regularly appearing on television. As well as presenting his own shows such as "Sporting triangles", he was a team Captain on BBCtv's "Question of Sport" for a number of years.

(Photo courtesy of: Liverpool Daily Post & Echo)

Roger Hunt, now running his own haulage firm.

HUGHES, Harry. *Southport, Chelsea, Bournemouth, Gillingham. (1950-1962).* Ran the Club shop at Spurs for eleven years, but Harry is now self-employed living in Guildford.

HUGHES, Ron. *Chester (1951-1961)* Veteran of over 400 games for Chester, now works for the Education department at Clwyd County Council.

HUGHES, William. *York (1951-1961)* Was forced to sell his two D.I.Y shops that he had in York 15 years ago due to serious back problems, Now retired but manages to play a golf and bowls.

HUGHTON, Chris. *Tottenham, West Ham, Brentford, (1979-1993).* Played almost 300 games for Spurs and won 53 full caps with Eire. Now on the coaching staff at White Hart Lane.

HUMPHRIES, Gerry. *Everton, C Palace, Crewe Alex. (1965-1976).* Gerry is now believed to be working as a Taxi driver in North Wales.

HUNT, David *Derby Co, Notts Co, Aston V, Mansfield T (1977-1989)* Played 300 plus games for Notts County. Now teaches at his soccer schools based in the Ashby-de-la-Zouch area.

HUNT, Ernie. *Swindon, Wolves, Everton, Coventry, Doncaster, Bristol C. (1959-1974)* **Lives in Gloucester, but a hip injury prevents Ernie from working. However, he is still jolly, and since quitting as a player has: run a pub, taught in a childrens home, worked in the Commercial departments at Gloucester City and Swindon and even had a spell cleaning windows.**

HUNT, Roger. *Liverpool, Bolton (1959-1971).* Hunt made a name for himself as a marksman while shooting Liverpool back into the first division in 1961-2 and topping the league scoring list with 41 goals. Won 34 England caps and had scored 245 goals in 401 League starts before ending his career at Bolton in 1971. Has been a member of the Pools Panel since 1974, and runs his own Road Haulage business on Merseyside.

HUNTER, Allan. *Oldham, Blackburn, Ipswich, Colchester. (1966-1982).* An Ireland Captain and centre half who started at Coleraine. His first English club was Oldham Athletic Signed for Ipswich Town in September 1971. Still lives in the area, and is a woodwork teacher at Belstead Special school. He keeps fit by playing golf and bowls.

(Photo courtesy : Yorkshire Post Newpspapers)

Norman Hunter, proudly displaying three of his twenty eight England Caps.

HUNTER, Norman. *Leeds Bristol C, Barnsley. (1962-1982).* Joined Leeds United during the 1959/60 season. As part of their "Glory days" team he played in over 700 games gaining winners medals for: two League Titles; the F.A. Cup; League Cup; and two European Fairs Cups triumphs. During his managerial career, Norman took Barnsley from the Third to the Second Division. He has also been manager of Rotherham, and Assistant Manager at West Brom and Bradford City. Internationally Norman has won 28 caps for England and was voted the first ever "Players Player of the Year" in 1973. Now a popular after dinner speaker and coach at local schools.

HURST, Geoff. *West Ham, Stoke, WBA, (1959-1975).* The only player ever to score a hat trick in a World Cup final, started his career at West Ham United, signing as a professional in April 1959. Over the next thirteen years he played over 400 league games, scoring 180 goals including one in the 1964 FA Cup final. By the time he retired in 1975 he had scored 24 goals for England and won 49 caps. Briefly managed Chelsea between 1979 and 1981, but has worked for a company selling Car Warranties for a number of years - where he is now the firms Managing Director.

HURST, Gordon. *Charlton (1946-1957).* Oldham born winger who notched up 369 league appearances for his only League Club, Charlton. Gordon died in 1980 at the age of 56.

Ian Hutchinson.

HURST, John. *Everton, Oldham, (1965-1980).* Played over 500 League games in defence for Everton and Oldham Athletic, winning nine England Under 23 caps before retiring in 1980. Now works as "B" Team Manager at Everton.

HUTCHINS, Don. *Leicester, Plymouth, Blackburn, Bradford C (1967-1980).* Former Bradford city winger (252 league appearances) Works for Leyland paints, first employed as a salesman, but now promoted to Sales Manager.

HUTCHINSON, Ian. *Chelsea, (1968-1975).* England Under 23 cap Ian scored 43 goals in his 112 league appearances and is remembered for his famous long throw ins. He has since helped out with the catering at Brentford FC and ran a pub in Windsor with his old team-mate Peter Osgood. They are still friends and sometimes appear together as an after dinner double act.

HUTCHINSON, Tommy. *Blackpool, Coventry, Man C, Burnley, Swansea. (1967-1990)* Ended up playing at Swansea City, where he became Player/Manager in until May 1986. Now employed as a Development officer with the P.F.A. at Merthyr & Taff Ely Borough Council working with school children, special needs schools, both mentally & physically handicapped and the unemployed. Also runs fun days during the summer holidays at a residential camp in Pontypridd.

HUTT, Geoff *Huddersfield, Blackburn, York, Halifax. (1968-1979)* Works in the customer services dept at Tibbett and Britten's, Huddersfield.

HUXFORD, Cliff. *Chelsea, Southampton, Exeter. (1958-1967).* Now works as a self employed painter & decorator, living outside Southampton. Manager of Brockenhurst in the Wessex League.

(Courtesy: Isle of Wight Press)

ICKE, David. *Coventry, Hereford (1969-1972).* **As a teenager he played in the same Leicester boys team as Peter Shilton, before joining Coventry City as an apprentice at the age of 15. Transferred to Hereford United in 1972 helping them to gain promotion from the Fourth to Third division. When his career was brought to an abrupt end by rheumatoid arthritis, David became a journalist in Leicester, going on to become a household name as a television sports presenter. Now lives in relative seclusion on the Isle of Wight and unfortunately has become better known for his unconventional beliefs which regularly hit the headlines.**

IMLACH, Mike *Peterboro, Tranmere (1982-1984).* Mike now works on a North Sea Oil rig.

INGHAM, Billy. *Burnley, Bradford C (1971-1981).* Midfielder who played over 200 games for Burnley, Billy still lives in the area and is currently employed locally as a bus driver.

INGHAM, Tony. *Leeds, QPR. (1947-1962).* Played over 500 games for Q.P.R. in a twelve stint ending in 1962. Now retired, but still helps out at the Loftus Road Club in various capacities.

IRVINE, Sammy. *Shrewsbury, Stoke (1972-1979)* Lives near Shrewsbury working as a groundsman, having previously experienced a variety of jobs including running a pub; selling insurance and a time as a laboratory technician.

IRWIN, Colin. *Liverpool, Swansea. (1979-1983).* **Colin only played 29 League games for Liverpool between 1979-1981, but in that time managed to win a European Cup Winners medal (although he didn't play in the final) and a League Cup winners medal in his first season. Was forced to quit through injury at the age of 27 following a £350,000 move to Swansea. Spent two years as Phil Neal's assistant at Bolton, but now lives close to the Indian Ocean in Perth, Western Australia where he supplies wines and spirits to liquor shops and hotels.**

JACKETT, Kenny. *Watford (1979-1989).* A Watford regular for ten years in the Eighties, during which time he was also capped 31 times by his country, Wales. Kenny was appointed Youth Coach at Vicarage Road in January 1991.

JACKSON, Barry *York (1958-1969)* Played almost 500 league games for York City and has worked for the Northern Electricity Board since finishing playing 25 years ago. He started as a pre-payment collector but since slot meters were done away with, has been a meter reader.

JACKSON, John. *C. Palace, Orient, Millwall, Ipswich, Hereford, (1964-1982).* Played nearly 350 League games for Palace before moving on to Orient. Now installs and fits Blinds in Brighton, also acts as goalkeeping coach for Brighton and the Sussex FA School of Excellence.

JACKSON, Tommy. *Everton, Notts F, Man U, (1967-1976).* Former Northern Ireland international who won 35 full caps went on to Manage several clubs in Northern Ireland after hanging up his boots. Now works as a self employed upholsterer for Bannon & Co back in Belfast.

JAMES, Glyn. *Blackpool (1960-1974).* **Played 393 games for Blackpool and qualified for his nine Welsh caps by being born to English parents, but in their nearest nursing home which happened to be just inside Wales!! Now runs his own laundry and dry cleaning business which can boast having the contract for cleaning the matchday shirts of his former club!**

JAMES, Leighton. *Burnley, Derby, QPR, Burnley, Swansea, Sunderland, Bury, Newport, Burnley. (1970-1988).* Ran a confectionery shop close to the Burnley ground and had a spell as Youth coach at Bradford City. Now manages Netherfield in the Northern Premier League.

JAMES, Robbie. *Swansea, Stoke, QPR, Leicester, Swansea, Bradford, (1972-1993).* With 47 Welsh caps and over 700 league games under his belt, Robbie is still playing, now for Barry Town.

JANKOVIC, Bozo. *Middlesboro (1979-1980).* **Played 42 games for Middlesborough after signing in February 1979. Born at Sarajevo in Yugoslavia and was capped for that country at both under-21 and full level. Previously played for Zeljeznicar of Yugoslavia, for whom he made close on 500 appearances. Returned home to set up his own Law Practice but sadly, was killed during the Bosnian/Serb conflict.**

JEFFREY, Billy *Oxford, Blackpool, Northampton. (1973-1983).* Has worked in Northampton as a Sales office manger with a Cane Office Furniture company for the past five years. Played for Kettering from 1983 until 1987. Managed Irthlingborough Diamonds and is currently Assistant Manager at Rushden & Diamonds.

JENNINGS, Nicky. *Plymouth, Portsmouth, Aldershot, Exeter. (1963-1977).* Now works as a Probation Officer in Dorset, where he also has had much experience managing non-league sides.

JENNINGS, Pat MBE, OBE. *Watford, Tottenham, Arsenal (1962-1984).* **Made 472 league appearances for Tottenham Hotspur and was PFA player of the year in 1976, before moving across North London to Arsenal. Pat won an incredible 119 caps for Northern Ireland and was awarded the M.B.E. in 1976, followed by the O.B.E. in 1987. Now shares his time between coaching the goalkeepers at White Hart Lane and making personal appearances.**

JENNSEN, Viggo *Hull (1948-1956)* Left sided Danish international who played over 300 games for Hull City before returning home to become coach at his former club Esbjerg. Now retired.

JOBLING, Keith *Grimsby (1953-1968)* Played 450 League games in his thirteen years at Blundells Park. Now an upholsterer in Grimsby.

JOHANNESON, Albert. *Leeds, York (1961-1971)* A naturally pacey winger who was recommended to Don Revie and Leeds United by an African schoolteacher. Albert's current whereabouts are still a mystery but he is thought to be living in the Chapeltown, area of Leeds.

JOHNS, Nicky. *Millwall, Sheff Utd, Charlton, QPR, Maidstone (1976-1990).* Experienced goalie who pulled on a Charlton jersey close to 300 times. Finished playing at Maidstone in 1990 but Nicky is now working as Football in The Community officer based at Crystal Palace FC.

Pat Jennings, showing off the hands that foiled so many forwards !

JOHNSON, David. *Everton, Ipswich, Liverpool, Everton, Barnsley, Man C, Preston (1970-1984).* England international striker who scored on four different competition debuts for Everton: Central League; Football League; FA Cup and European Cup. Now lives in Liverpool where he works for an insurance company and is a trustee of the North-West Sport Aid Foundation.

JOHNSON, Richard. *Tranmere (1971-1981)* The goalies at Liverpool FC, now benefit from the wisdom of this ex-Tranmere Rovers keeper, who played over 300 matches in his ten years at Prenton Park. As well as part time coaching, he now holds a senior post with the Sport and Community department of Liverpool City Council.

JOHNSON, Rob. *Luton, Leicester, Barnet (1979-1991).* Runs his own health club in Hitchin and is currently player/coach at Bedford Town.

JOHNSTON, Craig. *Middlesboro, Liverpool. (1977-1987).* **Born in Johannesburg in South Africa and signed for Middlesborough in February 1978. Made his name at Liverpool before returning to his native Australia after the 1988 Cup final. Now lives in Killiney, Northern Ireland and enjoys a full life as TV producer; TV star; writer; and inventor. His latest creation, the revolutionary 'PREDATOR' football boot has been launched by Addidas.**

JOHNSTON, John. *Blackpool, Halifax, Bradford, Southport, Halifax. (1968-1978).* Former Northern Irish Under 23 international midfielder is now sales representative for a paint company.

JOHNSTONE, Bobby. *Man C, Oldham (1954-1964).* Scottish international inside forward who won 17 caps Worked for many years as a controller in the Building industry, then edged into retirement by driving part-time for a local Seafood firm. Bobby is well known in the Oldham area for his ability as a very capable bowls player.

JOHNSTONE, Derek. *Chelsea (1983-1984).* A legend north of the border who moved to Chelsea for £35,000 in 1983 having been Scottish "Player of the Year" in 1978. Only played four league games for the "Blues" before moving back to Scotland where he became Manager of Partick Thistle in July 1986. Can now be seen on Sportscene, the Scottish version of Match of The Day and can also be heard on Radio Clyde.

JOHNSTON, Willie. *WBA, Birmingham, (1972-1979).* Very speedy winger who won 22 full Scottish caps and had seven years South of the Border, notably with West Bromwich Albion. Coached at Hearts, East Fife, Raith Rovers and Falkirk before becoming a Licensee in Kirkaldy.

JONES, Andy. *Port V, Charlton, Port V, Bristol C, Bournemouth, Leyton O. (1985-1993)* Welsh international striker, is still knocking in the goals, currently for BHL side, Havant Town.

JONES, Barrie. *Swansea, Plymouth, Cardiff (1959-1969).* Won Welsh Under 23 honours and fifteen full caps before retiring in 1969 whilst at Cardiff. Now works at Swansea Leisure Centre.

JONES, Cliff. *Swansea, Tottenham, Fulham (1952-1969).* Goalscoring winger whose talents were recognised by Wales, on 59 occasions. At one time, Cliff had a butchers shop but when the business failed he returned briefly to sheet metal working, a trade he had learnt as a 16 year old apprentice in Swansea dry dock. He then took employment at a sports centre before becoming games master at a London school. Now retired, living in Goffs Oak, Herts, although he does help out at Arsenal home games in their Legends Club.

JONES, David *Bournemouth, Notts F, Norwich C (1970-1979)* Welsh international defender, now works with Bournemouth's School of excellence.

JONES, George. *Bury, Blackburn, Bury, Oldham, Halifax, Southport. (1961-1977)* Has been employed by British Rail for the past sixteen years. His son, Alex now plays for Rochdale.

JONES, Gordon. *Middlesboro, Darlington (1960-1974)* Played 450 games in defence for Middlesborough and won 9 England Under 23 Caps. Now runs a general dealer shop in Stockton.

JONES, Joey. *Wrexham, Liverpool, Wrexham, Chelsea, Huddersfield, Wrexham. (1972-1991).* **Popular with the fans at all his clubs and was voted player of the year during his times at Chelsea, Huddersfield and Wrexham. He was appointed player/coach at Wrexham in November 1989 during his third spell with the club.**

JONES, Lyn. *Cardiff, Newport, Reading (1978-1992)* Now in his second spell as manager of Merthyr Tydfil. Welsh under 21 international, Lyn, also previously managed Inter Cardiff.

Mick Jones, now attacking the flowers in his garden! *(Courtesy: Yorkshire Post)*

JONES, Mick. *Sheff U, Leeds (1962-1973).* Centre forward during the Leeds United purple years of the sixties and seventies, Mick chalked up a total of over 350 league appearances and won three England caps to add to his nine at Under 23 level. Retired due to a knee injury in 1973 to become a representative for a sports goods company, then ran a sports shop in Maltby for the next fourteen years. Now runs a market stall with his son, selling sportswear in Nottingham and lives nearby, in his hometown of Worksop.

Joe Jordan.

JONES, Paul. *Bolton, Huddersfield, Oldham, Blackpool, Rochdale, Stockport Co, (1970-1989).* Spent twelve years with Bolton before taking in stops at five further clubs including Blackpool, for whom he now does some scouting.

JONES, Stan. *Walsall, WBA, Walsall. (1957-1972).* Has worked as a manufacturers agent in the sports trade since retiring from the game in 1972, after a total of more than 450 appearances.

JONES, Wayne. *Bristol R (1966-1972).* Became Huddersfield Town's physiotherapist in 1990. Now assistant manager at Notts County.

JORDAN, Joe. *Leeds, Man U, Southampton, Bristol C, (1971-1989).* Scottish international Joe's heyday came during spells with Leeds and Manchester United before moving to Italy to play for AC Milan, then Verona. Progressed into management with Bristol City (1988-1990) before successfully managing Hearts in Scotland. Returned South to briefly occupy the Stoke City Manager's position. Resigned in September 1994 but was quickly re-employed, joining Bristol City for a second spell in the following November.

JOYCE, Joe *Barnsley, Scunthorpe (1979-1991)* Held a regular berth at full back for Barnsley for over a decade (332 league starts), before ending at Scunthorpe United. Joe is currently a member of the Coaching staff at Carlisle United.

JUDD, Mike. *Southampton (1967-1969).* Mike is now living in the New Forest and working in the drinks industry as a sales manager.

KAMARA, Chris *Portsmouth, Swindon, Portsmouth, Brentford, Swindon, Stoke, Leeds, Luton, Sheff U, Bradford C (1975-1995)* Former dockyard apprentice who earned a crack at top flight soccer as a player with Leeds and Sheffield United.Was appointed Assistant Manager at Bradford City towards the end of the 1994/5 season.

KAY, Tony. *Sheff Wed, Everton. (1954-1963).* After being banned from soccer for alleged 'fixing' of matches whilst with Sheffield Wednesday, went abroad and is believed to be in Spain.

KAYE, John. *Scunthorpe, WBA, Hull (1960-1973).* A goal scoring forward who joined West Brom from Scunthorpe for a record transfer fee. After being converted into defence went on to make more than 360 appearances for Albion. Transferred to Hull in 1971, became coach, then manager before retiring to go into the hotel business. Currently a welder, working on gas rigs both onshore and offshore and coaching at Brigg Town.

KEEGAN, Ged. *Man C, Oldham, Mansfield, Rochdale. (1974-1985)* Former Manchester City apprentice who won one England Under 21 cap. Ged has worked as an insurance salesman since retiring in 1985, and enjoys a regular round of golf which he now plays off a nine handicap.

Kevin Keegan.

KEEGAN, Kevin. *Scunthorpe, Liverpool, Southampton, Newcastle. (1968-1983).* One of the great favourites of the modern game, Keegan, now a soccer millionaire, set an example to all aspiring youngsters. Plucked by Bill Shankly from Scunthorpe for £35,000 in May 1981, he became an immediate success, making a rapid rise to full international. With Liverpool he won two League Titles, FA Cup and European Cup winners medals. He left Liverpool during the summer of 1977 for S.V. Hamburg in Germany, to become "European Footballer of the Year" two years in succession. Retired at the end of the 1983/4 season after spells with Southampton and Newcastle to become an unofficial Soccer ambassador playing in exhibition matches throughout the World from his relaxing base on the Costa del Sol in Spain. The lure of management could be resisted no more, when in February 1992 he accepted the challenge of restoring glory to Newcastle United.

KEELAN, Kevin. *Aston V, Stockport, Wrexham, Norwich. (1959-1979).* **Formidable keeper, but it was at his fourth League club, Norwich, that Kevin made his mark, playing 571 League games before retiring in 1979. Now sells contact lenses for a living in Florida.**

KEELEY, Glen. *Ipswich, Newcastle, Blackburn, Everton, Oldham, Colchester, Bolton (1972-1988)* Played 365 games in defence for Blackburn Rovers. Now a publican, but uses his spare time to indulge in his passion for flying.

KEEN, Mike. *QPR, Luton, Watford. (1959-1974).* Now lives in High Wycombe, where he has managed "Sport & Ski" in the town since his own sports shop that he ran for 25 years went bust two years ago. Is Manager of Flackwell Heath in the Diadora League and coaches one night a week at West Ham's school of excellence in Slough. Mike's son Kevin now plays for Stoke.

KELLARD, Bobby. *Southend, C Palace, Ipswich, Portsmouth, Bristol C, Leicester, C Palace, Portsmouth, Hereford, Torquay. (1959-1975).* **This "have boots-will travel" midfielder, played for eight clubs before taking over as manger at Chelmsford, where he hit the headlines by signing a certain Jimmy Greaves! Ran a taxi business in Southend for several years, but now trades an Antiques dealer. Recently had a stint as joint manager at Harlow with Len Glover.**

KELLOCK, Billy. *Cardiff, Norwich, Millwall, Peterboro, Luton, Wolves, Southend, Port V, Halifax. (1972-1985).* Midfielder who turned out for nine clubs over 13 years. Lives in Kettering where he is manager of the Barndale Country Club.

KELLOW, Tony. *Exeter, Blackpool, Exeter, Plymouth, Swansea, Newport, Exeter. (1976-1987).* Tony held the post of Assistant manager at Exeter City, but now runs the "Centre Spot" Social Club at their St James Park ground

KELLY, Chris. *Millwall, (1974).* Chris shot to fame during Leatherhead's famous cup run of the early seventies, earning him a contract with Millwall. The "Leatherhead Lip" is now Chief Exec and Commercial Manager at Kingstonian.

KELLY, Eddie *Arsenal, QPR, Leicester, Notts Co, Bournemouth, Leicester, Torquay. (1968-1985).* The first substitute to score in an F.A. Cup final. Now making double glazed windows in Paignton, Devon and was appointed manager of Western League side Barnstaple in June 1995.

KELLY, Hugh. *Blackpool (1946-1959)* Joined Blackpool from the Scottish junior side, Jeanfield swifts in 1943. Unfortunate in missing the "Matthews final", as he had played in the two losing finals of 1948 and 1951, also playing one game for Scotland against the USA in 1952. He played over 400 games in fourteen years. He now owns a cafe in the North shore area of Blackpool.

KELLY, Mike. *QPR, Birmingham. (1967-1974)* Former England Amateur international goalie now works as an F.A. staff coach and helps with the coaching of England squad keepers.

KELSEY, Jack. *Arsenal (1950-1961).* After making his debut in 1951, he went on to become a great goalie for both club and country. The climax of his career was when Wales won through to the quarter finals of the World Cup, eventually losing to champions - Brazil. Gave over 40 years service to Arsenal, before his death in 1992.

KEMBER, Steve. *C Palace, Chelsea, Leicester, C Palace. (1965-1979).* England Under 23 international, whose fourteen year career started and finished at Crystal Palace. Owned a Wine Bar in Croydon, and managed Diadora League side Whyteleafe until 1992, but Steve is now employed back at Selhurst Park, as a scout.

David Kemp.

KEMP, David. *C Palace, Portsmouth, Carlisle, Plymouth, Gillingham, Brentford. (1974-1981)* A goal scoring forward in his day, David is now Assistant manager to Alan Smith at Wycombe Wanderers, having previously held the same post at Crystal Palace; coached at Wimbledon; and held the managers job at Plymouth Argyle.

KEMP, Fred *Wolves, Southampton, Blackpool, Halifax, Hereford. (1964-1974)* Born in Italy, but played for five League Clubs. now an office equipment salesman, living in Wolverhampton.

KENDALL, Howard. *Preston, Everton, Birmingham, Stoke, Blackburn, Everton. (1962-1981).* Kendall became an overnight sensation when becoming the youngest player to appear in a Wembley Cup final, where his team, Preston, lost to West Ham in 1963/4. He was unlucky not to be capped but did collect Football league and Under-23 honours. He later became Player/manager at Blackburn Rovers, before entering full management with Everton until 1987. In January 1995, he Gave up the sunshine of Greece, where he managed Xanthi, to return to a cold English winter and the managers post at Notts County. Unfortunately his reception at Meadow Lane was also somewhat frosty and his stay was terminated rather acrimoniously, within weeks.

KENDALL, Mark. *Tottenham, Chesterfield, Newport, Wolves, Swansea, Burnley, (1976-1992).* Former Tottenham Hotspur keeper and Welsh Under 21 cap, joined the Police Force three years ago, Mark is now stationed at Newport in Gwent

KENNEDY, Alan. *Newcastle, Liverpool, Sunderland, Hartlepool, Wigan, Wrexham. (1972-1990).* Joined Liverpool from Newcastle in August 1978 for £330,000 and won two England caps. Still playing, part time for Barrow in the Northern League. Lives in Ormskirk and regular contributes to programmes on Radio City, Liverpool, as well as running his own Soccer schools.

KENNEDY, Joe. *WBA, Chester. (1948-1961).* A solid, reliable England 'B' defender who had it not been for injuries would have won full England honours. Retired in 1966 but collapsed and died at his workplace in 1986 aged 60.

KENNEDY, Keith. *Newcastle U , Bury, Mansfield T. (1971-1982).* Made over 400 appearances for Bury as a reliable left back, before finishing his League career at Mansfield in 1982. Keith is now running a greetings card business.

KENNEDY, Ray. *Arsenal, Liverpool, Swansea, Hartlepool. (1969-1983).* **Great striker, who signed as a professional with Arsenal in November 1968, having served his apprenticeship at Port Vale. Less than three years later played a part in the Gunner's Double Winning triumph. Ray joined Liverpool in 1974 for £180,000 and won a total of seventeen England Caps to add to his six at Under 23 level. Finished in his native North-East with Hartlepool in 1983. Became a publican in Northumberland, but now sadly suffers from Parkinsons disease which severely limits his activities.**

KENNON, Sandy. *Huddersfield, Norwich, Colchester. (1956-1966).* Goalkeeper born in South Africa, who played for Bulawayo before coming to England to Huddersfield Town. After ten years and over 300 appearances for his three clubs, became a rep for a Whisky firm and then partner in a bookmakers prior his retirement.

KENWORTHY, Tony. *Sheff U Mansfield (1975-1989)* Although born in Leeds, Tony played most of his league soccer for another Yorkshire club - Sheffield United (281 starts). Now works for a Youth training Programme in Scotland.

KERR, George. *Barnsley, Bury, Oxford, Scunthorpe. (1961-1972).* Experienced manager, who held posts at Lincoln, Grimsby, Rotherham, and Boston. Although he has been unemployed since the change of management at Southampton - for whom he worked as a scout, George has travelled extensively from his home near Grimsby: taking in Venezuela (where he lived for six months); New York; and Houston, Texas

KETTLEBOROUGH, Keith. *Rotherham U, Sheff U, Newcastle, Doncaster, Chesterfield (1955-1968).* Made over 400 league starts before ending in 1958. Lives in Rotherham, and has been a sports master at a local private school since 1985

KEVAN, Derek. *Bradford P.A., WBA, Chelsea, Man C, C Palace, Peterboro, Luton, Stockport. (1952-1967).*Kevan made a terrific reputation with West Brom where teaming up with the great Ronnie Allen, he scored over 150 league goals. After Albion he went on a merry-go-round of clubs before retiring. Now living in Castle Vale, Birmingham and has worked as a drier for a Sign Company in Birmingham for the past six years.

KIDD, Brian. *Man U, Arsenal, Man C, Everton, Bolton. (1967-1981).* Won a European Cup winners medal at the age of 19 with Man Utd; won two England caps; and was transferred four times for six figure sums before hanging up his boots in 1981. Was assistant manager at Swindon, briefly managed Barrow and Preston, before returning to Old Trafford as Assistant Manager.

KIERNAN, Joe. *Sunderland, Northampton T.(1962-1971)* Wing half, veteran of 300 plus games for Northampton Town. Joe still lives in the town and works as a Painter and decorator.

KINDON, Steve. *Burnley, Wolves, Burnley, Huddersfield. (1968-1981).* Bustling centre forward who scored over 100 goals in a career which was ended by a serious knee injury in 1982 while at Huddersfield, where he stayed on as Promotions manager. Although he is now President of the "Town Supporters Club", for the past three years Steve has been the globe trotting sales manager at Rolyat, a firm of basketware importers.

KING, Alan. *Tranmere R, (1962-1971).* Wing half, Alan played 342 games for Tranmere Rovers. Now lives in Moreton on the Wirral, and works in the family scrap metals business.

KING, Andy. *Luton, Everton, QPR, WBA, Everton, Wolves, Luton, Aldershot. (1974-1986)* Everton paid a £35,000 fee to sign Andy from Luton, where he first appeared in 1975. Big money moves to Q.P.R and then West Brom then followed before re-joining Everton. Worked in the commercial department at Luton, before stepping into the vacant manager's job at Mansfield Town.

KING, Brian. *Millwall, Coventry (1967-1975)* **Brain was Millwall's regular goalkeeper for many years, after joining them from non-league Chelmsford City in 1967. Now works as a commentator for Norwegian Television.**

KING, Jake. *Shrewsbury, Wrexham, Cardiff C. (1971-1985)* Played 300 matches in a nine year stint at Shrewsbury. Stayed in the town, where he is now landlord of a pub. Jake is still involved with soccer, as assistant manager of Newton FC.

KING, John. *Everton, Bournemouth, Tranmere, Port V. (1957-1970)* One of the League's longest serving managers, John has been in charge at Tranmere Rovers since 1987. He had previously played almost 250 league games for the club.

KING, John. *Swansea (1950-1963).* Welsh international goalkeeper who played 368 League games for Swansea, died in 1982 aged 49.

KING, Peter *Cardiff (1961-1973)* Played for Cardiff for 12 years, appearing in their colours over 350 times. Now works in the prison service.

(Courtesy: Paul Willatts Photography)

KINNEAR, Joe. *Tottenham, Brighton. (1965-1975).* Dublin born Joe, won 25 caps for Eire and played at right back for Tottenham for nine years before ending his playing days at Brighton. Was Assistant Manager to Dave Mackay at Doncaster Rovers, eventually becoming manager. Joined Wimbledon in the same capacity in January 1991.

KINSEY, Noel. *Cardiff, Norwich, Birmingham, Port V. (1944-1960).* Scored for Birmingham City in the 1956 FA Cup final and is the proud owner of 7 Scotland Caps. Now retired from the Solicitors Office of Norwich Union Insurance.

KIRKMAN, Alan. *Man C, Rotherham U, Newcastle U, Scunthorpe U, Torquay U, Workington T. (1956-1967)* Former inside forward, Alan is now working as a Manager for a Transport company in his hometwon of Bolton, Lancashire.

KIRKUP, Joe *West Ham, Chelsea, Southampton. (1958-1973).* Former England Under 23 international full back, moved to South Africa in 1968 to play for Durban City, becoming their player/coach in 1974. Returned to England to run a pub in Alton, then owned "Cranleigh Sports" shop near Guildford. However, Joe is now runnning his own newsagency in Ewell, Surrey.,

KITCHEN, Peter. *Doncaster, Leyton O, Fulham, Cardiff, Leyton O, Chester (1970-1984).* Goalscoring forward who appeared for five league clubs before having a spell in Hong Kong with Happy Valley. Peter returned to these shores to manage the White Oak Leisure Centre in Kent

KITCHENER, Barry. *Millwall (1966-1981).* A long serving Millwall defender who made over 500 appearances for the London club in a fifteen year League career. Barry now owns Souvenir shops in Caistor and Great Yarmouth, Norfolk.

(Photo courtesy: Liverpool Daily Post & Echo)

John King (right) with fellow Merseyside managers **Roy Evans** and **Joe Royle.**

KNAPP, Tony. *Leicester, Southampton, Coventry, Tranmere. (1955-1970).* **Tony was Captain of the first ever Southampton side to reach the First Division. Now coaching in Norway, with second division club, Ulf-Sandnes. He had previously steered Viking Stavanger to League and Cup double success and was at one time, Manager of the Icelandic national team.**

KNIGHT, Ian. *Barnsley, Sheff Wed, Grimsby (1984-1995).* A serious leg injury seemed to have ended Ian's career whilst at Sheffield Wednesday, however he managed to recover to play for Grimsby, where he is now a Community Officer

KNOWLES, Cyril. *Middlesboro, Tottenham. (1962-1975).* **Cyril left Spurs after 400 league appearances in a 13 year stay which saw him pick up an FA Cup winners medal in 1967. In his heyday, the hit record "Nice One Cyril" was named after him. Became Manager of Torquay, but died at the age of only 47 in 1991**

(Courtesy: Express & Star, Wolverhampton)

KNOWLES, Peter. *Wolves. (1963-1969).* **Dramatically quit Wolves in 1969 to become a Jehovah's witness. Nowadays he works three days a week as a window cleaner, and the rest of the time preaching Jehovah gospel door to door. Lives a few minutes away from Molineux.**

KRUSZYNSKI, Detzi. *FC Hamburg, Wimbledon, Brentford, Peterboro, Coventry (1988-1994)* Detzi moved to England from German club FC 08 Hamburg in 1988. Now runs his own business in Hertfordshire and plays for St Albans City.

KRZYWICKI, Dick. *WBA, Huddersfield, Scunthorpe, Northampton, Lincoln. (1964-1975).* Although he sounds Polish, Dick was Welsh and won eight caps. Now works in the engineering industry and coaches youngsters in his spare time

LABONE, Brian. *Everton (1957-1971)* Turned professional in 1957 and went on to play over 450 league games before retiring. He was also capped 26 times by England. Forced to quit in 1972 Brian went into business on Merseyside. Moved into the insurance industry and now works in the Commercial office at Goodison Park.

LACEY, Bill. *Middlesboro, Aldershot, Reading. (1952-1962).* Was a Carpet department manager for the Co-Op in Reading prior to his death.

LACY, John. *Fulham, Tottenham, C Palace. (1972-1983).* John might have become a Liverpool or Everton player had he not left Merseyside to study at the London School of Economics. He was coached at the College team by England defender George Cohen and signed for Fulham in 1972. Moved to Tottenham in July 1978, then had spell at Crystal Palace. Became the Vauxhall-Opel League's first full time manager at Albans City, where he was until his resignation in June 1988. Now sells insurance.

(Courtesy: Portsmouth News)

Joe Laidlaw

LAIDLAW, Joe. *Middlesboro, Carlisle, Doncaster, Portsmouth, Hereford, Mansfield. (1967-1982)* Midfield dynamo initially with Middlesborough then with five more clubs. Lives in Portsmouth, where he works as a roofer. Manager of Portfield in the Sussex County League.

LAMBERT, Roy. *Rotherham, Barnsley. (1956-1965).* Played over 300 games for Rotherham United, now works for Garrard industries as a machinist, but still in Rotherham.

LAMPARD, Frank. *West Ham, Southend, (1967-1985).* With the exception of a brief stint at Southend United as player/coach in 1985, Frank has been at West Ham United for close on thirty years. As a player, made the right back berth his own for over 600 games, winning Under 23 honours and two full caps along he way. Currently working as Assistant Manager to his friend and old Hammers team-mate, Harry Redknapp.

LANGAN, David. *Derby, Birmingham, Oxford, Leicester, Bournemouth, Peterboro. (1976-1988).* Dublin born, David now lives in Peterborough, but has been forced to give up work due to a back injury sustained during his playing days. Latterly had been employed in the security industry. As a player, won 25 caps for the Republic of Ireland and played over 300 league games.

LANGLEY, Jimmy. *Leeds, Brighton, Fulham, QPR. (1952-1966).* Speedy attacking England full back, who won three full caps in 1958 whilst on the books at Fulham. Starred at Caven Cottage for eight years before a £4,000 move took him across London to Queens Park Rangers where he finished his career two years later. Went on to Manage Hillingdon Borough and was coach at Crystal Palace after his playing days were over. Now living in West Drayton, Middlesex, where he is Steward of the local British Legion Club.

LARGE, Frank. *Halifax, Q.P.R, Northampton, Swindon, Carlisle, Oldham, Leicester, Fulham, Northampton, Chesterfield. (1958-1973).* In a league career with eleven clubs he scored 210 goals from 563 games. Frank is now working as a farmer in County Mayo, Ireland.

LATCHFORD, Bob, *Birmingham, Everton, Swansea, Coventry, Lincoln, Newport. (1968-1985).* England international forward served his apprenticeship with Birmingham City but hit the heights with Everton, Swansea City and then Coventry City. Bob owned a children's clothes shop in Swansea, but now has moved back to live in the Midlands. He lives in Redditch, Worcestershire, and worked for a firm selling nuts and bolts, but is now employed as a marketing manager by Ladbrokes Bookmakers, working from their headquarters in Uxbridge, North London.

(Courtesy: Solihull News)

LATCHFORD, Dave. *Birmingham, Bury. (1968-1978).* Former Birmingham City goalkeeper. Now lives in Solihull and runs the Widney Manor Cemetery in Bentley Heath, Birmingham.

LATCHFORD, Peter. *WBA (1972-1974).* An England Under 23 goalkeeper. Joined Celtic from West Brom in 1975, where he won medals in League and Cup competitions. Was the Glasgow club's 'Player of the Year' in 1977-8. Retired in 1988, and now lives on a farm in Mauchline.

LAVERICK, Mick. *Mansfield, Southend, Huddersfield, York, Huddersfield. (1972-1982).* Now a Prison Officer living in Nottinghamshire.

Denis Law

(Courtesy: Manchester Evening News)

LAW, Denis. *Huddersfield, Man C, Man U, Man C. (1956-1973).* **Law was signed by the great Bill Shankly as a skinny bespectacled youngster for Huddersfield. He developed into one of the most dangerous forwards in the game. In a cup game against Luton in 1966, Denis had already scored six goals when the game was abandoned. Amazingly enough, they lost the replay! He moved to Torino in Italy for a season before joining Man Utd, helping them to win two League Titles and an FA Cup final in 1963. He returned to Maine Road to end his illustrious career as undoubtedly one of soccer's great personalities. Since leaving the playing side has worked as a commentator on both television and radio and a popular after dinner speaker. Lives in Bowden, Cheshire.**

LAWRENCE, Lennie. *Plymouth, Charlton (player/Manager)* Lennie Managed Plymouth, worked wonders at Charlton, and then had a short lived term of office at Middlesborough before accepting the post offered by Bradford City in 1994

LAWRENCE, Tommy. *Liverpool, Tranmere. (1962-1973)* Affectionately nicknamed "The Flying Pig" by the Kop due to his rather portly stature, Tommy kept goal for Liverpool in 300 league games and for almost a decade. He won three full caps for his native Scotland, won League Championship medals in 1964 and 1966 and an FA Cup Winners Medal in 1965. Finally finished in 1973, having played a further 80 games for neighbours Tranmere Rovers. He now works on night shift at a wire factory in Warrington, Cheshire.

LAWRENSON, Mark. *Preston, Brighton., Liverpool. (1974-1987).* The son of a former Preston forward, started his career like his father at Deepdale. The £100,000 that Brighton paid for his services in 1977 was rewarded by starring performances and then by a very healthy profit when Liverpool parted with £900,000 to take him to Anfield. A Republic of Ireland International (38 Caps) moved into management with Oxford, then Peterborough - but is now developing a media career with the BBC and Sky Television.

LAWRIE, Sam. *Middlesborough, Charlton Ath, Bradford P.A. (1951-1965).* Goalscoring winger during a 14 year career. Died in 1979.

LAWS, Brian. *Burnley, Huddersfield, Middlesboro, Notts F, Grimsby (1979-1995).* England "B" international, who after fifteen years as a player was offered his first managerial opportunity by Grimsby Town in November 1994.

LAWSON, Alan. *Oldham (1964-1969)* Alan was a central defender who in 1965, became the first ever substitute to score a goal. He is now back in Scotland, living near Motherwell ands currently works as a maintenance engineer.

LAWTON, Bill *Oldham, Chester (1946-1949)* **Oldham wing half of the late 40's and husband of actress, Dora Bryan. Now lives on the South Coast at Brighton where they took an hotel.**

(Courtesy: Evening Post, Nottingham)

LAWTON, Tommy. *Burnley, Everton, Chelsea, Notts Co, Brentford, Arsenal. (1935-1955)* One of the greatest ever centre forwards. Made his mark at the age of 17, becoming the youngest player to score a hat-trick. Won 23 full caps and scored goals galore for all of his six league clubs. After spells as manager at Kettering and Notts County, Tommy became a publican in Lowdham but is now retired and lives in Nottingham. Writes a regular column in the Nottingham Evening Post.

LAYNE, David. *Rotherham, Swindon, Bradford C, Sheff Wed, Hereford. (1957-1972).* Retired in 1972 with an incredible goalscoring ratio, having netted 128 times in 194 league games. David is now a Publican in Chesterfield.

LAYTON, John. *Hereford, Newport (1974-1983).* Central defender who originally signed for Hereford from Gloucester City in 1974, later became Manager at Edgar Street until August 1995

LEA, Cyril. *Leyton O, Ipswich. (1957-1968).* Wrexham born wing half who won two full Welsh caps during an eleven year playing career in England, is now Youth team coach at West Brom.

LEACH, Mick. *QPR, Cambridge. (1964-1978).* Died in 1992 after a long illness. Spent 13 years at Loftus Road, playing 313 League games.

Colin Lee

LEADBETTER, James. *Chelsea, Brighton, Ipswich (1951-1966).* Played 344 League games for Ipswich Town as an outside left. Worked as a newsagent, then as a salesman with Cadburys in Suffolk. Returned to Scotland in 1971 to work for the Scotsman publications - retiring in 1993.

LEARY, Stuart. *Charlton, QPR. (1951-1965).* **Former England Under 23 centre forward, Stuart committed suicide in 1988, by jumping out of a cable car near the top of Table mountain in his native South Africa. He was also an accomplished cricketer, who played for Kent.**

LEE, Colin. *Bristol C, Hereford, Torquay, Tottenham, Chelsea, Brentford. (1974-1988).* Was Youth Coach at Brentford, then took the same post at Watford, where he later became Manager. Joined Reading as Assistant to Mark McGee: following him to Leicester in December 1994

LEE, Francis. *Bolton Man C, Derby. (1960-1975).* **Man City signed "Frannie" from Bolton for £60,000 in 1967. With City he won the League; FA Cup; and European Cup Winners Cup. He finished with Derby County, retiring in May 1976, going into business full time. Made a fortune with diverse business interests which included owning/training racehorses, and building up a recycled paper business. Returned to Maine Road in 1993, heralded as a saviour when he headed a consortium that took control of the Manchester Club.**

(Courtesy Manchester Evening News)

Francis Lee, hoping to add to the Silverware at Manchester City.

LEE, Jeff. *Halifax, Peterboro (1964-1977).* Having enjoyed a thirteen year career as a player, Jeff is currently Assistant manager of Hull City.

LEE, Sammy. *Liverpool, QPR, Southampton, Bolton (1977-1990)* Developed through Liverpool's junior ranks to become a first team regular and full England International (14 caps) before moving onto Queens Park Rangers and then abroad for a spell in Spain with Osasuna. Returned to play for Bolton Wanderers, where fe finished in 1990, but Sammy is now back at Anfield working as their reserve team manager.

LEEK, Ken. *Northampton, Leicester, Newcastle, Birmingham, Northampton, Bradford C. (1955-1967).* Lives in Northampton and works for Ford Motor Company in Daventry. In 1963 Ken scored twice in the last three minutes for Wales against Scotland to win the game 3-2 !

LEGGAT, Graham. *Fulham, Birmingham, Rotherham (1958-1968)* **Scottish international winger (18 full caps), and scored one of the fastest hat-tricks on record (4 mins 33 secs.). Graham left the U.K. in 1971 to set up home in Canada, where he now hosts his own soccer show for a Toronto based television station.**

LEIGH, Dennis. *Doncaster, Rotherham, Lincoln. (1966-1978).* Battling left back, stayed in Lincoln after a six year stint with the 'Imps'. Now Advertising manager at the Lincolnshire Echo.

LEIVERS, W.E. *Chesterfield, Man C, Doncaster. (1951-1965).* Played 250 matches for Manchester City before going into management. Was in Charge at Cambridge United when they won admission to the League in 1971. Now General Manager of neighbours Cambridge City.

LELLO, Cyril *Lincoln, Everton, Rochdale. (1944-1956).* Played over 200 games for Everton after the War, before becoming player/manager of Runcorn, then coach to New Brighton. Worked for a Contract Electricians, but is now in a Liverpool nursing home having suffered a stroke.

LEONARD, Carleton. *Shrewsbury, Hereford, Cardiff. (1975-1985)* First choice full back for Rotherham in the 70's, has returned to his home town of Oswestry where he is now a publican.

LESLIE, John. *Wimbledon, Gillingham, Millwall. (1977-1986).* **Finished playing for non-league Dartford, in December 1994, and now works for a central heating company in Lewisham. He has lived in the same house for many years, in fact it was Dave Bassett who sold him the insurance policy when it was purchased. Also spent his wedding night with "Harry" in a Huddersfield hotel, after getting married the day before a game, and was then driven up to Yorkshire in Ron Noades' Rolls Royce.**

LESLIE, Steve. *Colchester (1970-1983).* Played over 400 matches for his only club, Colchester. Now works for Brentwood Council.

LEWINGTON, Ray. *Chelsea, Wimbledon, Fulham, Sheff U, Fulham. (1975-1989).* Best remembered for his days at Chelsea, Ray went over to Canada to help Vancouver Whitecaps win the North American Soccer Bowl before returning to London for spells with Wimbledon and then Fulham. Became Manager at Craven Cottage and is now on the coaching staff at Crystal Palace.

LEWIS, Brian. *C Palace, Portsmouth, Coventry, Luton, Oxford, Colchester, Portsmouth. (1960-1974)* Lewis was a member of the giant killing Colchester team that stunned the then mighty Leeds. He now works as a salesman in a furniture showroom in Bournemouth but is still involved with football running an Under-16 side.

Dave Leworthy

LEWIS, Russell. *Swindon, Northamptn. (1976-1985).* Defender who spent almost a decade in the League after joining Swindon from Bridgend in 1976. Now a bricklayer in Northampton.

LEWORTHY, Dave. *Portsmouth, Tottenham, Oxford, Shrewsbury, Reading (1981-1993)* Three years after being discarded by home town club, Portsmouth, Dave was snapped up from non-league soccer by Tottenham in 1984. Went on to play for three other clubs before returning to the lower leagues where he is with currently with Dover Athletic . Was their top scorer in 1993/4 earning him England semi-pro honours.

LEY, George. *Exeter, Portsmouth, Brighton., Gillingham (1963-1975).* **Left back who once topped a poll for best looking footballer, beating off the challenge of other players such as George Best! Had a spell as Luton Town Youth Coach before emigrating to the United States.**

LEYLAND, Harry. *Everton, Blackburn, Tranmere. (1951-1965).* Former Blackburn and Tranmere goalkeeper, Harry is now a shop owner and market trader, living in Moels, Merseyside.

LIDDELL, Billy. *Liverpool, (1946-1960).* Scottish international who scored 216 goals for his only club, Liverpool, despite being a winger. Worked in an accountants office throughout his career and continued once he had hung up his boots. Went on to become bursar at Liverpool University and a J.P. in the City. Billy is now aged 73 and sadly suffering from altzheimers disease.

LINDSAY, John. *Everton, Bury. (1951-1956).* Full back who joined Everton from Glasgow Rangers in 1951. Stayed in the area, John lives on Merseyside and works in Walton hospital.

LINEKER, Gary. *Leicester, Everton, Tottenham, (1978-1993).* The second most successful England International striker with 48 goals in from his 60 games. Started his career with home town club Leicester City in 1978 where he established himself as a prolific marksman, moving to Everton in 1985 for £800,000. After only a season at Goodison Park, Terry Venables took him to Spanish giants, Barcelona in a £2.75m move. Spells with Tottenham Hotspur and Japanese club Grampus followed, before he quit in 1994 to join the BBC, working on their television programmes and hosting his own Sunday show on Radio 5.

(Courtesy: Raymonds Press Agency)

Gary Lineker, paying a return visit to Filbert Street.

LINES, Barry. *Northampton. (1960-1969).* Northampton winger throughout the sixties, Barry is now working as a sports equipment salesman.

LISHMAN, Doug. *Walsall, Arsenal, Notts F (1946-1956).* Goalscoring inside forward who hit the back of the net 125 times in 226 games for Arsenal. Won England 'B' honours before ending at Notts Forest in 1956. Returned to manage his family furniture business in Stoke-on-Trent, but died on December 21st 1994 aged 71

LITTLE, Alan. *Aston V, Southend, Barnsley, Doncaster, Torquay, Halifax, Hartlepool. (1974-1985).* Played in midfield for seven clubs. Then coached at Hartlepool until moving on to become Assistant Manager at York City.

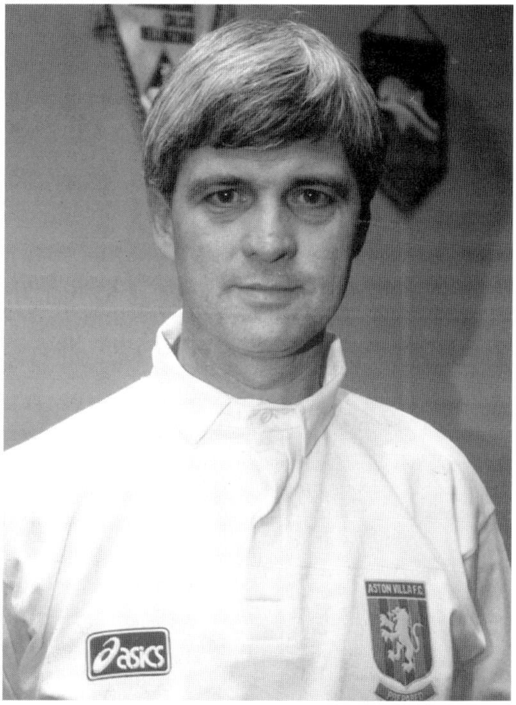

LITTLE, Brian. *Aston Villa (1971-1979).* Played all his career at Villa until he was forced to quit through injury aged 26. Gained coaching experience at Wolves, Middlesborough and then in 1989 was appointed manager at Darlington leading them to the GM Vauxhall Conference title and back into the Football league in 1990. He then took them to the fourth Division championship in 1991, before taking the helm at Leicester City. Resigned from Filbert Street in November 1994 and caused a storm by taking over at Aston Villa after strongly denying that he would.

(Photo courtesy: Evening Post, Nottingham)

Larry Lloyd

LIVERMORE, Doug. *Liverpool, Norwich, Bournemouth, Cardiff, Chester. (1967-1978).* Former Liverpool junior who went on to play for four more clubs. Coached at Cardiff, Norwich and Swansea and was Assistant Manager to Mike England for the Welsh National side. Now finally back at Anfield where he is first team coach.

LLOYD, Barry. *Chelsea, Fulham, Hereford, Brentford (1966-1977).* England Youth international started at Chelsea, but had most success a little further down the Kings Road at Fulham. Manager of Brighton from 1987 until 1994.

LLOYD, Brian. *Stockport, Southend, Wrexham, Chester, Port V, Stockport. (1967-1982)* Wrexham's first choice keeper in the 1970's. Whilst at Stockport County, studied Building design, gaining an HND, which has allowed him to pursue a career in the field since retiring in 1982.

LLOYD, Cliff. *Wrexham, Fulham (1937-1946)* Made only a handful of League appearances, but will always be remembered for his contribution to the PFA where he was Secretary between 1953 and 1981, now lives in retirement near Chester.

LLOYD, Larry. *Bristol R, Liverpool, Coventry, Notts F, Wigan. (1968-1982).* Won only four England caps, but was a commanding defender who enjoyed success with Liverpool and Nottingham Forest. Joined the Anfield club from Bristol Rovers for £50,000 in 1969 and in the next five years won Championship and EUFA Cup winners medals. After a spell at Coventry, he bcame a central figure in Nottingham Forest's European Cup triumphs of 1979 and 1980. Larry went on to coach at Wigan and manage at Notts County before leaving soccer in October 1984. Now Licensee of "The Stage Door" club in Nottingham.

LOCHHEAD, Andy. *Burnley, Leicester, Aston V, Oldham. (1960-1974).* Scottish Under 23 attacker who scored an average of almost every other game for Burnley in the sixties. After returning from America he coached Oldham for a number of years before scouting for several clubs including Burnley. He now acts as a steward at the Ighton Mount bowling club outside the town.

LOCK, Kevin. *West Ham, Fulham, Southend (1971-1985).* After six years in the claret and Blue of West Ham, Kevin moved to West London to play over 200 games for Fulham. Won Under 23 caps with England and ended at Southend United, where he is now a member of the coaching staff.

(Courtesy: Bolton Evening News)

Nat Lofthouse - 'The Lion of Vienna'

LOFTHOUSE, Nat. *Bolton W (1946-1960).* One of the all time greats, earned the nickname "The Lion of Vienna" following a game against Austria in which his style and bravery were dominant. Won 33 caps and scored 255 goals in 452 games for his only league club Bolton. Was "Footballer of the year" in 1953. A dedicated Wanderers man, Nat has served the club as player; Reserve Coach; Chief Coach; Manager; General manager; Chief Scout; and now Club President.

LORD, Frank. *Rochdale, Crewe A, Plymouth A, Stockport Co, Blackburn R, Chesterfield, Plymouth A. (1953-1968).* Frank scored goals from the centre forward position for a total of seven clubs, averaging almost a goal every other game. In September 1991 took over as Director of Coaching for Western Province in South Africa.

LORIMER, Peter. *Leeds, York, Leeds. (1963-1985).* A Scottish international who played a total of 676 times for Leeds United, making his debut at the age of 15 which is still a club record. Reputed to have had the hardest shot in his day, Peter had spells in Canada and Israel before finally retiring in 1985. Now landlord of the Commercial Inn public house in Holbeck, Leeds and also helps to run the Leeds ex-professionals team.

LOVELL, Steve. *C Palace, Stockport, Millwall, Swansea, Gillingham. (1980-1992).* Former Crystal Palace junior went on to win six full caps for Wales and play for five league clubs. Left Hastings Town in February 1995 to become player/manager of Sittingbourne Town FC.

Peter Lorimer
(Courtesy: Yorkshire Post Newspapers)

LOVETT, Graham. *WBA, Southampton. (1964-1971).* Won an FA Cup winners medal in 1968 with West Bromwich Albion after surviving two horrific car crashes. Sadly, the injuries that he received eventually forced him to give up league soccer in 1986 at the early age of 26. Now a Newspaper executive in the West Midlands.

LOWNDES, Steve. *Newport, Millwall, Barnsley, Hereford, (1977-1993)* Won 12 caps for the Wales and played over 400 league games for his four clubs. Now physio to the Welsh national team and plays for Newport AFC in the B.H.L.

LUCAS, Mal. *Leyton O, Norwich, Torquay (1958-1973).* Wing half who was plucked from Local league side Bradley by Leyton Orient in 1978. Played professionally for the next fifteen years and won four Welsh Caps. Now an Account executive/collector for Brent Leisure Services Ltd.

LUMBY, Jim *Grimsby, Scunthorpe, Carlisle, Tranmere, Mansfield (1973-1981)* Licensee of the "Hainton" pub in Grimsby, having previously worked as a pipefitter at the Conoco oil refinery.

LYALL, John. *West Ham (1959-1962).* Only played 31 League games but made his name in management. John was appointed Assistant-Manager at West Ham in 1971, team manager in 1974 and manager in 1977. Moved to East Anglia, to become manager at Ipswich until December 1994.

LYNEX, Steve. *WBA, Birmingham, Leicester, Birmingham, WBA, Cardiff. (1976-1989)* **Winger who served his apprenticeship at home club, W.B.A, but played most of his soccer with Leicester. Now runs the Red Lion pub in West Bromwich, which sadly hit the headlines in 1994, due to a fatal bonfire night accident.**

LYNN, Stan. *Accrington S, Aston V, Birmingham. (1946-1965).* Found fame in the Midlands with Birmingham and Aston Villa. Retired from Soccer in 1968, now lives in Shirley, West Midlands and works in the toolroom stores at Lucas.

LYONS, Mick. *Everton, Sheff Wed, Grimsby. (1970-1986).* Played 389 league games for Everton and appeared in three FA Cup finals, unfortunately losing side each time. Gained coaching and managerial experience at Grimsby, Everton, and then Huddersfield before accepting the post of Coach to the Brunei national team.

McALLE, John. *Wolves, Sheff U, Derby. (1967-1983)* John now runs his own landscape gardening business based on the outskirts of Dudley, West Midlands. Made over 500 appearances for Wolves in his fourteen years at Molineux.

McANDREW, Tony. *Middlesboro, Chelsea, Middlesboro, Darlington, Hartlepool, (1973-1988).* Glasgow born defender who spent eight years in the centre of the Middlesborough defence. Held the post of Joint youth team coach at Leicester until early 1995 when he joined Aston Villa.

McANEARNEY, Tom. *Sheff Wed, Peterboro, Aldershot, (1952-1968).* Former Aldershot Manager who made over 350 appearances for Sheffield Wednesday in the fifties. Joined the 'Owls' from Dundee St Stephens in his native Scotland. Now retired in the Aldershot area of Hampshire.

McCAFFERY, Jim. *Notts F, Mansfield, Huddersfield, Portsmouth, Northampton. (1969-1979).* Former England Youth international winger who played for five clubs, ending at Northampton Town in 1978. Jim is now a newsagent.

McCALL, Steve. *Ipswich T, Sheff Wed, Carlisle U , Plymouth A, (1979-1995).* Former England Under 23 defender, Steve briefly took over as manager of Plymouth Argyle in January 1995, having joined them from Sheffield Wednesday in March 1992. However, he relinquished the post within two months to concentrate on playing.

McCALLIOG, Jim. *Chelsea, Sheff Wed, Wolves, Man U, Southampton, Lincoln. (1964-1978).* Scottish international midfielder whose trophy cabinet includes five full caps. Appeared in the 1966 Cup final with Wolves, and then ten years later was on the winning side with Southampton. Played in Norway in the 1977/8 season before joining Lincoln as player/coach in September 1978. Had spells as manager at Halifax Town Runcorn but is now a journalist and publican, running the 'County Hotel' in Harrogate.

(Courtesy: Portsmouth News)

McCANN, Albert *Luton, Coventry, Portsmouth (1959-1973)* Long serving Pompey midfielder, 'Albie' is now a rest home proprietor in Emsworth, Hampshire, having previously run a newsagents in Southsea for many years.

McCARTHY, Bob. *Southampton (1967-1974).* Former Saints full back is now an Area Manager for Beer Seller Ltd, an independent wholesaler. Having previously worked for major brewers.

McCARTHY, Mick. *Barnsley, Man City, Millwall (1977-1994).* Appointed Millwall Manager in April 1992 following a spell as caretaker boss, after Bruce Rioch left for Bolton Wanderers. He started his career with home town club, Barnsley, playing 272 times before a £200,000 move took him to Manchester City. From Maine Road he went North of the border to Celtic and then to Lyon in France. Mick skippered the Republic of Ireland in the 1990 World Cup finals, and played a total of 57 games for his country.

McCARTNEY, Mike. *W.B.A, Carlisle, Southampton, Plymouth, Carlisle. (1971-1986).* Mike made his first, and then thirteen years later, his last league appearance - in a Carlisle United shirt. Now player, manager/groundsman at Gretna in the Northern Premier League Division One.

McCLAREN, Steve. *Hull, Derby, Lincoln, Bristol C, Oxford, (1979-1981).* Reserve team coach at his last playing club, Oxford United until June 1995 when he returned to another former club, Derby County to become First team coach.

McCLELLAND, John. *Arsenal, Fulham, Lincoln (1960-1968).* Irish international goalkeeper (6 caps), died from a brain haemorrhage after a brief illness in 1976 aged 36. His son, John now works in the Accounts department at Arsenal.

McCREADIE, Eddie. *Chelsea (1962-1973).* Chelsea skipper in the seventies, Eddie picked up 23 Scottish caps during his 13 years as a player at Stamford Bridge. Retired in 1975, when he was appointed the Club's Manager, a post held until July 1977. Moved to the America in 1978 to manage Memphis Rogues, and is still living there, now working as a painter and decorator.

McCREERY, David. *Man U, QPR, Newcastle, Hartlepool. (1974-1995)* Man United snapped up this Dublin born midfielder as a youngster in 1974, but it was at Newcastle some eight years later that he really became a first team regular. He made 67 appearances for Northern Ireland and finally finished at Hartlepool where he became Manager, from September 1994 until April 1995

McCROHAN, Roy. *Reading, Norwich, Colchester, Bristol R. (1949-1964)* Played 384 games for Norwich in the fifties, now believed to be living in Tampa, Florida and coaching youngsters.

McCULLOCH, Andy *Q.P.R., Cardiff, Oxford, Brentford, Sheff W, C. Palace, Aldershot (1970-1984)* Andy's career lasted 14 years and took in seven clubs, ending at Aldershot in 1984. Now owns a cleaning business based in Hampton Court, where his wife also runs an antiques shop.

McCULLOCH, Iain. *Notts Co (1978-1983).* Former Scottish Under 21 winger Now Lifeline co-ordinator at Notts County, his only League club as a player. Iain is also joint manager of Arnold Town in the North East Counties League.

McCULLOCH, William. *Arsenal, Millwall (1958-1966).* Arsenal's regular left back in the late fifties/early sixties. Won 10 caps for Northern Ireland, and later managed Cork Celtic and then Derry City. Upon retirement from soccer, he worked as an electrical engineer in his father-in-law's factory based in Woodford, Essex.

McDERMOTT, Brian. *Arsenal, Fulham, Oxford, Huddersfield, Cardiff, Exeter (1978-1990)* Served his apprenticeship at Arsenal before making league appearances for six clubs. Currently playing for Stamco in the Sussex League and acts as Community Officer at Slough Town.

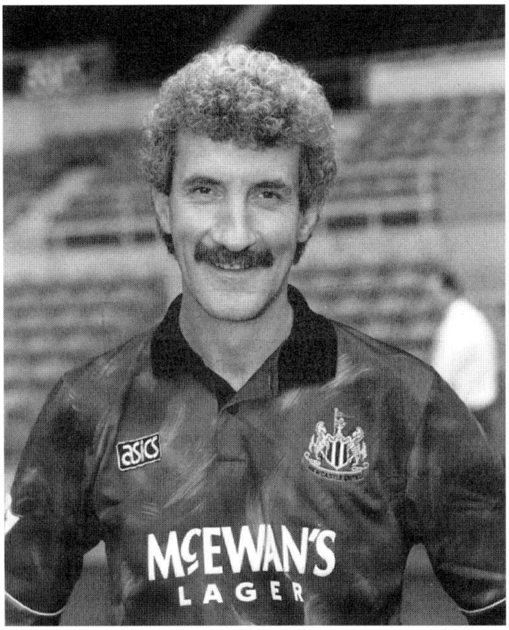

Terry McDermott

McDERMOTT, Terry. *Bury, Newcastle, Liverpool, Newcastle. (1969-1983).* Kevin Keegan's sidekick at Newcastle, was capped by England 25 times during his time at Liverpool, where he also won every honour in the game except an FA Cup winners medal. Voted PFA and Football Writers Association 'Player of the Year in 1980', the first time a player had won both awards.

McDONALD, Ian. *Barrow, Workington, Liverpool, Colchester, Mansfield, York, Aldershot, (1970-1988).* Ian sampled league soccer with seven clubs in over 500 games, although he didn't appear for the first team during a spell at Liverpool (1974). Now Reserve team coach at Millwall.

McDONALD, Kevin. *Leicester, Liverpool, Leicester, Coventry, Cardiff, Walsall, (1980-1993).* Joined Leicester in 1980 fromInverness Caledonians. Spent three years at Liverpool but only made 40 starts before moving on to three further clubs. Returned to Filbert Street as youth team coach until 1995, when he followed Brian Little to Aston Villa to take up a similar post.

MacDONALD, Malcolm. *Fulham, Luton T, Newcastle, Arsenal (1968-1978).* **Malcolm was originally a full back, until Fulham converted him to a centre forward with deadly effect. They allowed him to join Luton Town in 1969, where he scored 49 goals from 88 games in two sensational seasons. However, finances forced the Kenilworth Road club to sell him to Newcastle for a record fee of £185,000. Amazingly in his 14 England matches he only scored on one occasion, but netted five times against Cyprus in that match. Arsenal signed this still dynamic sharpshooter in 1976, but within three years, injuries forced him to quit. He later returned to his first club, Fulham, as manager and then on to Huddersfield Town in the same capacity. Moved to Italy in 1991, now lives in Milan and works for Audiotel setting up the equivalent of our 0891 service. Still does occasional scouting for British clubs and is a regular contributor to Channel 4's Football Italia.**

McDONOUGH, Jim. *Rotherham, Bolton, Everton, Bolton, Notts Co, Birmingham, Gillingham, Sunderland, Scarborough, Huddersfield, Charlton. (1970-1988).* Managed Derry City in Ireland until May 1989. Now in the insurance business and playing for Arnold Town and Ilkeston Vets in the Umbro Vets Competition.

McDONOUGH, Roy. *Birmingham, Walsall, Chelsea, Colchester, Southend, Exeter, Cambridge, Southend. (1976-1989)* **Manager of Colchester until May 1994. He is son-in-law of Gordon Parker, the Colchester Chairman, who had to dismiss him! Now playing for Dagenham & Redbridge in the Vauxhall Conference.**

MacDOUGALL, Ted. *Liverpool, York, Bournemouth, Man U, West Ham, Norwich, Southampton, Bournemouth, Blackpool (1966-1980).* After scoring a hatful of goals for all his clubs Ted was appointed player/coach at Blackpool between February and October 1980, then retired. Came out of retirement in August 1981 to play a few games for Salisbury, moving to Poole Town in the following December and Gosport Borough in 1982. Became the owner of sports shops in Bournemouth and a licensee of a public house near Romsey, Hampshire. Emigrated to Canada with his French/Canadian wife, where he has become a wealthy property developer. Based in Vancouver, he still follows the progress of AFC Bournemouth, and was the centre of takeover speculation during the Summer of 1994.

McDOWELL, John. *West Ham, Norwich. (1970-1980)* Right back, John won thirteen England Under 23 caps, and played almost 250 league games for the Hammers before ending his career in Norfolk with Norwich. Retired in 1980 and went on to become a publican in Essex.

McEWAN, Billy. *Blackpool, Brighton., Chesterfield, Mansfield, Peterborough, Rotherham. (1973-1983).* Manager at Rotherham between 1988 and 1991, before becoming Coach at Derby.

MacEWAN, Jimmy. *Aston V, Walsall. (1959-1966).* Scottish Winger who spent six years at Villa Park following a move from Raith Rovers in 1959. Two knee replacement operations in 1991 forced Jimmy to retire from the job that he had held in the civil service for nine years.

McEVOY, Don. *Huddersfield, Sheff Wed, Lincoln, Barrow. (1949-1961)* After his playing days, Don had spells as manager at Halifax Town, Barrow, Grimsby Town, and Southport. Now runs the Crown Hotel in Brighouse, North Yorkshire.

(Photo courtesy: Bournemouth Echo)

Ted MacDougall, during a return to Bournemouth from his adopted home of Canada.

McFARLAND, Roy. *Tranmere, Derby, Bradford C, Derby. (1966-1983).* A classic centre back, who had it not been for injuries would have played for England on many more occasions than his total of 28. Became manger at Derby in late 1993. Failure to achieve promotion despite many inherited big money signings resulted in his dismissal at the end of the 1994/5 season. However he was installed as boss at Bolton only weeks later.

McFARLANE, Ian. *Chelsea, Leicester, (1956-1958).* Scottish full back who moved South to play for Chelsea and Leicester in the fifties. Ian is now Assistant manager at Leeds United.

Willie McFAUL
(Courtesy: Newcastle Chronicle)

McFAUL, Willie. *Newcastle (1966-1974)* After completing almost 300 appearances for Newcastle, he went on to become their manager from August 1985 until December 1988. Now lives in Northern Ireland and is part of the Bryan Hamilton's national side management set up.

McGARRY, Bill. *Port Vale, Huddersfield, Bournemouth. (1946-1962)* Won four England caps as a player, whilst also notching up over 500 league appearances at wing half. Became player/manager at his last club, Bournemouth, before managing Watford, Ipswich, Newcastle and Wolves. In 1976 took over as Saudi Arabia's national team manager, but Bill is now thought to be coaching in Bopnutbuswanana, South Africa.

McGARVEY, Scott. *Man U, Wolves, Portsmouth, Carlisle, Grimsby, Bristol C, Oldham, Wigan. (1980-1989).* Former Man United junior and Scottish Under 23 striker. Played for eight league clubs, before quitting in 1989. Scott has set up his own company, Moneystone, which sells sand to sports clubs and agricultural concerns from their base at Levenseat Quarry, Glasgow.

McGHEE, Mark. *Newcastle, Reading.* A well travelled striker who won four full caps for Scotland, during a career which took in stops at Celtic, Aberdeen, and SV Hamburg in Germany. His football league experience consisted of two spells at Newcastle United before moving to Reading as player manager in 1991. After four years, and having guided the Berkshire club to their highest ever league placing, Mark accepted the manager's job at Leicester City in January 1995.

McGILL, James. *Arsenal, Huddersfield, Hull, Halifax. (1965-1976).* Upon finally leaving football having managed several clubs in Denmark, Jimmy took a job with ICI based in Huddersfield,

McGIVEN, Mick *Sunderland, West Ham, (1969-1977).* Central defender with Sunderland and West Ham, Mick was appointed Football development manager at Ipswich in May 1995.

McGOVERN, John. *Hartlepool, Derby, Leeds, Notts F, Bolton. (1965-1983).* The backbone of many a Brian Clough side, he started with Hartlepool, before following his boss to Derby County, Leeds and then Nottingham Forest. Ended his playing days at Bolton as player/manager prior to leaving these shores to enjoy the sun, sand, and sea of Tenerife. Became Assistant Manager to Peter Shilton at Plymouth until September 1994, when he took on the same post at Rotherham United - offered by another of his former Forest colleagues, Archie Gemmill.

McGRATH, Chris *Tottenham, Millwall, Man U. (1973-1980).* Belfast born Chris played less than 75 league games for his three clubs, but won 21 full caps with Northern Ireland. Now lives in Harrow, and works at an Armaments factory.

McGRATH, John. *Bury, Newcastle, Southampton, Brighton. (1956-1972).* Fearsome central defender, John won one England Under 23 cap. After almost 500 games, hung up his boots in 1973 and then Managed Port Vale, Chester City, Preston North End, and Halifax Town. However he is now a most popular after dinner speaker.

McGUINNESS, Wilf. *Man U (1955-1959)* A broken leg prevented Wilf from fulfilling his early promise which had already earned him two full England caps before his 23rd birthday. Has since held coaching or scouting posts for a host of clubs including Everton, Manchester United, York, Hull, Bury and the England Youth team (1963-1969). Now lives in Timperley, Cheshire and is a regular on the after dinner speaking circuit.

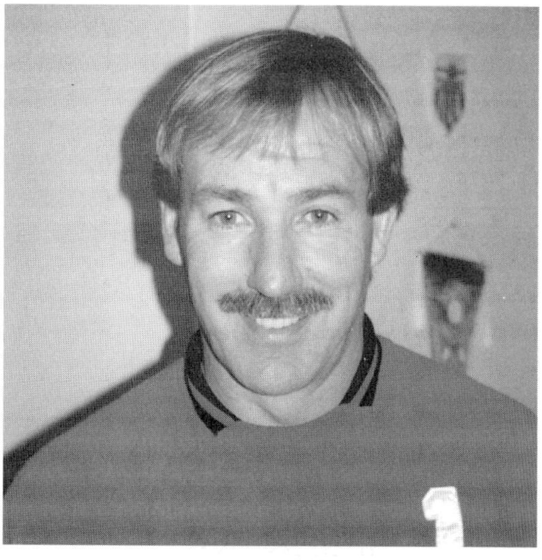

Ray McHale

McGUIRE, Mick. *Coventry, Norwich, Barnsley, Oldham. (1971-1986).* Blackpool born midfielder who played for four clubs in a 350 plus game career. Now works as a director of the P.F.A.

McHALE, Kevin. *Huddersfield, Crewe, Chester (1956-1971).* Spent eleven years on the wing for Huddersfield in the fifties and sixties. Kevin now works at David Browns in the town.

McHALE, Ray. *Chesterfield, Halifax, Swindon, Brighton., Barnsley, Sheff U, Bury, Swansea, Rochdale, Scarboro. (1971-1987).* Returned to manage Scarborough in December 1994, 21 months after being sacked from the same position. Managed Guisley Town in the interim.

McILMOYLE, Hugh. *Leicester, Rotherham, Carlisle, Wolves, Bristol C, Carlisle, Middlesboro, Preston, Carlisle, (1959-1974).* Prolific goalscorer during his fourteen year career which included three spells with Carlisle United. Now lives in Leicester, and works for the Walkers Crisps company in their warehouse.

McILROY, Jimmy. *Burnley, Stoke, Oldham. (1950-1967).* Won a championship medal with Burnley in 1959-60, and 55 Northern Ireland caps. Jimmy wrote his own column in the local paper whilst a player and became a journalist with the Lancashire Evening Telegraph. Then after nine years with the Burnley Express, he took early retirement which now allows him to play golf and attend Art School three times a week.

Sammy McIlroy
(Courtesy: Manchester Evening News)

McILROY, Sammy. *Man U, Stoke, Man C, Bury, Preston. (1971-1989).* Belfast born midfielder, Sammy joined Manchester United as an apprentice in 1969, and played in their cup final teams of 1976, 1977, and 1979. Was a regular in the Northern Ireland team, winning a total of 88 caps. Now fast gaining a reputation as a talented manager with Macclesfield Town. Unfortunate to miss out on promotion to the Football League due to ground standards regulations after winning the Vauxhall Conference in 1995.

MACKAY, Dave. *Tottenham, Derby, Swindon. (1958-1971).* Dave started with Hearts, where he won the first of his 22 Scottish caps. Transferred to Tottenham Hotspur for a give-away fee and went on to become one of the finest hard tackling wing halves in Britain. He joined Derby County when Brian Clough signed him to lead them back into the first division. While at the Baseball ground, he was recognised as "Footballer of the Year", and later managed Derby to the First Division title in 1974-5. His leadership qualities also led to management posts at Swindon Town; Nottingham Forest; Walsall; Arabic Sporting Club (Kuwait) Doncaster Rovers, Birmingham City, and currently holds a coaching post in Qatar.

McKECHNIE, Ian. *Arsenal, Southend U, Hull C. (1961-1973)* **Ian was originally signed by Arsenal as an outside left, but went on to play over 300 league games and became a New Zealand international as a goalkeeper. Hung up his boots in 1974 after seven years with Hull City. Initially took a job as a prison officer, but has since worked for many years at British Aerospace in Brough. Had a two week spell as manager of Nuneaton Borough and later took over as team boss at Sligo Rovers.**

McKENZIE, Duncan. *Notts F, Mansfield, Leeds, Everton, Chelsea, Blackburn. (1968-1980).* **One of the classiest players to grace the League during the seventies, although never capped by his country. He made his name at Notts Forest and went on to play for several of the top clubs of the day including a spell with Anderlecht in Belgium. Now works for "Football in the Community" at Everton, Duncan lives in Newton-le-Willow, Merseyside. As well as owning a delicatessen, he is a familiar face on the after dinner circuit where he has become an accomplished, entertaining speaker.**

MacKENZIE, Steve. *C Palace, Man C, WBA, Charlton, Sheff Wed, Shrewsbury.* Scored one of the most spectacular goals seen in a Wembley FA Cup final for Manchester City against Spurs. He had joined City in 1979 for £250,000, before making even one first team appearance for Crystal Palace. Steve is still playing in non-league soccer, currently turning out for Stafford Rangers.

McKINLAY, Bobby. *Notts F (1951-1969).* Made 611 appearances for Nottingham Forest, which is still a club record. Now a retired prison officer living in a village outside the city.

McLAREN, Ross. *Shrewsbury, Derby, Swindon. (1980-1992)* Scottish born utility player who played over 400 League matches before taking over as Reserve team coach at Swindon Town

McLAREN, Thomas. *Port V (1967-1976).* Port Vale stalwart, who played for the Valiants for nine years. Died in 1978 aged only 29.

McLEAN, Derek *Middlesboro, Hartlepool (1955-1963).* Derek was a goalscoring inside forward for Middlesborough and Hartlepool in the fifties. Still working in the North East for Middlesborough Council Planning department.

McLELLAND, John. *Portsmouth* Now works as a technician at a Hayling Island school, close to his home. Previously had worked at Pompey's Fratton Park as a maintenance officer.

McLEOD, John. *Arsenal, Aston V, (1961-1967)* Scottish international winger (4 full caps) who joined Arsenal from Hibernian in 1961 for £40,000. Also played for Aston Villa and Mechelen in Belgium. Recently moved back to Scotland after working for Guardian Royal Exchange in Birmingham for many years.

McLINTOCK, Frank. M.B.E. *Leicester C, Arsenal, QPR. (1959-1976).* **Signed by Arsenal from Leicester City in 1964 for £80,000. He became their captain and regular centre-half, winning the coveted double in 1970-1. He represented Scotland nine times, was "Footballer of the year" in 1971 and awarded the M.B.E. in 1972. Spells in Management/coaching at Leicester City, Q.P.R. and then Brentford followed. Went on to become Assistant manager at Millwall, before leaving the game to become a players agent. Together with boxing promoter, Frank Warren, he set up an ill fated restaurant in the Barbican, London, however recent business interests which include running three 'Cash Converter' shops (one in partnership with former boxer Dave 'Boy' Green) have more than compensated for that setback. Frank also keeps busy as an after dinner speaker; Capital Gold match summariser; and is a regular golf partner to his former Arsenal colleagues George Graham and John Radford.**

McMANUS, Eric. *Coventry, Notts C, Stoke, Lincoln, Bradford, Middlesboro, Peterborough, Tranmere. (1969-1986).* Northern Ireland amateur goalkeeper who played most of his League games for Notts County. Now Supervisor for "Football in the Community" at Bradford City".

McMAHON, Pat. *Aston Villa (1969-1974).* Left Aston Villa in 1976 to join the NASL club Portland Timbers, later playing for the now defunct Caribous of Colorado, and Atlanta. McMahon is still in America, working as a partner in a company supplying aluminium to industry.

McMAHON, Steve. *Everton, Aston Villa, Liverpool, Man C, Swindon, (1979-1995).* Hard tackling midfield general, Steve started at Everton but achieved much of his success at neighbours, Liverpool where he won seventeen England caps and a host of domestic and European honours. Appointed manager of Swindon Town in early 1995

McMILLAN, Sammy. *Man U, Wrexham, Southend, Chester, Stockport. (1961-1971).* Northern Ireland international forward who moved across the water to join Manchester United in 1959. Retired in 1971 and is now a process worker, living and working near Wrexham.

McMORDIE, Eric. *Middlesboro, Sheff Wed, York, Hartlepool (1947-1957)* Won 21 caps for Northern Ireland to add to his Under 23 cap. Retired in 1977 whilst with Hartlepool and now runs a chain of greengrocers based on Teeside.

McNAB, Bob. *Huddersfield, Arsenal, Wolves. (1963-1975).* **Emigrated, initially to manage Vancouver Whitecaps and then Tacoma stars. Bob opened the Vancouver Racquets Club, which once established, he sold in 1988. Now lives on Americas West Coast, in Agoura Hills, California, running his own executive recruitment agency His daughter, having already appeared in films, is tipped to be a star actress.**

McNAB, Neil. *Tottenham, Bolton, Brighton, Leeds, Man C, Tranmere, Huddersfield, Darlington, (1974-1993).* Moved South in 1973 to join Tottenham from Morton, but achieved most success during his six years with Manchester City in the 1980's. Scottish under 21 cap, Neil is now back at Maine Road as Youth Team manager.

McNAUGHT, Ken. *Everton, Aston Villa, WBA, Man C, Sheff U. (1974-1985)* **Forced to retire through injury at the age of 31 in 1986 having played in 438 matches for his five professional clubs. In 1987 he became coach to Dunfermline but can now be found working at he Pro shop at the famous Gleneagles Golf Course.**

McNEILL, Alan. *Middlesboro, Huddersfield, Oldham, Stockport (1967-1976).* Joined Kirklees Council as a sports centre supervisor in 1977, and has now progressed to become Operations manager, responsible for six sports centres in the area.

Dixie McNeill

McNEILL, Dixie. *Leicester C, Exeter C, Northampton T, Lincoln C, Hereford U, Wrexham, Hereford U. (1964-1982).* A much travelled bustling centre-forward. Best known for his goal scoring exploits with Hereford United, where he also later became manager. Dixie is now at the helm of Flint Town United in the Konica Welsh League.

McNEILL, Ian. *Leicester, Brighton, Southend, (1956-1963).* Joined Leicester from Aberdeen in 1955 and played League soccer for the next eight years. Now Chief scout at Bolton Wanderers.

McNICHOL, Johnny. *Luton, Brentford, Exeter, Torquay, Exeter, Torquay. (1976-1991).* Scottish under 23 defender who made over 400 league appearances before ending at Torquay United in the early nineties. Now still living in Devon, and is landlord of the London Inn at Ashburton.

McPARLAND, Peter. *Aston Villa, Wolves, Plymouth. (1952-1963).* One of Aston Villa's greatest post-war goalscorers, who earned the first of his 34 Northern Ireland caps before he was 20, scoring twice on his debut against Wales in 1954. Managed Glentoran (1970-1) then moved to Bournemouth in 1972 and during the past 15 years has coached in Cyprus, Kuwait, and Hong Kong from his home base in the Dorset town.

Gordon McQueen

McPHEE, John. *Blackpool, Barnsley, Southport (1962-1972).* Scottish wing half who played over 250 games for Blackpool in the 1960's. Now owns the Hotel Sheraton in the town.

McQUEEN, Gordon. *Leeds, Man U. (1972-1984).* **Scottish international defender, who starred for Leeds and Man Utd in the 1970's and 1980's. After spending a season with Seiko in Hong Kong, was bedridden and on the danger list with a combination of typhoid and septicaemia. Now fully recovered and managed Airdrie in the Scottish first division as well as working for STV, before taking up the post of Reserve Team Coach at Middlesborough.**

McSHANE, Harry. *Blackburn R, Huddersfield, Bolton, Man Utd, Oldham A. (1937-1954).* **Footballing father of Ian, star of the BBC series "Lovejoy". Harry still does some scouting for Manchester United and can list Andy Ritchie, and more recently, Nicky Butt among his notable discoveries. Lives in Urmston and had previously spent sixteen years working for Massey Fergusons until his retirement.**

MCVAY, Dave. *Notts Co, Torquay, Peterboro, Lincoln, (1973-1981).* Former Notts County defender, Dave has now returned to the City after spells with Torquay and Peterborough to become a journalist with the Nottingham Evening Post.

McVITIE, George. *Carlisle, WBA, Oldham, Carlisle. (1965-1980).* Carlisle born winger, George started and ended his career with his hometown club, United, taking in stops at Oldham and West Brom in the interim. Became a milkman when he hung up his boots in 1980, but now runs his own sub post office outside Carlisle.

Kevin Mabbutt (and family) in California.

MABBUTT, Kevin. *Bristol C, C Palace (1977-1984).* Bristol born Kevin made his name at Bristol City before moving to Selhurst Park in 1981. Although injured, Kevin continued to play after leaving Crystal Palace, firstly for Vancouver in Canada, then Beveren in Belgium, and finally in Cyprus. Now lives in California, USA, where he runs his own family restaurant called, "Delicias".

MABBUTT, Ray. *Bristol R, Newport Co. (1957-1970).* Father of Kevin (see above) and Gary (Spurs). Played almost 500 games for Bristol Rovers and once wrote a book entitled "You can be a soccer star". Now runs his own Financial Advice Business in the Bristol Area.

MACARI, Lou. *Man U, Swindon. (1972-1985).* Scottish international striker (24 caps) joined Manchester United in 1973 for £200,000 from Celtic. Went on to play over 300 League games for the Reds before accepting the post of player/manager at Swindon Town in 1984. Spells at West Ham, Stoke City, and Celtic followed before returning to the Potteries in October 1993 to rejoin Stoke, whom he has managed to date.

MACEY, John. *Bristol C, Grimsby, Newport. (1965-1975).* Bristol born keeper who minded the goal for Newport County in the early to mid 1970's. Now owns the John Macey Sports shops in Newport and Chepstow, both in Gwent.

MACHIN, Mel. *Port Vale, Gillingham, Bournemouth, Norwich. (1962-1977).* Mel had fifteen years as player, ending at Norwich in 1977 before moving into coaching. Managed Manchester City and Barnsley before being appointed Manager at Bournemouth in September 1994.

MADDEN, Craig. *Bury, W.B.A, Blackpool, Wrexham, York. (1977-1989).* Forward who scored over 150 goals from his 350 plus league appearances. Now works with Football in the Community at Blackpool and plays for Blackpool Rovers in the Carling North West Counties League.

MADDREN, Willie. *Middlesboro (1968-1977).* England Under 23 defender who played almost 300 league gamcs for his only club, Middlesborough. Willie went on to run a sports shop on Teesside, but now works for an Insurance company and is still living in the area.

MAHONEY, John. *Crewe, Stoke, Middlesboro, Swansea (1965-1982).* As well as playing in over 400 league matches, John won 51 full Welsh Caps as a bustling midfielder. He returned to Wales to end his playing days at Swansea and to become manager of Bangor City.

MANCINI, Terry. *Watford, Leyton O, QPR, Arsenal, Aldershot. (1961-1976).* Since finishing in 1976, Terry has had a stint at Luton Town as Asssitant Manager; owned a sports shop in Harrow; run a pub in Hammersmith; and is currently living in New Malden where he is involved with the running of a car hire business in the area.

(Photograph courtesy: Yorkshire Post Newspapers)

MADELEY, Paul. *Leeds (1963-1980)* Capped by England, Paul had an illustrious career, appearing over 500 times in a Leeds shirt and won almost honour domestically and in Europe. He and his brothers sold their chain of 26 D.I.Y stores for £27 million in 1987. In 1992 he successfully underwent an operation to remove a brain tumour. Now acts as a property consultant, based in Yorkshire.

MANN, Arthur. *Man C, Blackpool, Notts Co, Shrewsbury, Mansfield. (1968-1981).* Joined Manchester City from Hearts in 1968, but made most impact during his six years at Notts County, where he made over 250 appearances. Became Youth and reserve team coach at Grimsby Town, before moving to West Bromwich Albion with Alan Buckley, as his assistant manager.

MANNING, John. *Tranmere, Shrewsbury, Norwich, Bolton, Walsall, Tranmere, Crewe, Barnsley, Crewe . (1962-1976)* **Lives in West Derby, and works as a sales manager for a chemical company. When he retired from playing in 1976, became National coach in Saudi Arabia for three years. Upon his return to England, coached Brighton under Jimmy Melia reaching the FA Cup final in 1982/3.**

MANNION, Wilf. *Middlesboro, Hull. (1936-1954).* Mannion was an inside forward who spent most of his career at Middlesborough, where his magnificent scheming earned him 26 England caps. Now although retired and living in Redcar, Wilf can still be seen at Ayresome Park where he acts as an ambassador for his former club.

MAPSON, Johnny *Reading, Sunderland (1935-1952)*. Sunderland's regular keeper before and after the War. Johnny is now retired, living in Swindon, having been a self employed manufacturers agent, then 20 years as a manager.

MARCH, Zillwood 'Zac' Was the oldest surviving ex-pro until his death in September 1994, a month short of his 102nd birthday ! Played for Portsmouth and Brighton, he once turned down the opportunity to join Manchester United, preferring to stay on the South Coast.

(Photograph courtesy: Evening Gazette, Teeside)

Wilf Mannion (centre) with fellow Boro' legends, **Harold Shepherdson** and **George Hardwick.**

(Courtesy: Bournemouth Echo)

MARGERRISON, John. *Tottenham, Fulham, Leyton O. (1972-1981).* John now lives in Borehamwood, Herts and works as a telephone engineer. Managed Dunstable until 1994.

MARINELLO, Peter. *Arsenal, Portsmouth, Fulham. (1969-1979).* **Moved to Arsenal from Hibernian in 1969 amid a blaze of publicity before moving on to Portsmouth Later played for Motherwell, Fulham and in America. In 1983 he swapped running at defenders to running a pub, "Marinello's", in Edinburgh. However, Peter is now living in Bournemouth, unemployed, and was officially declared bankrupt by the local County Court in March 1995**

MARINER, Paul. *Plymouth, Ipswich, Arsenal, Portsmouth. (1973-1987)* England striker (35 caps), While at Ipswich Paul caught the eye of the England management team, and Arsenal, who paid £150,000 in 1984 to take him to Highbury. Ended at Portsmouth in 1976 and briefly became Commercial Manager at Colchester. Now coaches in the U.S.A., but when home, commentates for Radio, and Cable Television as well as helping train youngsters at a Private school in Lancashire

MARSH, John. *Stoke (1967-1978).* John occupied the right back berth at Stoke for almost a decade after making his debut in 1967. Now lives in Stoke and works as a sales representative.

MARSH, Rodney. *Fulham, QPR, Man C, Fulham. (1962-1976).* **One of the games most entertaining players to watch. Scored over 100 goals in his 211 league games for Q.P.R. but like so many other "characters" of his ilk, was never really given a chance to repeat this internationally (winning only 9 caps) Became General manager of Tampa Bay Rowdies in Florida for eleven years. But in 1994, Rodney took a year off , which enabled him to tour the U.K. with George Best in a soccer roadshow**

MARSHALL, Frank. *Rotherham, Scunthorpe, Doncaster. (1951-1961).* Gained his league experience as a wing half in the fifties. Frank is now coaching La Holm FC in the Swedish League.

MARTIN, Eric. *Southampton (1966-1974).* Eric kept goals for the "Saints" in almost 250 league games, following his move from Dunfermline in 1967. He retired in 1974 and moved to America to coach in Washington where he still lives, working for an American mailing company.

MARTIN, Mick. *Man Utd, WBA, Newcastle U, Cardiff , Peterborough, Rotherham, Preston. (1972-1985).* Retired after well over 500 games as a professional footballer. He made 52 appearances for the Republic of Ireland. Mick became coach at Newcastle United (1987) and moved up to Scotland to take on a similar role with Celtic.

MARUSTIK, Chris. *Swansea, Cardiff. (1978-1986).* Swansea born midfielder, who played for his home club for seven years (1978-1985). Won seven Under 23 caps and six full caps with Wales. Chris now runs a wine bar with his brother.

MARWOOD, Brian *Hull, Sheff Wed, Arsenal, Sheff U, Middlesboro Barnet (1979-1994)* Winger who caught the eye playing for Hull City. Went on to play for both Sheffield Clubs and had two years with Arsenal, winning one England cap. Brian is now an executive with the P.F.A.

MASON, Bobby *Wolves, Leyton O (1955-1963)* Inside forward who quit at the age of 27 whilst with Orient. Bobby now lives in Bournemouth where he is employed by a local holiday village, having formerly worked as an H.G.V. driver.

MASON, Stuart. *Wrexham, Liverpool, Chester, Rochdale, Crewe. (1965-1977)* Full back who played over 300 league games, although he never made the first team during a spell with Liverpool. Stuart now owns a sports shop in Wrexham.

MASSEY, Steve. *Stockport, Bournemth, Peterboro, Northpton, Hull, Camb U, Wrexham. (1974-1987)* Steve played for seven clubs during his 12 years as a pro. Now runs two holiday camps in Cornwall: the St Martin's Holiday Park near Looe and the Mullion Holiday Park near Helston.

MASSIE, Les. *Huddersfield, Darlington, Halifax, Bradford P.A., Workington (1956-1970)* A Huddersfield Town regular for 10 years and over 300 league games. Went into the haulage business . Later took a job at Hoslets in Huddersfield.

MASSON, Don. *Middlesboro, Notts Co, QPR, Derby, Notts Co. (1964-1981).* Don played over 600 league games and won 17 full caps with Scotland after the age of 30. Ended his days at Notts County, where he later managed the sports complex. Now owns the Gallery Hotel in the City

MATHIAS, Ray. *Tranmere. (1967-1984).* As a player, Ray served Tranmere for 17 years, and his total of 636 games broke the club's appearance record. Managed Wigan before becoming returning to Prenton Park as Reserve Team Coach.

MATTHEWS, Reginald D *Coventry, Chelsea, Derby (1950-1967)* Goalkeeper, who won five full England caps, as a Third Division player. Later worked at Massey Ferguson Ltd for 20 years.

MAUCHLEN, Ally. *Leicester (1985-1991).* Ally joined Leicester from Motherwell in 1985 and starred in their midfield through in to the 1990's. Now with Glenavon in Northern Ireland.

MAY, Eddie *Southend, Wrexham, Swansea (1964-1990)* Although born in Epping, Eddie has made his mark in Wales, firstly a player with Wrexham and Swansea, then as a manager with Cardiff. Reinstated as manager at Ninian Park in March 1995, when a proposed take-over of the club failed: the consortium had included Terry Yorath, who was their manager at the time.

(Courtesy: Portsmouth News)

MAY, Larry. *Leicester, Barnsley, Sheff Wed, Brighton (1976-1988).* Midfielder who made more than 300 league appearances before becoming Youth Team Coach at Brighton, his last playing club. Moved along the Coast to take on the same role at Portsmouth in February 1995.

(Photograph courtesy: Evening Sentinel, Stoke.)

MATTHEWS, Sir Stanley. *Stoke, Blackpool, Stoke (1931-1964)* "The Wizard of dribble", Sir Stanley ranks as one of football's greatest living legends, achieving world wide acclaim during a career that spanned 33 years. Son of a boxer, he started at his home town club, Stoke City as a brilliant schoolboy prodigy. He was sensationally transferred to Blackpool in 1947 for £11,500. After gaining two Cup final runners up medals, he achieved a lifetimes ambition by helping them beat Bolton in the 1952-3 final, now known as the "Matthews Final". He returned to Stoke, assisting them back to the First Division, and still playing in that league past the age of 50. His contribution to the game was formally recognised when awarded the C.B.E. in 1957 and knighted in the 1965 New Years Honours. He was Footballer of the year in 1953 and 1963; and voted European Footballer of the Year in 1957, one year after being named King of Soccer in Ghana ! Went to live Ontario in Canada to retire, but the lure of his native "Potteries" proved too much to resist, and finally returned. Hit the headlines again in 1995, with a number of functions arranged to celebrate his 80th Birthday.

MAYO, Joe. *Walsall, WBA, Leyton O, Cambridge U, Blackpool (1972-1982).*Walsall plucked Joe from non-league Dudley in 1972 and in the following ten years he played over 275 games for his five clubs. Now works as a hotelier in Crriccieth, Wales, where he runs the "Plas Isa".

MEAGAN, Mick. *Everton, Huddersfield, Halifax. (1957-1968).* Republic of Ireland international full back (17 caps) who spent ten years with Everton and Huddersfield Town. Then after one season with Halifax, Mick returned to his native Ireland. He was involved in management and coaching with Drogheda, Shamrock Rovers and Bray, as well as working in a Dublin Hospital.

MEDHURST, Harry. *West Ham, Chelsea, Brighton . (1938-1952).* Former West Ham, Chelsea, and Brighton goalkeeper, Harry died in 1984

MEDLEY, Les. *Tottenham. (1946-1952).* Scored 45 goals from his 150 league games for Tottenham immediately after the war, earning him six England caps. Having played all his soccer in the capital, Les is now retired in another London - in Ontario, Canada. He had originally emigrated in 1946, but returned to England to pursue his career, leaving for Canada again in 1953.

MEDWIN, Terry. *Swansea, Tottenham (1951-1962)* Swansea born winger, who played on the wing for the local club before being snapped up by Tottenham Hotspur in 1956. Won 30 full Welsh caps and played almost 200 league games for Spurs before returning to Wales. Now back home in Swansea, unfortunately Terry has been unable to work since 1983 due to a nervous disorder.

MEE, Bertie Played as a winger, but in 1960 joined Arsenal as trainer and physiotherapist, becoming manager in 1966-7. Under his leadership they won the European Fairs Cup and the famous 'Double' triumph of 1971-2. He retired in 1976, but after a break from the game, joined Watford as General manager. Upon his final retirement in 1986, he remained a director of the Vicarage Road club.

MEEK, George. *Leeds, Walsall, Leicester, Walsall. (1952-1964).* Spent twelve years in the league following his move from Hamilton Accademicals to Leeds United in 1952. Now a postman living in Walsall whose family are following his sporting footsteps: George's son plays his golf off a handicap of two, and his daughter is a Midland County Rugby Union player.

Sir Stanley - proving why he was crowned King of Soccer in Ghana !

MEGSON, Don. *Sheff Wed, Bristol R (1959-1970)* Sheffield Wednesday's first choice right back for over decade, during which time he played 386 games and won England League representative honours. Although now technically retired, Don still does some scouting for Norwich City.

MEGSON, Gary. *Plymouth, Everton, Sheff Wed, Notts F, Newcastle, Sheff Wed, Man C, Norwich (1977-1995)* Well travelled midfielder, who played for seven league clubs, including two spells at Sheffield Wednesday. Became Assistant, then manager at Norwich until the Summer of 1995.

MEHMET, Dave. *Millwall, Charlton, Gillingham Millwall, (1976-1987).* Started and ended at Millwall and had a spell in the States with Tampa Bay Rowdies. Dave is now Manager of Fisher 93, in the Beazer Homes League.

MELIA, Jimmy. *Liverpool, Wolves, Southampton, Aldershot, Crewe (1955-1971)* Played 269 games for Liverpool and won two England caps, but is probably better known as the manager who took Brighton to the FA Cup final in 1983. Since then he has managed Belenenses (Portugal), Stockport County, and coached in Kuwait. His most recent travels have taken him to Dallas in America to coach in their indoor soccer league.

MELLOR, Ian. *Man C, Norwich, Brighton., Chester, Sheff Wed, Bradford C. (1970-1983).* Former Man City winger has been an executive with the P.F.A. for the past two years, handling commercial deals, having previously worked for sports manufacturers "Puma" and "Gola".

(Courtesy: Mike Jones)

MELLOR, Peter. *Burnley, Chesterfield, Fulham, Hereford, Portsmouth. (1969-1980).* **Popular goalkeeper, who ended at Portsmouth in 1980 after making a total of over 400 league appearances. Peter then moved over to America where he has prospered selling and fitting fireplaces, as well as maintaining gardens and swimming pools. Lives in some splendour in Florida and is the proud owner of a £15,000 boat. He is Florida state goalkeeping coach and trains keepers throughout the States.**

(Courtesy: Portsmouth News)

MELLOWS, Micky. *Reading, Portsmouth. (1970-1977).* Ex-amateur international who won 16 caps and a place in the 1972 Olympic team. Made almost 200 appearances for Portsmouth in five years after persuading manger, John Mortimore to give him a trial. Now lives in Portsmouth where he runs an annual international tournament for youngsters from around the world.

MENDHAM, Peter. *Norwich (1988-1986).* Born in Kings Lynn and played 200 plus games for nearby Norwich City, where he now works as Football in the Community officer. Peter is still turning out for Diss Town in the Eastern League.

MERCER, Joe. O.B.E. *Everton, Arsenal. (1932-1953).* **Joe suffered a double leg fracture in 1954 after a playing career with Everton and Arsenal. Moved into management with Sheffield Wednesday and then Aston Villa. He briefly retired due to ill health before returning to Soccer with Manchester City, striking up a very successful partnership with Malcolm Allison and bringing a decade of glory to Maine Road. Departed in 1972 to become general manager at Coventry and in 1977 took temporary control of the England team. He resigned as a Coventry director in 1981 after nine years on the board and sadly died in 1990 aged 76.**

MEREDITH, Trevor. *Burnley, Shrewsbury, (1959-1971).* Winger who spent seven years as a winger with Shrewsbury before retiring in 1971. Trevor is now a school teacher in Preston.

MERRICK, Alan. *WBA, Peterboro. (1968-1975)* Former West Brom and Peterborough full back who quit in 1975 aged only 25. Alan then went over to America to Coach in Minnesota.

MERRINGTON, Dave. *Burnley, Bristol C. (1964-1971).* Former centre half, coached at both of his playing clubs, Burnley and Bristol City. Was Assistant Manager at Leeds United then Sunderland. Then became a popular Youth Coach at Southampton, responsible for the development of many stars including Alan Shearer and Matthew Le Tissier. This success resulted in his promotion to first team manager at te Dell in July 1995.

METCALF, Micky. *Wrexham, Chester. (1957-1968).* Inside forward who played over 300 games in the 1950's and 1960's. Is now area manager with a Manchester based scientific company.

METGOD, Johnny. *Notts F, Tottenham, (1984-1987).* Dutch international midfielder who joined Nottingham Forest from Real Madrid in 1984. Played over 100 games for Forest and a handful of matches for Tottenham before returning home to Holland where he is now working as a Youth development Officer with Feyenoord FC.

METHLEY, Irvin. *Wolves, Walsall. (1946-1950).* Former Walsall full back, now runs a fish and chip shop in the West Midlands town.

MIDDLEMASS, Clive. *Leeds, Workington (1962-1969).* Made 186 appearances in the league with Workington in the 1960's as a defender, Clive is now Assistant manager at Burnley.

Statue erected in Newcastle as a tribute to **Jackie Milburn.** *(Courtesy: Newcastle Chronicle)*

MIELCZAREK, Ray. *Wrexham, Huddersfield, Rotherham. (1964-1973).* Central defender who was capped once by his native Wales during his nine years as a professional. Ray now lives near Wrexham and works as a Security Officer.

MILBURN, Jackie. *Newcastle, (1946-1956).* **"Wor Jackie" died at his Northumberland home in 1988 just months after learning that he had cancer. A real tyneside folk hero, he played in the three Newcastle cup successes in the fifties and scored the fastest Cup final goal after only 45 seconds in 1953. Capped by England, Jackie became coach at Linfield in Ireland before succeeding Alf Ramsey as Ipswich boss in 1963. Returned home to the North East to become a football writer with the News of the World for 24 years until his retirement shortly before his death . A statue remains in the City as a reminder of his contribtution.**

(Courtesy: Portsmouth News)

MILKINS, John. *Portsmouth, Oxford. (1960-1978).* Milkins made 344 league appearances for Portsmouth and was their first choice goalkeeper for well over a decade before moving to Oxford. He was player/manager at Waterlooville, but is now General Manager of a company that owns four snooker clubs along the South Coast.

MILLAR, Alistair. *Barnsley, York, (1970-1980).* Scottish midfielder who played almost 300 league games during his nine years with Barnsley. Now works as a machine operator for PMC Redfern glass, and lives in Barnsley.

MILLARD, Len. *WBA. (1946-1957).* Captained West Bromwich Albion to win the F.A. Cup in 1954. Made 436 league appearances as a full back in his decade at the Hawthorns, before retiring in 1957. Now retired living in an Old Peoples Home in Coseley, West Midlands.

MILLER, Brian. *Burnley (1955-1966).* Played one game for England and 379 for his only club, Burnley. Had two spells at Turf Moor as the Club's Manager but is now their Chief Scout.

MILLER, Ian. *Bury, Notts F, Doncaster, Swindon, Blackburn, Port V, Scunthorpe. (1973-1990).* Coached at Port Vale until November 1994, when he became Reserve Team Manager at Wolves.

MILLER, Keith. *West Ham, Bournemouth (1968-1979).* Former West Ham junior who went on to play 381 games for Bournemouth. Keith is now Manager of Poole Town and works as a sales manager with a computer typesetting company.

MILLER, Paul. *Tottenham, Charlton, Watford, Bournemouth, Brentford, Swansea C. (1978-1990)* Paul spent nine years at White Hart Lane, before appearing for five more clubs in quick succession prior to his retirement in 1990. Now lives in Hampstead and works as a business development manager for an Employment Consultancy.

MILLINGTON, Anthony. *W.B.A., C.Palace, Peterborough, Swansea (1961-1973).* Former Welsh international goalkeeper (21 caps), now helps run the Wrexham Disabled supporters club.

MILLINGTON, Grenville. *Chester, Wrexham(1968-1983).* Takes weekly coaching sessions at the Racecourse Ground, helping Wrexham's goalkeepers. Grenville is employed by the Cheshire Probation Service and works in Chester as a Community Services Officer.

MILLINGTON, Ralph. *Tranmere (1950-1960).* Wing half who made 357 appearances for Tranmere Rovers. Ralph is now living in Hesweall, Wirral,where he works as a self employed building and joinery contractor.

MILLS, David. *Middlesboro, WBA, Newcastle, Sheff Wed, Newcastle, Middlesboro, Darlington. (1968-1986).* Mills was Britain's costliest player when he joined Ron Atkinson at West Brom in 1979. Retired in 1986 after a series of niggling injuries, and became player/commercial manager at Whitby Town. Works as a freelance journalist for local press, T.V. and radio, and has been a print consultant since 1986.

MILLS, Don. *Q.P.R. Torquay, Q.P.R., Cardiff, Leeds U, Torquay (1946-1961).* Clocked up over 400 appearances after the War, most of them for Torquay. Don sadly died in the town in 1994.

MILLS, Mick. *Ipswich, Southampton, Stoke. (1965-1987).* England 42 caps. Mick settled down in the Ipswich defence, having originally played in midfield after being released by Portsmouth . Mick went on to captain both Ipswich and England. Gained a UEFA Cup medal, and highlighted his career when he led Ipswich to victory in the 1978 F.A. Cup final. Became manager of Stoke before a proposed move to Kuwait was thwarted by the Iraqi invasion. Now lives in Staffordshire and is Chief Scout for Sheffield Wednesday.

MILLS, Roly. *Northampton (1954-1963).* A Northampton regular for a decade, Roly is now in promotions and lives in Harpole, Northants.

MILLS, Steve. *Soton (1972-1976).* **Steve was an outstanding prospect with the Saints and England Under 23's, before his career was cruelly cut short by injury. Died in 1988 of Leukaemia. However, a Charity was formed in his memory to raise funds for Leukaemia research.**

MILNE, Gordon. *Preston, Liverpool, Blackpool (1956-1969).* Manager of Grampus in Japan, (the club that Gary Lineker played for), until September 1994. Became Chief Executive of the Managers & Secretary's Association in June 1995.

MILNE, Ralph. *Charlton, Bristol C, Man Utd (1986-1989)* Ralph appeared to have a big future ahead of him when his £170,000 move from Bristol City made him one of Alex Fergusons first signings. However, he was quickly released following a press interview in which he made various claims about the personal lives of his teammates. A brief spell at Bury was followed by a time in Hong Kong, but he has now been unemployed in for several years, living in Bristol.

MITCHELL, Arnold. *Notts Co, Exeter. (1948-1965).* Wing half who played 495 league games for Exeter, now retired and still living in the city.

MITCHELL, Bobby. *Sunderland, Blackburn, Grimsby, Carlisle, Rotherham, Lincoln. (1973-1986).* Now working with the Community programme at former club, Grimsby Town FC.

MITCHELL, John. *Fulham, Millwall. (1972-1980).* **Runs a promotions company in London's West End. Currently lives in Harpenden and in 1994 made a take-over bid for Luton Town**

MOBLEY, Vic. *Sheffield W, Q.P. R. (1963-1970).* Former "Owls" defender, who despite winning 13 under 23 caps for England, never won a full cap. Vic is now living in New Zealand.

MONEY, Richard. *Scunthorpe U, Fulham, Liverpool, Derby Co, Luton T, Portsmouth, Scunthorpe U. (1973-1989).* Experienced central defender, Richard was manager at Scunthorpe until March 1994. Then appointed first team coach at Nottingham Forest in June 1994.

(Courtesy: Ian Wright, Rufus Abajas)

MONTGOMERY, Jim. *Sunderland, Southampton, Birmingham C, Notts F, Sunderland. (1961-1980).* Montgomery was one of the top class young goalkeepers of the sixties. His greatest moment of glory came when, against all the odds, as a Second Division side, Sunderland won the 1973 F.A. Cup final against Leeds. After spells at Birmingham and Notts Forest, he returned to the Sunderland area, to work as Director of Youth at Roker Park. A post held until the summer of 1995.

(Photograph courtesy: Newcastle Chronicle)

MONCUR, Bobby. *Newcastle U, Sunderland, Carlisle U. (1962-1976).* Former Newcastle central defender, became player/manager at Carlisle in November 1976 and player only from September 1977. Heart of Midlothian manager February 1980; Plymouth manager June 1981 until September 1983. Returned to work on Tyneside and had a brief spell coaching Whitley Bay FC. Now runs his own yacht charter business in Newcastle. His interest in Sailing started while managing Hearts, and has since sailed in the Round Britain Race; Transatlantic Race; and the Fastnet race of 1987.

MOORE, Bobby. *West Ham U, Fulham. (1958-1976).* **A brilliant youthful prodigy in the central defenders position, who went on to captain club and country and won 108 full caps. He collected an FA Cup winners medal in 1964, but in the twighlight of his career when playing for Fulham, was on the losing side at Wembley in 1975 against his old team mates, West Ham. Was Footballer of the year in 1964, and when he retired after more than 650 league appearances he had achieved a world-wide reputation as one of the best players of all time. Sadly did not manage to repeat his success off the field and after brief associations with Oxford City and Southend United, decided to concentrate on journalism and broadcasting. Remaining a fine ambassador for the game. Died of cancer on February 24th 1993 aged only 51.**

MOORE, Dave. *Grimsby T, Carlisle U, Blackpool, Grimsby T, Darlington. (1978-1988).* Grimsby born defender, brother of Kevin (playing with Fulham), Dave was the youngest manager in the League when appointed to the position at Scunthorpe United in June 1994.

MOORE, Eric. *Everton, Chesterfield, Tranmere R. (1949-1957).* First choice full back at Everton for several years after the War, Eric retired in 1957 and is now a publican in Atherton.

MOORE, Graham. *Cardiff C, Chelsea, Manchester U, Northampton T, Charlton Ath, Doncaster R. (1958-1973).* Welsh international midfielder with 21 full caps to his name. Now running a sub post office in Scarborough.

MOORE, Jon. *Millwall, Bournemouth (1974-1980)* Full back who spent 4 years with Millwall, but ended at Bournemouth aged only 25. Now works in the City of London for Tullett & Tokyo.

MOORE, Ronnie. *Tranmere R, Cardiff C, Rotherham U, Charlton Ath, Rochdale, Tranmere R (1971-1988).* Now a Coach at Tranmere, where he started and ended his 17 year playing career during which time he made over 600 appearances.

MORAN, Kevin. *Man U, Blackburn R, (1978-1994).* Republic of Ireland defender, moved to England to join Manchester United in 1978 from Gaelic soccer side Pegasus. After a spell with Sporting Gijon in Spain, Kevin became a central figure in the Blackburn Rovers revival story. Finally retired in 1994 to concentrate on the Sports Promotion business that he runs with his former Manchester United team-mate, Jesper Olsen.

MORAN, Ronnie. *Liverpool (1952-1964).* Made 342 appearances in his twelve playing years at Liverpool. Then after many years as a valuable member of the backroom staff, Ronnie progressed to his current role of first team coach.

MORELAND, Vic. *Derby Co.(1978-1979).* Northern Ireland international midfielder who spent a time in the League with Derby County, after joining them from Glentoran in 1978. Now Manager of Tulsa's Expo Pavilion in America.

MORGAN, Roger. *Queens Park R, Tottenham H. (1964-1971).* England Under 23 international winger who played over 250 games for his two London clubs before quitting in 1971 aged only 25. Roger now lives in Chingford and worked as a Recreation Officer for Haringey Council before becoming a Community Officer at West Ham.

(Courtesy: Jim Tamplin, Dorset Evening Echo)

MORGAN, Stuart. *West Ham U, Torquay U, Reading, Colchester U, Bournemouth (1967-1976)* Manager of Dorchester having previously held posts at Weymouth (Manager), AFC Bournemouth (Assistant Manager), Brentford (Coach).

MORGAN, Trevor. *Bournemouth, Mansfield, Bristol C, Exeter C, Bristol R, Bolton W, Colchester U, Exeter C (1980-1990)* Ten years in the league took in stops at seven clubs including two spells at Bournemouth; Bristol City and Exeter, where went on to become Assistant Manager.

MORGAN, Willie. *Burnley, Man U, Burnley, Bolton, Blackpool. (1962-1981).* Dashing winger, who provided the crosses for the likes of Bobby Charlton and Dennis Law. Won 21 caps for Scotland and made over 600 League starts before hanging up his boots in 1982. Retired from the game having invested his money in a chain of laundrettes. Briefly opened a sports shop in Altrincham, but now concentrates on the marketing/promotions firm in which he is a partner.

MORLEY, Tony. *Preston N.E., Burnley, Aston Villa, W.B.A., Birmingham C, W.B.A, Burnley. (1972-1988).* England 'B' International ended his playing days in America with Tampa Bay Rowdies in 1989, then with Hamran Spartans in Malta in 1990. Following a very brief stop at Bromsgrove Rovers in January 1995, as player/coach, moved to play for Stratford Town FC.

(Courtesy: Salisbury Journal)

MORRELL, Paul *Bournemouth (1983-1993)* Paul was a first team regular for Bournemouth for most of the 1980's. Returned in late 1994 from a spell in Hong Kong to join Salisbury in the BHL.

MORRIS, Peter. *Mansfield T, Ipswich T, Norwich C, Mansfield T, Peterborough U. (1960-1979).* Peter played over 600 league games before progressing into coaching roles. Manager at Boston until Summer 1994 and then Assistant Manager at Northampton until February 1995.

MORRITT, Gordon. *Rotherham U, Doncaster R, Northampton T, York C, Rochdale, Darlington. (1961-1973).* Having enjoyed a twelve year career as a goalie for six league clubs Gordon now works as a Security manager in York.

MORRISSEY, John. *Liverpool, Everton, Oldham Ath. (1957-1972).* Played for both Liverpool clubs, then after a brief stint at Oldham, his career was ended by injury. Stayed on Merseyside and is now a successful businessman.

MORTENSEN, Henrik. *Norwich C, (1989-1990)* Made 18 appearances for Norwich City in 1989-1990, but Henrik is now back in his Danish homeland, playing for his local side, Aarhus.

MORTENSEN, Stan. *Blackpool, Hull C, Southport. (1946-1957).* **Played either as a centre forward or inside forward, Stan recovered from an aeroplane crash in a Wellington and then proceeded to score four goals on his England debut. He will forever be associated with great comebacks and although the 1953 Cup final is remembered as the "Matthews final", Morty scored a hat-trick. Apart from that he played in two other finals, but ended up on the losing side, however he did score 24 goals in 25 internationals. Managed Blackpool in the late 1960's before going into business. Died 1991.**

MORTIMER, Dennis. *Coventry C, Aston Villa, Sheffield U, Brighton & H.A., Birmingham C. (1969-1986).* When he retired from professional football, he had played over 700 competitive matches for a total of five league clubs. Was player/manager at Redditch FC. before becoming Football in the Community Officer at West Bromwich Albion in 1990, then Assistant manager at the Hawthorns until October 1994

MORTIMORE, Charlie. *Aldershot, Portsmouth, Aldershot. (1949-1955).* England amateur international, who played for three league clubs, all as an amateur. Charlie is now Retired form his role as deputy head of Cove Comprehensive school. Lives in Farnborough. Youth development officer at Farnborough Town FC.

MORTIMORE, John. *Chelsea, Queens Park R. (1955-1965).* Was dismissed by Benfica in 1987 after steering them to a Portuguese League and Cup double. Had previously spent two years at Southampton as Assistant but quickly earned another place in the sun with Real Betis. John is now back at the Dell as Assistant manager.

MOSS, David. *Swindon T, Luton T, Swindon T. (1971-1985)* Dave was a goalscoring winger who played over 400 league matches before becoming assistant manager at Swindon. and then the same post at Manchester City until the Summer of 1995.

MOSS, Ernie. *Chesterfield, Peterboro, Mansfield T, , Port V, Lincoln, Doncaster, Chesterfield, Stockport, Scarboro, Rochdale. (1968-1987).* Ernie played 271 games for Chesterfield in seven years, but then remarkably went on to play for ten more clubs before retiring in 1987. Now a sports outfitter in Chesterfield and manager of Gainsborough Trinity since May 1995.

Dave Moss

MOSS, Frank. *Sheffield Wed, Aston Villa. (1936-1954).* He coached at Aston Villa where he had previously played at centre half either side of the war. Frank then left the club to concentrate on his newsagents business at Kingstanding, later retiring to the Cornish resort of Looe

MUDIE, Jackie. *Blackpool, Stoke C, Port Vale. (1949-1966).* Scottish international striker (17 caps) who scored 143 goals for Blackpool during the 1950's. Jackie went on to run his own successful painting and decorating business in the Potteries area before his death in 1992

MUHREN, Arnold. ***Ipswich T, Manchester U (1978-1984)*** **Arnold spent six successful years in England with Ipswich and then Manchester United following his from Dutch side Twente Enschade in 1978. He now lives back in Holland in Volendam and is employed by a Dutch Football Magazine to train youngsters. Still plays for the ex-Ajax and ex-Holland teams.**

MULHEARN, Ken. *Everton, Stockport Co, Man C, Shrewsbury T, Crewe A (1963-1981).* After finishing his playing career at 37 years of age having minded goal in over 600 league games, Ken bought a pub in the Shrewsbury area.

MULLEN, Jimmy *Sheffield Wed, Rotherham U, Preston N.E., Cardiff C, Newport Co (1970-1986.)* Former centre back, Jimmy held managerial posts at Newport County, Aberdeen and Blackpool, before joining Burnley as assistant to Frank Capser. Taking over as Manager in 1991.

MULLEN, Jimmy. *Wolves (1938-1958)* Mullen joined Wolves straight from School in 1937, and made his debut in 1939, when only 16. Played in two World cups, winning twelve full England caps as well as Football League and F.A. Cup medals. He formed one of the great wing partnerships of he day with Johnny Hancocks. Retired from soccer in the fifties and died aged 64 in 1987.

MULLERY, Alan. *Fulham, Tottenham H, Fulham, (1958-1975).* Two spells at Fulham were separated by eight years with Spurs where he established himself as one of the best wing-halves of his day. Alan won 35 caps, was Player of the Year in 1975 and awarded the M.B.E. the following year upon his retirement from the game. He then tried his hand at Management with spells at Brighton (twice), Charlton, and Q.P.R. before joining an Insurance company. Also acts as a football presenter on Capital Gold Radio in London.

MULLIGAN, Paddy. *Chelsea, Crystal Palace, W.B.A. (1969-1977).* An attacking right back who won 51 full Caps for the Irish Republic and was a member of Chelsea's League Cup final team of 1972. After a spell as assistant manager to Panathinaikos in Greece, retired in 1982 to become an insurance agent in West London.

MUNDY, Albert. *Portsmouth, Brighton & H.A., Aldershot. (1950-1960)* Former inside for Now working for Charringtons in Portsmouth.

MUNKS, David. *Sheff U, Portsmouth, Swindon T, Exeter C (1965-1975)* Sheffield born defender now lives in Bedhampton, near Portsmouth and took a management job in a Southampton Sports centre after hanging up his boots.

MUNRO, Francis. *Wolves. (1967-1976).* Won nine Scottish caps and played almost 300 games in defence for Wolves before moving to Celtic in 1976. Francis went on to coach and manag football in Australian between 1981 and 1989 then worked as a salesman for a garden furniture company. In January 1993, Francis suffered a from a severe stroke which has left him unable to work and now has to walk with the aid of a stick.

MURDOCH, Bobby. *Middlesbro (1973-1975).* Bobby who was a midfielder in his playing days, made 12 appearances in the full Scottish international team when with Celtic. Was a member of their team that won the European Cup in 1967. Early in season 1973-4, moved South to join Middlesborough. He was an immediate success and played a big part in the club's second division championship success and return to Division One. Became Youth Team Coach and then Manager at Ayresome Park before returning to Glasgow where he is now running a public house.

MURPHY, Barry *Barnsley (1962-1977)* After clocking up 509 league appearances for Barnsley Barry became their Youth team coach, then coach to the First Team. After spending four years in the same post at Leeds United, left the game to work for Barnsley Borough Council firstly as a sports development officer, now in his current role as manager of Penistone Leisure Centre.

MURPHY, Colin Former Lincoln City boss, was working as manager of Shelbourne in Ireland before returning to England to join Notts County as General Manager in June 1995.

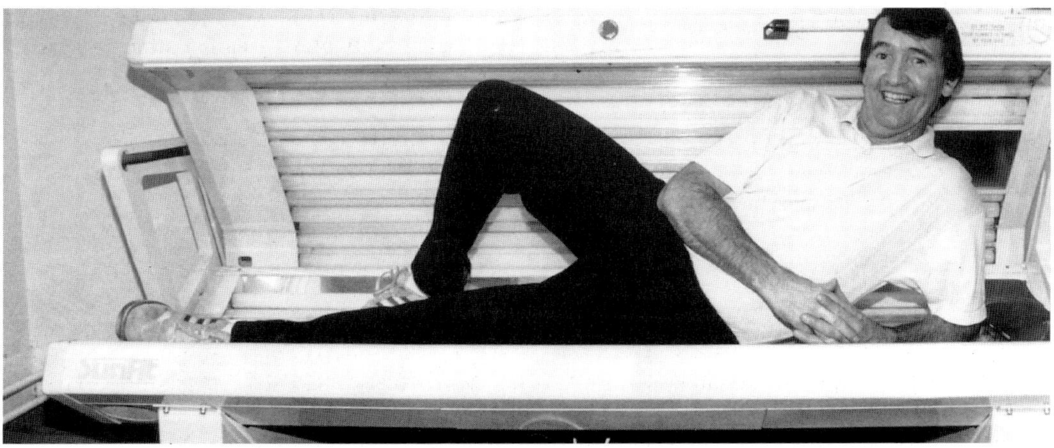

Barry Murphy

MURRAY, Bob. *Stockport Co (1952-1963)* Stockport County was Scotsman Bob 's only Football League club, but during an eleven year stay between 1951 and 1963. He was to set an appearance record of 465 games that would stand for 29 years. Worked at British Aerospace as an aircraft interior finisher before retiring in 1993, aged 61.

MURRAY, Jimmy. *Wolves, Man C, Walsall. (1955-1968).* Hotshot centre forward, who netted over 200 goals from his 400 games in the league. Won two Under 23 caps with England and Football League honours before retiring in 1968. Jimmy is now a greengrocer in Tamworth.

MUSGROVE, Malcolm. *West Ham, Leyton O. (1953-1965).* Former West Ham wingman who played over 350 league games in the 1950's and 1960's. Now a very experienced coach Malcolm is into his 42nd year in the game, currently employed as Physio/coach at Shrewsbury Town.

(Courtesy: Newcastle Chronicle)

NATTRASS, Irving. *Newcastle, Middlesboro (1970-1985).* Former England Under 23 right back, went on to run his own clothes shop in Chester-le-Street, but Irving is now believed to be breeding horses in the north east.

NAYIM, Mohammed. *Tottenham, (1988-1992).* Moroccan international Nayim, who joined Spurs from Spanish giants Barcelona in 1988, is now playing for Real Zaragoza back in Spain.

NAYLOR, Terry. *Tottenham H, Charlton A. (1969-1983).* Former Spurs defender Terry went on to run the "Pickwick" public house in South East London, having finished playing in 1983.

NEAL, John. *Hull, Swindon, Aston V, Southend. (1949-1965).* When he hung up his boots after 416 league games, John managed Wrexham, Middlesborough, then Chelsea (1981- 1985) Now retired but still doing some scouting for Charlton and Shrewsbury from his Edinburgh home.

NEAL, Phil. *Northampton, Liverpool, Bolton. (1968-1988).* Played 455 League games for Liverpool before becoming player-manager, then manager at Bolton. Managed Coventry City until February 1995, having previously been Graham Taylor's England team assistant.

NEALE, Phil. *Lincoln. (1974-1984)* Left back who combined his left back role at Lincoln City (335 appearances) with his career as a County Cricketer. Now playing for Worcestershire C.C.C.

NEATE, Gordon. *Reading (1958-1965).* Now working as groundsman at Elm Park, Reading, home of his only league club as a player.

NEEDHAM, Dave. *Notts C, QPR, Notts F. (1965-1981).* **Central defender who played over 400 games for Notts Co, before ending at neighbours Forest in 1981 - Now a successful businessman in his home town of Leicester. His son Ben is currently on the books at Meadow Lane.**

NEIGHBOUR, Jimmy. *Tottenham H, Norwich C, West Ham U, AFC Bournemouth. (1970-1982).* Jimmy ran a sports shop in Chingford as well as coaching at Wimbledon, and then was at Doncaster Rovers until December 1994. Now returned to his roots to live back in Woodford, Essex.

NEIL, Pat. *Portsmouth, Wolves Portsmouth (1955-1962).* Former England Amateur international is now living in Purbrook, Hampshire and is a teacher at Midhurst Intermediate school.

NEILL, Terry. *Arsenal, Hull (1960-1972).* **Captain of both club and country, Neill won 59 Irish caps before moving into club management with Hull City. Took over at Arsenal in July 1976, and during his seven years in office led them to three successive FA Cup finals. Now runs his own Wine Bar in central London, called - the Terry Neill Sports Bar & Brasserie.**

NELSON, Sammy. *Arsenal, Brighton. (1969-1982).* Belfast born left back who won 51 caps for Northern Ireland and starred in the Arsenal double winning side, now works for Save & Prosper Insurance Company, and lives in Brighton.

NETHERCOTT, Ken. *Norwich, (1947-1958).* England 'B' international keeper who played 378 games between the posts for his only club, Norwich. Now retired, still living in the City.

NEWMAN, John. *Birmingham C, Leicester C, Plymouth, Exeter. (1951-1971)* Wing half who made almost 300 league appearances for Plymouth Argyle in the 1960's. John went on to manage neighbours Exeter City but is currently working as Assistant manager at Burton Albion.

Henry Newton

(Courtesy: Derby Evening Telegraph)

NEWMAN, Ron. *Portsmouth, Leyton O, C Palace, Gillingham. (1954-1965).* Ron has been coaching in America for some years, with Dallas Tornado, Fort Lauderdale, and latterly with San Diego sockers, where he is now general manager.

NEWTON, Henry. *Notts F, Everton, Derby, Walsall. (1963-1977).* Henry established himself as regular with Notts Forest before moving on to Everton, then Derby. Won four England Under 23 caps and Football League honours before retiring in 1977. Now combines his love of golf with his duties as a postmaster in the Derby area.

(Courtesy: Howard Talbot Photography)

NEWTON, Keith. *Blackburn, Everton, Burnley. (1960-1977).* An England full back who joined Everton from Blackburn rovers mid way through the 1969-70 season. Had a second crack at the First Division after winning promotion with Burnley. Then went on to play non-league soccer with Morecambe, and Clitheroe where he was player/manager. Later set up a sports trophy business, and ran a newsagents in Blackburn. Now working with a local garage group in the town.

NICHOLAS, Peter. *Crystal Palace, Arsenal, C Palace, Luton, Chelsea, Watford (1977-1993)* Welsh international who won a total of 73 full caps for his country. Peter is now working as Youth team manager at Crystal Palace, where he had previously enjoyed two spells as a player.

NICHOLL, Chris. *Burnley, Halifax, Luton, Aston V, Southampton, Grimsby. (1965-1984).* Centre half who had a splendid career in first class football before being appointed manager at Southampton in July 1985. In 17 years he had amassed 754 league and cup appearances and 51 caps for Northern Ireland. Joined Walsall as their Manager in September 1994, having had a few years break after leaving Southampton in 1991

NICHOLL, Jimmy. *Man U, Sunderland, WBA (1974-1985).* Former Manchester United apprentice who although born in Canada, played 73 international matches for Northern Ireland. Jimmy is now manager at Raith Rovers in Scotland.

NICHOLLS, Johnny. *WBA, Cardiff Exeter. (1951-1958).* One of the great goal 'poachers' of his day, he had formed a great partnership with Ronnie Allen. Was a member of the 'Baggies' side that won the FA Cup in 1953/4 and so nearly won the double. Died in April 1995, aged 64

NICHOLSON, Bill. *Tottenham H. (1938-1954).* **A war-time signing who made 306 appearances at Wing half between 1946-1954, won one England Cap and three at 'B' level. Was appointed Spurs manager in 1958 and led them to their double success in 1961, also to two other FA Cup victories. Having established himself as one of the all time great managers, Bill left the job in 1974 but is still very much involved with the club, currently as President.**

NICHOLSON, Jimmy. *Man U, Huddersfield, Bury. (1960-1975).* Northern Irish international played 58 games for Man United before moving to Huddersfield in 1964, where he stayed for the next nine years and 300 games. Now Assistant Manager of Sale Sports Centre in Cheshire.

NICHOLSON, Peter. *Blackpool, Bolton, Rochdale, Carlisle, (1970-1983).* Works part time for Bolton Wanderers helping with the coaching and commercial activities. As a player he had been at Burnden Park for ten years in the seventies and played in more than 300 league games.

NIEDZWIEKI, Eddie. *Wrexham, Chelsea. (1977-1987).* Forced to retire after six operations on his knee, became youth team coach at Chelsea. In 1990 Eddie went as coach to Reading and later became assistant to Ian Porterfield at Elm Park. When the Berkshire club decided that they could not afford an assistant manager, he returned to Chelsea, where he is reserve team manager.

NIGHTINGALE, Albert. *Sheff U, Huddersfield, Blackburn, Leeds. (1946-1956).* Inside forward who enjoyed a ten year career immediately after the war. Now a retired golfing greenkeeper.

NILLSON, Roland. *Sheff Wed, (1989-1993).* Swedish international Roland, joined Sheffield Wednesday from I.F.K. Gothenburg in November 1989. However for family reasons, he returned to Sweden to play for Helsingborg in 1994.

David Nish
(Courtesy: Raymonds Press Agency)

NISBET, Gordon. *WBA, Hull, Plymouth, Exeter. (1969-1987).* England Under 23 international who normally played at right back, **however he did make one appearance in goal while at West Brom**. Played for Ottery St Mary and then coached Plymouth. Became a Company director of the Bealon Group in charge of property but is now with the Devon & Cornwall Police and playing for the Police team in the local league.

NISH, David. *Leicester, Derby. (1966-1978).* Former full back David won five full caps with England and was only 21 when he captained Leicester in the 1969 FA Cup final. After spells in America with Tulsa and Seattle. Went on to run a Post Office in Derby but was appointed Youth team coach at Middlesborough in 1988. He currently holds the same post at Leicester City.

NIXON, Jon. *Derby Co, Notts Co, Peterborough U, Shrewsbury T, Barnsley, Halifax T, (1965-1978).* **Former Derby County and Notts County winger is now working for his old team-mate, Dave Needham, in a company specialising in the selling of personalised number plates.**

NOBLE, Norman. *Rotherham (1948-1957).* Played over 300 league games for Rotherham United, his only club. Died in 1973 aged 50.

NOBLE, Peter. *Newcastle, Swindon, Burnley, Blackpool. (1965-1982).* Enjoyed a seventeen year career which included Swindon's League Cup win. Has since run his own stall in Burnley Market selling sports goods for the past eighteen years.

NORMAN, Maurice. *Norwich, Tottenham (1954-1965).* Made over 350 appearances for Spurs and was capped 23 times by England before retiring through injury in 1967. Became assistant manager of a London garage, then opened a wool shop with his wife in Frinton-on-sea. Now works as a landscape gardener in Suffolk.

NORMAN, Richie. *Leicester, Peterboro. (1959-1968).* Played over 300 games for Leicester City in the 1960's. Now runs his own Health clinic and acts as physio to Kettering Town.

NORTHCOTT, Tom. *Torquay, Cardiff, Lincoln, Torquay. (1948-1965).* Scored 125 league goals for Torquay during his eight years at Plainmoor. Tom still lives in the Devon seaside town where he currently works as a builder.

NURSE, Mel. *Swansea, Middlesboro, Swindon, Swansea. (1955-1970).* Welsh international centre half (12 full caps) who started as a junior with home town club Swansea in 1955. After spells with Middlesborough and Swindon, finished 15 years later, back at the Vetch Field. Now a Business man and property owner running a boarding house in Wales. As a director of Swansea, was involved in their survival battle in 1985/6.

NUTT, Gordon. *Coventry, Cardiff, Arsenal, Southend. (1951-1960).* Winger who played for four league clubs in the fifties, including a four year stint with Arsenal. Went over to Australia to play for Corinthians of Sydney, and stayed !

NUTTON, Mike. *Chelsea, Reading, Millwall (1978-1985).* Former Chelsea and Millwall defender, Mike is now playing with Fisher Athletic

O' BRIEN, George. *Leeds, Southampton, Leyton O, Aldershot. (1956-1967).* George scored a most impressive tally of 154 goals in his 244 games for Southampton following his move from Leeds United in 1959. Now a publican in the City, running the Star & Garter, Freemantle.

O' BRIEN, Gerry. *Southampton, Bristol R, Swindon. (1969-1976).* Returned to the Clydebank area of Scotland to resume work as a bricklayer - his trade prior to becoming a professional.

O'BRIEN, Ray. *Man U, Notts Co, Derby. (1973-1983).* Ray now works as a reprographics manager with Nottinghamshire County Council. Living in Nottingham, he is Joint manager of Arnold Town in the NE Counties League.

O'CALLAGHAN, Brendan. *Doncaster R, Stoke C, Oldham Ath. (1973-1985).* Was a manager with the PFA but then decided to study for a degree in Business Administration at the University of Dublin. Also helps out with sports programmes on local radio in the Stoke area.

O'DRISCOLL, Jack. *Swansea. (1947-1951).* Northern Ireland international who joined Swansea City from Cork City in 1947. Jack went on to become a bookmaker prior to his death.

O'DRISCOLL, Sean. *Fulham, Bournemouth, (1979-1994).* Won three caps for the Republic of Ireland during his 500 plus games league career. Sean is now Physio/coach at AFC Bournemouth, where he has been since his transfer in 1984.

O'FARRELL, Frank. *West Ham, Preston. (1950-1960).* **Now retired, living in Torquay. He remembers with amusement an incident that occurred whilst managing non-League Weymouth. They had reached the fourth round of the F.A. Cup, but urgently needed a goalkeeper of their forthcoming tie at Preston North End. Through his contacts, Frank managed to acquire the services of 42 year old Billy Bly, who had recently retired from Hull City. The weather on the day of the match was appalling, thick fog and very poor visibility - although the game was started, eventually the referee was forced to order the players off the pitch. It was sometime later in the dressing room that it became apparent that Billy was missing - a subsequent search found him dutifully still guarding his goal blissfully unaware of the abandonment. When asked about it afterwards, he said "I just assumed we were putting Preston under pressure at the other end!"**

O'FLANAGAN, Dr Kevin. *Arsenal, Brentford, (1945-1949).* **An all round sportsman who represented the Republic of Ireland at both football and rugby, as well as winning sprint and long jump championships in Ireland. After his playing days with Arsenal, he resumed a career in medicine firstly at a hospital in Ruislip, then back in Ireland, where he also acted as Doctor for the Irish Olympic teams**

O'GRADY, Mike *Huddersfield, Leeds, Wolves, Birmingham, Rotherham (1959-1973)* A Don Revie buy who was capped once by England. Worked as a grip for Yorkshire TV for 18 years until being made redundant. Now works behind the bar of the Royal Oak public house in Abbaford, Wetherby, and still plays for the Ex-Leeds side.

O'HARE, John. *Sunderland, Derby, Leeds, Notts F. (1964-1979).* Left the first class game in 1981 and spent a season with Belper Town, after giving up playing he managed Ockbrook FC. Was a licensee in Derby before taking up an appointment with a combustion firm in 1981. Now works as a stock controller with a Derby Car dealer.

O'KANE, Liam. *Notts F, (1968-1975).* Notts Forest persuaded Irish international defender (20 caps), Liam to cross the Water from Derry in 1968, and he has been at the City Ground ever since. Currently employed as First team coach.

O'KEEFE, Vince. *Birmingham Walsall, Exeter, Torquay, Blackburn, Bury, Blackpool, Wrexham (1975-1993)* Having failed to make the first team with his first two league clubs, goalkeeper Vince finally proved his ability by playing over 300 league appearances. Now works as a financial advisor for the P.F.A. based in Birmingham.

O'NEILL Brian. *Burnley, Southampton, Huddersfield. (1962-1975).* Speedy winger who won England Under 23 and League representative honours. Brian was a Civil Engineer, until a serious accident left Brian unable to work. Lives in Hedge End just outside Southampton.

O'NEILL, John. *Leicester, QPR, Norwich. (1978-1987).* **His career was cut short as a result of a now famous clash with John Fashanu which resulted in a much publicised court case in 1994. He has now returned to Derry where he is in charge of a wines and spirits business.**

O'NEILL, Martin. *Notts F, Norwich, Man C, Norwich, Notts Co. (1971-1984).* A former Northern Ireland international captain, who joined Notts Forest from Derry City. During his ten years at the City Ground, he won a host of medals. Moved into management with Grantham and Shepshed Charterhouse before business commitments forced him to quit. Wycombe Wanderers lured him back in February 1990, and he lead them into the League in 1993. Despite resisting many approaches from larger clubs, Martin finally could not resist the offer to return to one of his former clubs, Norwich City, in June 1995.

(Photograph courtesy: Southampton Evening Echo)

OSGOOD, Peter. *Chelsea, Southampton, Norwich C, Chelsea. (1964-1979).* Windsor born Peter is still held in godlike status at Stamford Bridge where he starred as a deadly centre forward for ten years from 1964. Surprisingly, he only won four full England caps to add to his six at Under 23 level, but despite this, is widely accepted as one of the games all time great strikers. After spells in America and a brief return to Chelsea, Peter retired in 1979 to run a public house in his home town of Windsor with former team-mate Ian Hutchinson. Later became Youth team coach at Portsmouth, but now lives near Southampton and is a very popular after dinner speaker (occassionally again with "Hutch"); acts as match day host at Chelsea; runs a successful business which organises celebrity golfing breaks ; as well as being able to find time to give expert match analysis for Sky Sports Soccer programmes.

O'RIORDAN, Don. *Derby Co, Doncaster R, Preston N.E., Carlisle U, Middlesboro, Grimsby T, Notts Co, Mansfield T. (1976-1989).* Dublin born Irish Under 23 international, Don was appointed manager of Torquay United in May 1993.

O'ROURKE, John. *Chelsea, Luton, Middlesboro, Ipswich, Coventry, QPR, Bournemouth, (1962-1974).* England Under 23 forward and former Chelsea apprentice who scored an incredible 64 goals in 84 games for his next club, Luton. Netted plenty more for his next five teams before finishing in 1974. John now lives in Bournemouth, where he runs a newsagents.

O'SHEA, Danny *Arsenal, Charlton Ath, Exeter C, Southend U, Camb U, Northampton (1982-1995)* Now player/coach at Northampton Town and manager of Arsenal Reserves - Ladies side !! who play in the London Women's League.

O'SULLIVAN, Peter. *Man U, Brighton., Fulham, Charlton, Reading, Aldershot. (1968-1983).* Peter played for Brighton for ten years (1970-1980), notching up over 400 league appearances and three full Welsh caps. Now working as an insurance salesman, from his Sussex home.

OAKES, Alan. *Man C, Chester C, Port V. (1959-1983).* Alan made his debut for Manchester City in 1959, and was still going strong 22 years later at Chester City. He was one of the cornerstones in the great Mercer and Allison sides, which during a four year period collected the Football League Championship, FA Cup, European Cup Winners Cup, and Football League Cup. He represented the Football League, before joining Chester City in July 1976 in a player/manager role. Now back at Sealand Road as a coach.

OGLEY, Alan. *Barnsley, Man City, Stockport, Darlington (1962-1976).* Stockport County's first choice goalkeeper for many years in the 1960's and 1970's. Alan is now living in Barnsley, where he works with a local haulage contractor.

OLSEN, Jesper. *Man U, (1984-1988).* **Danish international winger who joined Manchester United in 1984 from Ajax of Amsterdam. Retired in 1988 at the peak of his career, although only aged 27. Jesper now lives in Alderley Edge, Cheshire, and runs a sports management and promotions company with his former United team-mate Kevin Moran.**

ORMSBY, Brendan. *Aston V, Leeds, Shrewsbury, Doncaster, (1978-1993).* Former Villa and Leeds United defender, Brendan is Currently playing for Garforth Town, having previously been assistant manager at Farsley Athletic and had a spell as manager of Waterford in Ireland.

OSBORNE, John. *Chesterfield, WBA, Walsall. (1960-1972).* A product of Chesterfield's great goalkeeping 'academy', Osborne kept goal for West Brom for almost ten years. Once ran a sports wear business with Jim Cumbes, and in later years worked in the promotions department of the Sandwell & Birmingham Evening Mail. Now Commercial Manager at Worcestershire C.C.C.

OSBORNE, Roger. *Ipswich T, Colchester Utd. (1973-1985).* Scored the winner in the 1978 FA Cup final for Ipswich. Now drives a fruit and veg lorry for one of his brothers. Roger is still playing, now back at his very first club, Westerfield United. Also helps out at Portman Road's School of excellence a few hours each week.

OSMAN, Russell. *Ipswich, Leicester, Southampton, Bristol C (1977-1994)* England international (11 caps) starred at Ipswich before transfers took him to Leicester (£220,000 in 1985) and Southampton (£325,000 in 1988). Russell was appointed Manager of Bristol City in January 1993. Despite saving them from relegation in his first year, his contract was terminated in November 1994. He then briefly acted as advisor to Plymouth Argyle until the end of the 1994-5 season.

Russell Osman.

OTTO, Heine *Middlesboro, (1981-1984).* Dutch international midfielder who spent three years with Middlesborough having signed from Twente Enschade in 1981. Was an executive with Den Haag FC, back home in Holland. Now coaching the youth team at Ajax of Amsterdam.

OWEN, Brian. *Watford, Colchester, Wolves. (1962-1972).* Former Watford winger, Brian was Reserve team manager at Ipswich Town, but now working as physiotherapist at Colchester United.

Graham Paddon

OWEN, Gary. *Man C, WBA, Sheff Wed. (1975-1987).* **A skilled midfield player whose career was marred by a series of injuries. During his time with Manchester City, he won England recognition at Youth, 'B' and Under 21 levels and holds the record for most Under 21 caps (22). Had a spell in Cyprus after being released by Sheffield Wednesday, then retired in 1989 to become an art dealer, running the 'Gary Owen Fine Art Co' from his Manchester base.**

PADDON, Graham. *Coventry, Norwich, West Ham, Norwich, Millwall. (1968-1981)* Stylish England under 23 midfielder. Held posts at Portsmouth and Stoke. His second spell as Assistant Manager at Pompey lasted until February 1995.

PAGE, Malcolm. *Birmingham, Oxford. (1964-1982).* Long serving Birmingham City defender who won 28 Welsh caps during his eighteen year playing career. Malcolm retired in 1982 and went on to become an insurance representative.

(Courtesy: Southampton Evening Echo)

PAINE, Terry. *Southampton, Hereford. (1956-1976).* Played a massive 713 League games for Southampton between 1956 and 1973 during which time he was capped 19 times by England. He signed as player/coach at Hereford United in August 1974, but has now been a football coach in South Africa for several years, only interrupted by a brief return to Coventry City in the 1980's.

PAISLEY, Bob. *Liverpool. (1946-1953).* Bob is a one club man who gave Liverpool sterling service. It was as long ago as 1939 that he joined the Merseysiders as a player from Bishop Auckland. After his war duties, Bob returned to Anfield and remained as a player with the club until 1954, when he was appointed to Liverpool's training staff. Succeeded the late Bill Shankly as Liverpool's manager in 1974 and enjoyed spectacular success until his retirement in 1983.

PALIN, Leigh. *Shrewsbury T, Notts For, Bradford C, Stoke C, Hull C, Rochdale, (1983-1992).* Leigh is now Promotions officer and player for Immingham Town in South Humberside.

PALIOS, Mark. *Tranmere, Crewe, Tranmere R. (1973-1984).* Former midfielder. Now a Chartered Accountant working for a firm of liquidators, and living in Lode, near Cambridge.

PALMER, Geoff. *Wolves, Burnley, Wolves, (1973-1986).* Geoff won 12 England under 23 caps and played 400 games for Wolves. Now a Police Constable stationed at Darlaston, having joined the West Midlands force in October 1986.

PARDOE, Glyn. *Man C. (1961-1974).* Former Manchester City defender, who occupied the right back berth for almost thirteen years, and won four England Under 23 caps. Glyn is still at Maine Road, now working on the coaching staff.

PARK, Terry *Stockport, Man C, Bury (1974-1983)* Bought and run a Post Office for seven years, but in 1990 joined a Liverpool haulage firm.

PARKER, Albert. *Crewe, Wrexham (1948-1958).* Wrexham defender of the fifties. Became the club's groundsman and a Town Councillor. Now retired but still living in the town.

PARKER, Alex. *Everton, Southport. (1958-1967).* **Scottish international right back who was Scotland's "Player of the Year" in 1957, prior to his move South to Everton. Managed Southport and also had a brief spell in management in Ireland, before taking a pub called "The Swinging Sporron". Then returned to his native Scotland to run a pub in Gretna Green.**

PARKER, Bobbie. *Coventry, Carlisle (1969-1983).* Played over 400 League games for Coventry and Carlisle before becoming a Health & Safety officer for a foods firm in Carlisle.

PARKER, Cliff *Doncaster R, Portsmouth (1931-1950).* Winger with Pompey during the thirties and forties. Died in 1983 at the age of 70.

PARKER, Derrick. *Burnley, Southend, Barnsley, Oldham, Doncaster, Burnley, Rochdale. (1974-1987).* Derrick is now living in Barnsley and works as a salesman for a brick manufacturing company. Has been in sales since 1989, previously Doncaster Rovers's Community Officer.

PARKER, John Willie. *Everton, Bury. (1950-1958).* After five years at Everton, went to Bury in 1956, but eventually returned to Merseyside where he worked in a pub. Died 1988

Tommy Parker

PARKER, Tommy. *Ipswich, (1946-1956).* Long serving, player and captain for Ipswich, for whom he notched up 493 appearances. Became a publican and worked in a timber merchants before returning to Portman Road as Commercial Manager for 19 years until his retirement.

PARKES, Harry. *Aston V (1946-1954).* Played 320 games for Aston Villa before retiring in 1955 to concentrate on his flourishing sports-outfitters business, which still trades today in Corporation Street, Birmingham. He was appointed to the Villa board of Directors and later elected to the board of neighbours, Birmingham City.

PARKES, Phil. *Walsall, QPR, West Ham, Ipswich. (1968-1990)* West Ham broke the transfer record for a goalkeeper to take Phil across London in 1979 for £560,000. Ironically, he went on play 344 league games for the Hammers, exactly the same total that he had amassed while with Q.P.R. Returned to Loftus Road in September 1991 as goalkeeping coach and has also helped out in the same capacity at Ipswich Town.

PARKIN, Derek. *Huddersfield T, Wolves, Stoke. (1964-1982).* Wolverhampton Wanderers long serving left-back was signed from Huddersfield the fee of £80,000 set a record for a full back. Lives in Wheaton Aston near Bridgenorth and works as a professional landscape gardener.

PARKIN, Tim *Blackburn, Bristol R, Swindon T, Port Vale, Shrewsbury T, (1976-1992).* Former central defender Tim became Football in the Community Officer at Middlesborough before deciding to leave the club to join the Police force.

PARLANE, Derek. *Leeds U, Man C, Swansea, Rochdale. (1979-1987).* Derek joined Leeds from Rangers in 1980 for £160,00, having already become a full Scottish international. Over the next seven years he played for three more clubs and enjoyed two spells in Hong Kong before retiring in 1987. Now a sportswear agent in the North West of England, living in Wilmslow, Cheshire.

PARSONS, Lindsay. *Bristol R, Torquay, (1963-1978).* Held his place in the Bristol defence for almost thirteen years before ending at Torquay in 1978. Lindsay has been Manager of Cheltenham Town in the BHL League since 1992.

PARTRIDGE, Malcolm. *Mansfield, Leicester, Charlton, Grimsby, Scunthorpe. (1967-1981)* Malcolm ended his playing days in 1981 and is now running the Millfields Hotel in Grimsby.

PASHLEY, Terry. *Burnley, Blackpool, Bury (1973-1988).* Former left back who played in more than 200 league games for both Blackpool and Bury, Terry is now Youth team coach at Burnley.

PATE, Alex (Sandy). *Watford, Mansfield. (1964-1977).* Veteran of over 400 games at Mansfield. Now runs "The Travellers Rest in Ashfield.

PATES, Colin. *Chelsea, Charlton, Arsenal, Brighton, (1979-1994)* Former Chelsea apprentice who played in the Blues' defence for close to a decade. Forced to quit in December 1994 due to a knee injury, Colin joined Crawley and was appointed as their manager in May 1995. Also helped out at the Arsenal School of Excellence.

PAUL, Roy. *Swansea, Man C, (1944-1956).* **Joined Swansea during the War and played 160 League games before making the unusual move to South America to join Bogota. Returned to the U.K. to lead Manchester City to their FA Cup success in 1956. Capped 33 times by Wales, Roy is now retired from his job as lorry driver and lives in Gelli, Mid Glamorgan.**

PAYNE, George. *Tranmere R, (1946-1960).* Goalkeeper who played over 400 League games for Tranmere Rovers until 1960. Now deceased.

PEACH, David. *Gillingham, Southampton, Swindon T, Leyton Orient. (1969-1982).* Former England Under 23 full back. Has now worked in the building trade for many years, and is living in Milford on Sea, near Lymington, Hampshire.

PEACOCK, Alan. *Middlesboro, Leeds U, Plymouth Arg, (1955-1967).* Scorer of 153 goals in 284 league games, most for Middlesborough in the 1950's and 1960's, Alan was rewarded with six full England caps.Went on to run a newsagency in Middlesborough but is now co-owner of a cleaning products business in the area.

PEACOCK, Keith. *Charlton. (1962-1978).* Keith's sixteen year career was exclusively spent at Charlton Athletic, for whom he appeared in over 500 matches. Now working at the Valley as Reserve Team coach. Father of Gavin (Chelsea.)

PEAKE, Andy. *Leicester, Grimsby, Charlton, Middlesboro, (1978-1992).* England Under 23 cap who after a stint as manager of Ayssriska (Sweden), is now training for the Police force.

PEARCE, Jimmy. *Tottenham. (1968-1972)* England youth winger who finished playing at the age of only 25, now works in the "Rag Trade".

PEARSON, Jim. *Everton, Newcastle, (1974-1979).* Scottish Under 23 international who moved South to join Everton from St Johnstone in 1974. Now works for NIKE in the north east.

PEARSON, Lawrie. *Hull C, Bristol C, Port Vale, (1984-1987).* Former Hull City full back, is now working as Football in the community officer at Ayresmoe Park with Middlesborough.

PEARSON, Stan. *Man U, Bury, Chester C, (1937-1958).* One of the early Busby stars with Manchester United in the forties, who played eight games for England. After almost 500 games, ended at Chester in 1958. Now a retired newsagent living in Prestbury, Lancashire.

PEARSON, Stuart.. *Hull C, Man U, West Ham. (1969-1981).* Began his pro career at Hull City and moved to Manchester United in 1974 for £200,000, scored 55 goals in 139 league games and won 15 England Caps. Since ending his career at West Ham, Stuart has held coaching and managerial posts at Stockport, Northwich Victoria, West Brom, and more recently was Assistant Manager at Bradford City. Lives in Sale, Cheshire and is now looking for a new challenge.

PEJIC, Mike. *Stoke C, Hereford U, Wrexham. (1968-1979).* Long serving Stoke City defender who won four full England Caps whoile at the Victoria Ground. Had spells as assistant manager of Port Vale and coaching in Kuwait before becoming manager of Chester City in 1994. However, Mike was sacked in the following January.

Mike Pejic.

PENDREY, Gary. *Birmingham, WBA, Torquay, Bristol R, Walsall. (1966-1982).* Managed former club Birmingham City, where he had previously made over 300 League appearances. Then worked at Wolves as a coach until the arrival of Graham Taylor and the subsequent change of staff. Now acts as a coach at Coventry City.

PENK, Harry. *Portsmouth, Plymouth, Southampton. (1955-1963).* Former Plymouth and 'Saints' winger now lives in Southampton and is working as a painter and decorator in the area.

PENMAN, Willie *Newcastle, Swindon, Walsall (1962-1972).* Scottish midfielder who joined Newcastle form Glasgow Rangers in 1963. Now lives in the West Midlands and sells for sports firms.

PENNYFATHER, Glenn. *Southend, C. Palace, Ipswich, (1980-1994).* Glenn spent seven years with Southend in the 1980's making 238 appearances. Now playing for Canvey Island.

PERRIN, Steve. *C Palace, Plymouth, Portsmouth, Northampton. (1976-1982).* Midfielder who moved into League Soccer with Crystal Palace relatively late, having caught the eye whilst playing for Hillingdon. Deputy head at a Primary School in Bushey, Herts, living in Hemel Hempstead and is P.T instructor with Hillingdon FC.

PERRY, Bill. *Blackpool, Southport (1949-1962)* Bill is South African but an England International. Joined Blackpool from Johannesburg in 1949 and went to star for the northern side for the next twelve years. Scorer of the winning goal in the 1953 Cup final. Now in business as a match manufacturer (promotional book matches) near Preston, but still lives in Blackpool.

PERRYMAN, Steve. *Tottenham H, Oxford U, Brentford. (1969-1989).* Steve won only one England Cap but proudly holds the Spurs record for the most number of League games played - 653. Was Manager of Brentford and Watford before returning to Tottenham Hotspur as Assistant manager then briefly caretaker manager, prior to Gerry Francis's arrival at White Hart Lane.

PETERS, Gary. *Reading, Fulham, Wimbledon, Aldershot, Reading, Fulham. (1975-1989)* Former defender who played all his league soccer for four Southern clubs, is now Manager of Preston N.E.

PETERS, Martin. *West Ham, Tottenham, Norwich, Sheff U. (1961-1980).* **Peters was one of the great talent of the modern game and was once described by the England tam manager, Alf Ramsey, as "ten years ahead of his time". He was a member of the 1966 World Cup winning side before signing for Spurs in March 1970 to become Britain's first £200,000 player. Later he played for Norwich and in 1980 became player/manager to Sheffield United. Now lives in Essex and works for the same Motor Insurance Company as his former West Ham and England striking partner, Geoff Hurst.**

PEYTON, Gerry, *Burnley, Fulham, Southend, Bournemouth, Everton, Bolton, (1975-1993).* Republic of Ireland keeper who played 33 times for his country. Appeared in over 600 league games before taking up a coaching role in Japan. Gerry is now believed to be in Hong Kong.

PHILLIPS, Brendan. *Leicester, Peterboro U, Mansfield. (1972-1980).* England semi-pro international midfielder, despite being born in the West Indies. Brendan was manager of Stafford Rangers for 18 months until November 1994.

PHILLIPS, Ernie. *Man C, Hull, York. (1948-1957).* Ernie was captain of the famous York team that reached the 1954 F.A. Cup semi-final. Now retired but can be found playing indoor bowls.

(Photograph courtesy: Raymonds Press Agency)

Martin Peters (right) with former England strike partner and current work colleague **Geoff Hurst.**

PHILLIPS, John. *Shrewsbury, Aston V, Chelsea, Crewe, Brighton., Charlton , C Palace (1968-1983).* Welsh international keeper who played 125 games for Chelsea in the seventies. Now runs the motor factors company that he set up in Mitcham, while still playing at Crystal Palace in the 1980's.

PHILLIPS, Leighton. *Cardiff, Aston V, Swansea, Charlton, Exeter. (1967-1982).* Welsh international defender who won 58 full caps. Leighton made his league debut for Cardiff in 1967 and went on to play almost 500 games over the next 15 years until his retirement in 1982. Lives in Neath and has worked for Confederation life since retiring where he is now a senior life underwriter.

PHILLIPS, Len. *Portsmouth (1946-1954).* Inside forward for Portsmouth for eight post war years who won three England caps. Worked for an Engineering firm in the city from 1959 but is now retired, living in Hilsea, Hampshire.

PHILLIPS, Steve. *Birmingham, Torquay, Northampton, Brentford, Northampton, Southend, Torquay, Peterboro, (1971-1987).* Took to selling double glazing in the Peterborough area after his eight year career finished in 1987.

Leighton Phillips

PHILPOTTS, Dave. *Coventry, Southport, Tranmere. (1971-1984).*Central defender whose two spells with Tranmere were separated by a six year stint in Carolina, USA. Now Youth team coach at Stockport County, living in Bebington.

PICKERING, Fred. *Blackburn R, Everton, Birmingham C, Blackpool, Blackburn R. (1959-1970)* Fred won three England caps before retiring from soccer in 1971. Now lives in his home town of Blackburn and works at a local factory, where he currently drives a fork lift truck.

(Photograph courtesy: Portsmouth News)

Pompey legend **Len Phillips,** proudly showing off his two championship medals.

PICKERING, John. *Newcastle, Halifax, Barnsley (1963-1974).* First team coach at Middlesborough, having previously coached at Blackburn; Bolton; Carlisle; then Newcastle.

PIERCE, Gary. *Huddersfield, Wolves, Barnsley, Blackpool. (1971-1983).* Returned to play non-league football for his first club, Mosseley. Now living near Bolton, Gary is currently unemployed and sadly having to rely on invalidity benefit as a result of back trouble.

PIPER, Norman. *Plymouth, Portsmouth (1964-1977).* After signing from Plymouth, this stylish England under 23 international gave Portsmouth senior service for more than 350 matches. Moved over to America to play for Fort Lauderdale and then on to become Assistant Coach for the Wichita Wings. Now believed to be living in Canada.

PIPER, Steve. *Brighton., Portsmouth. (1972-1978).* Former Brighton and Portsmouth defender, Steve became a Mortgage and Insurance Broker, and now living in Southwick, West Sussex.

PLATT, Jim. *Middlesboro, Hartlepool, Cardiff C. (1971-1978).* Middlesborough's keeper for over ten years following his move from Ballymena in 1970. Won 22 full caps with Northern Ireland Jim is now running a rag trade business back in his native Ballymena, Northern Ireland.

PLATT, John. *Oldham, Bury, Bolton, Tranmere, Preston. (1975-1985).* Now lives in Ashton-under-Lyne, Lancs and still plays for Stalybridge Celtic. Works for the M.S.C. programme attatched to Oldham Athletic, where he had previously appeared in goal as a player.

David Pleat

PLEAT, David. *Notts F, Luton, Shrewsbury, Exeter, Peterborough. (1961-1970)* Won England Schoolboy and youth honours as a player, but made his name in Management initially by guiding Luton Town to the first division in 1978. Spells at Tottenham Hotspur, Leicester City and a second stint at Luton Town followed, before David eventually joined Sheffield Wednesday in June 1995 following a bitter fight between Club Chairmen over compensation payments.

PLUMMER, Calvin. *Notts Forest, Chesterfield, Derby Co, Barnsley, Plymouth Argyle, Chesterfield (1981-1990).* Since 1990 Calvin has had spells with Gainsborough Trinity, Shepshed Albion, Corby Town and has been registered as a player for Nuneaton Borough since July 1994.

PLUMMER, Norman. *Leicester, Mansfield. (1947-1955).* Centre half who captained Leicester's 1949 Cup final side that lost 3-1 to Wolves. Norman ran a ladies, gents and childrens clothes shop until his retirement. Still lives in Leicester.

PODD, Ces. *Bradford, Halifax, Scarboro, (1970-1987).* Ces was born on the island of St Kitts, but played most of his soccer in the sunshine (?) of Bradford. Now works for Bradford City as a Community Officer having previously managed Eccleshill in N.E. Counties League.

POINTER, Ray. *Burnley, Bury, Coventry, Portsmouth. (1957-1972).* Centre forward, Ray won a league championship medal in 1960, and three England caps during his time with Burnley. Went on to coach at Blackpool, worked as Burnley's Commercial manager and became youth coach at Bury before retiring in 1990 aged only 54.

POOLE, Terry. *Huddersfield, Bolton, Sheff U. (1968-1979).* Former Man Utd apprentice, Terry became a permanent fixture between the posts for Huddersfield. Now lives near Chesterfield and is manager of a cash & carry video wholesalers.

PORTERFIELD, Ian. *Sunderland, Reading, Sheff Wed (1967-1979)* Ian scored the winning goal in the 1973 FA Cup final for Sunderland, whom he had joined from Raith Rovers in 1967. Went on to manage Chelsea (1991to 1993) and then became National team manager to Zambia, who lost eighteen of their players in a disastrous air crash in 1993. Most recently was coaching in the Middle East with club side Al Ittihad.

PORTEUS, Trevor. *Hull City, Stockport County (1951-1964)* Trevor became deputy officer at an Elderly persons home in Stockport. Despite undergoing heart bypass surgery in 1990, he is now fully recovered and is a regular visitor to Stockport County, where during his 40 year love affair with the club he had been sacked three times and left on his own accord more than once!!

PORTWOOD, Cliff. *Preston N.E., Port Vale, Grimsby T, Portsmouth, (1955-1968).* **Former insied forward Cliff, who played for Grimsby and Pompey in the 1960's, reached the final of the BBC television programme "Rising Stars" in 1980 - as a singer ! These days, he makes his living as a licensee, in Alton, Hampshire.**

POTTS, Harry. *Burnley, Everton. (1946-1955)* Harry became an outstanding manager for Burnley, guiding them to the League Championship title in 1960. Continues to live in the town and still keeps in touch with the Turf Moor Club.

POUNTNEY, Ron. *Walsall, Port V, Southend, (1973-1984).* Played one game for Walsall before becoming a regular fixture in Southend United's midfield. Played almost 350 games for the Shrimpers before retiring in 1984. Now works as a Painter & decorator in the Southend area.

POWELL, Barry. *Wolves, Coventry, Derby, Burnley, Swansea, Wolves. (1972-1987).* England under 23 midfielder who turned out for six clubs and had two spells in Hong Kong during the 1980's. Now an Officer with Football in the Community based at Coventry having previously been first team coach at Wolves from 1987 to 1991.

POWELL, Colin. *Charlton, Gillingham. (1972-1982).* A time with New England Teamen in America separated Colin's two periods with Charlton Athletic. Was Coach and Assistant manager at Bromley. Now back at the Valley working for his old club as their groundsman.

POWELL, David *Wrexham, Sheff U, Cardiff (1962-1974).* Dave played eleven times for Wales in the 1960's and finished with Cardiff in 1974 when he joined the police force at Bridgend.

POWELL, Steve. *Derby (1971-1984).* Like his father, Steve was Derby county man, who played over 350 matches. Manages a Sports Centre in the Derby area. His son is following the tradition and is now on the books at the Baseball Ground.

POWELL, Thomas. *Derby (1948-1961).* Father of Steve (see above), and former winger who tormented defences for Derby from 1948 to 1961. Still lives in Derby and is a keen Rams follower.

POWER, Paul. *Man C, Everton (1975-1987).* Paul joined Man City from Leeds Polytechnic in 1973 and proceeded to notch up over 350 appearances in their colours, before leaving for Everton in 1986. Coached at Everton, then joined the P.F.A as a Football in the Community Officer, but is now working for them as a Coaching Secretary.

PRATT, John. *Tottenham, (1968-1979).* John played over 300 games in midfield for his only club, Tottenham before retiring in 1979. When dismissed from his post as Assistant manager at Spurs in 1986, he left League soccer. Landed a coaching job in Nigeria, but returned to Chigwell to set up his own cleaning business. Briefly joined the backroom staff at Stevenage Borough in 1994

PRESLAND, Eddie. *West Ham, C Palace, Colchester (1964-1969).* Former West Ham and Crystal Palace defender now lives in Chelmsford and is a Games instructor at a school in Mile End.

PRICE, David. *Arsenal, Peterboro, C Palace, Leyton O. (1972-1982).* David was an Arsenal apprentice who made over 100 appearances for the Gunners. Joined Crystal Palace in 1981, but was forced to quit less than two years later aged 27. Now a mini cab driver and plays for West Wickham in the Southern Amateur league.

PRICE, Johnny *Burnley, Stockport, Blackburn, Stockport (1960-1975)* Licensee of the Grey Horse public house in Heaton Norris near Stockport, where he had played the majority of his league career. Had two spells at Edgerley Park, separated by two years at Blackburn Rovers (1973-5).

PRICE, Neil *Watford, Plymouth, Blackpool, Swansea, (1983-1985).* Managed Diadora League side, Walton & Hersham until February 1995.

PRICE, Paul. *Luton, Tottenham, Swansea, Peterboro. (1971-1987).* A solid central defender who played 25 matches for Wales. After making his name at Luton, Price joined Tottenham for £200,000 in 1981, currently with Hitchin Town.

PRING, Keith. *Newport, Rotherham, Notts Co, Southport (1961-1970)* Now a representative for Bass Charrington in West Lancashire.

PRITCHARD, Roy. *Wolves, Aston Villa, Notts Co, Port Vale (1946-1959).* Wolverhampton Wanderers full back from 1946-1954, who made over 200 league appearances. Now deceased.

PROBERT, Eric. *Burnley, Notts Co, Darlington (1968-1979).* Eric was a Burnley regular, before retiring in 1979 to become the landlord of a public house in North Yorkshire.

PROVAN, David. *C. Palace, Plymouth, (1970-1974).* Scottish international defender who ventured South from Glasgow Rangers to play initially for Crystal Palace, then spent four years on the Devon Coast with Plymouth Argyle. Dave is now back in Scotland, based at Morton FC where he works as Scottish Youth Development Officer.

PUCKETT, Dave. *Southampton, Bournemouth, Stoke, Swansea, Aldershot, Bournemouth (1980-1992).* Gained experience with seven league clubs before dropping into non-league soccer. Played for Woking in their FA Vase victory but now a player with Newport (IOW) in the BHL.

PUGH Graham. *Sheff Wed, Huddersfield, Chester, Barnsley, Scunthorpe. (1965-1980).* Graham won England Under 23 honours and enjoyed a fifteen year career following his debut with Sheffield Wednesday in 1965. Now a licensee of a pub in Sheffield, close to Hillsborough.

PULIS, Tony *Bristol R, Newport Co, AFC Bournemouth, Gillingham, Bournemouth, (1975-1994).* Tony played for five clubs including two spells at both Bristol Rovers and AFC Bournemouth. Became manager at Dean Court until August 1994, but was then appointed Manager of Gillingham in Kent the following Summer.

(Photograph courtesy: Sheffield Newspapers Ltd)

Johnny Quinn (far right) pulling on a Sheffield Wednesday shirt again after almost thirty years.

PURDIE, Bernard. *Wrexham, Chester, Crewe, Huddersfield, Crewe, (1968-1982).* Played over league 200 games for Crewe Alexandra, but now works as a postman back in his home town of Wrexham, where also started his soccer career.

QUAIRNEY, John. *Rotherham. (1948-1959).* Goalie who played over 260 games for Rotherham, works for Charlton Bros. in Scotland.

QUINN, Jimmy *Swindon, Blackburn, Swindon, Leicester, Bradford C, West Ham, Bournemouth, Reading. (1981-1995)* Goalscoring Northern Ireland international striker. Jimmy was appointed joint player/manager at Reading in January 1995.

QUINN, Johnny. *Sheff Wed, Rotherham, Halifax. (1959-1974).* One of Sheffield Wednesdays's stars of the 1960's, is now running a sports outfitting business in Hillsborough, Sheffield.

QUIXHALL, Albert. *Sheff Wed, Man U, Oldham, Stockport. (1950-1966).* Manchester United broke the British transfer record to take England international Albert to Old Trafford from Sheffield Wednesday for £45,000 in 1958. Now a scrap dealer in the Manchester area.

RADFORD, John. *Arsenal, West Ham, Blackburn. (1963-1978).* Part of Arsenal's deadly strike force in the early 1970's. John won two England caps while with the Gunners, before moving on to West Ham in 1976, and finishing at Blackburn Rovers two years later. Became a publican in Essex, and then in Hertfordshire, but is now general manager of Bishops Stortford FC.

RADFORD, Ron. *Leeds, Newport, Hereford. (1961-1973).* Scorer of a famous F.A. Cup goal for Hereford against Newcastle United, Ronnie now lives in Wakefield where he now runs his own joinery business. Manager of Ossett Albion.

RAFFERTY, Billy. *Coventry, Blackpool, Plymouth, Carlisle, Wolves, Newcastle, Portsmouth, Bournemouth. (1969-1984).* Played in Portugal for several years , and at the age of 37 scored 20 goals in the 1987-8 season to spark Loultanos's bid for promotion to the Portuguese first division. Now runs health and fitness club in Carlisle.

RAFFERTY, Ron. *Portsmouth, Grimsby, Hull, Aldershot. (1954-1968)* Ron scored 145 goals in his 264 league appearances for Grimsby (1956-1962). Now medically retired through arthritis, and he is now living in Aldershot, Hampshire.

RAMSAY, Sir Alf. *Southampton, Tottenham. (1946-1954).* **Started his career at Southampton but moved to Spurs in 1949, where he helped them to Second and First Division titles in successive years. Was appointed England manager in 1963, and three years later led them to World Cup glory, earning him a knighthood the following year. Sir Alf remained manager until 1974 and is now enjoying his well earned retirement in Suffolk.**

RANDALL, Kevin. *Bury, Chesterfield, Notts Co, Mansfield, York. (1965-1980).* A fifteen year career as a player ended in 1980 and Kevin is currently Assistant manager at Chesterfield.

RANDALL, Paul. *Bristol R, Stoke, Bristol R. (1977-1985).* Spent two spells at Bristol Rovers as a prolific goalscorer before being forced to quit through injury at the age of 27. Now in the building industry, living in Glastonbury, Somerset.

RANKIN, Andy. *Everton, Watford, Huddersfield. (1963-1981).* England Under 23 goalie who was understudy at Everton for seven years in the 1960's before establishing himself as first choice at Watford in the 1970's. Now a warehouseman for a Huddersfield firm that makes wage packets.

RANKMORE, Frank. *Cardiff, Peterboro, Northampton. (1961-1970).* Centre half who won one Welsh cap. Now a publican in Cardiff, his birthplace, and also the home of his first club.

RANSON, Ray. *Man C, Birmingham, Newcastle. (1978-1994)* Ray won ten caps forthe England Under 23 team during his time as a young defender with Manchester City. Appointed player/manager at Witton Albion in May 1995

REANEY, Paul. *Leeds, Bradford C, (1962-1979).* Stylish defender who played over 745 games for Leeds United and won three full England caps before moving to Bradford City in 1978. Paul then ventured down under, for a spell with Australian side, Newcastle UB United where in 1980, he was voted Australia's "Player of the Year". Now lives near Knaresborough and runs coaching courses for the World in Sport organisation as well as being a partner in the Classic Portrait Company, who kindly supplied his pic.

REAGAN, Martin. *York, Hull, Middlesboro, Shrewsbury, Portsmouth, Norwich. (1946-1955).* **Winger who appeared for six league clubs during the 1950's was Manager of the England Ladies team until his resignation in 1994.**

REDKNAPP, Harry. *West Ham, Bournemouth, Brentford, Bournemouth. (1965-1982).* Poplar born Harry played on the wing at West Ham for six years before moving down to the South Coast to play for Bournemouth. He became manager at Dean Court in 1982 and held the post until accepting the role of Assistant manager at West Ham in 1992, where went on to take over as manager in 1994, after the departure of Billy Bonds.

REECE, Gil. *Cardiff, Newport, Sheff U, Cardiff Swansea. (1961-1976).* Remembered for his time at Sheffield Utd, Gil ended his days back in Wales (for whom he won 29 caps), before setting up a successful plumbing & heating business with his brother. Now runs a hotel in Cardiff.

REES, Ronnie. *Coventry, WBA, Notts F, Swansea. (1962-1974).* Retired in 1975 and worked behind the scenes at Cardiff City before taking a job with a large car manufacturer in Bridgend.

REEVES, Derek. *Southampton, AFC Bournemouth. (1954-1964).* Scorer of 39 goals in 1959/60, which is still a Southampton record. He topped the clubs goal charts in four consecutive seasons. Moved to Bournemouth in 1962, where he continued to live and work as a Sales Representative. Died of cancer in May 1995 at the age of 60.

REEVES, Kevin. *Bournemouth, Norwich City, Man City, Burnley. (1974-1983).* Skilful striker who joined the 'Million Pound Club' when sold by John Bond, then manager of Norwich City, to Manchester City in March 1980 for £1,250,000. An England international (2 Caps) who began with AFC Bournemouth and moved to Norwich City for £50,000 in February 1977. Now holds the post of Assistant manager at Wrexham.

REID, Duggie. *Stockport, Portsmouth, (1936-1955).* Former Pompey inside forward, Duggie is now retired in Widley, Portsmouth, having been groundsman at Fratton Park for 20 years.

REID, John. *Bradford C, Northampton, Luton, Torquay, Rochdale. (1957-1967).* Scottish forward who joined Bradford City in 1957 from Hamilton Accedemicals. Now a newsagent in Bradford.

REID, Peter. *Bolton W, Everton, QPR, Man C, Southampton, Bolton W, Sunderland (1971-1995).* After starring in the Bolton Wanderers midfield for several years, Peter joined Everton in 1982 for a meagre £60,000, but went on to become one of their most popular players of the time. Won the "Player of the Year" award in 1985 having won the FA Cup in 1984 and reached the final the following year. Coached at Goodison Park, and then had a brief spell as manager of Manchester City. Appointed player/manager at first division Sunderland in March 1995.

REILLY, George. *Northampton, Camb U, Watford, Newcastle, WBA, Camb U, (1976-1988).* Intimidating forward who scored goals galore during a 12 year career which ended in 1988 while at Cambridge United. George now runs his own building firm in nearby Ely, Cambridgeshire.

RELISH, John. *Chester, Newport. (1972-1986)* Made the left back position his own during twelve years with Newport County from 1974. Now works as Y.T.S. training officer for Football in the Community based in Newport, Gwent.

(Courtesy: Portsmouth News)

RENYOLDS, Ritchie. *Plymouth, Portsmouth. (1964-1975).* Former Plymouth and Pompey striker owned a fish and chip shop in Portsmouth. also had a spell as manager of Fareham Town. Now runs a sandwich bar in Fratton, Portsmouth.

REVIE, Don. *Leicester C, Hull C, Man City, Sunderland, Leeds U. (1946-1961).* **Died in May 1989 after a long fight against motor neurone disease. In an extremely successful management career he won two League titles, League Cup, FA Cup and the European Fairs Cup with Leeds. Despite being banned from English Football for ten years after giving up the England Managers job to take a lucrative post in the U.A.E, he will always be remembered as one of the all time great motivators. Shortly before his death he asked that his ashes be strewn over the Leeds pitch and in 1994 his wife Elsie opened the new Don Revie North Stand at Elland Road, named in his memory.**

RHOADES-BROWN, Peter. *Chelsea, Oxford Utd, (1979-1988).* Peter now works in the commercial office at Oxford United. Also player/manager at Marlow FC and ironically was a member of their side which knocked his employers out in the first round of the 1994/5 F.A. Cup!

RICE, Pat. *Arsenal, Watford. (1967-1983).* Belfast born, Rice came through the Highbury junior ranks, to turn professional in 1966, and went on to play nearly 400 league games for the 'Gunners' also gaining 49 caps for his country. Honours achieved at Arsenal include the 'Double' in 1970-1 and a further F.A. Cup winners medal in 1979. Pat then joined Watford in 1980 for a fee of £20,000 where he enjoyed promotion to the First Division in 1981-2 and then the next season finishing runners up to Liverpool. Returned to Arsenal as Youth Team Coach and is still on the coaching staff of the North London outfit.

(Courtesy: Express & Star, Wolverhampton)

RICHARDS, John. *Wolves, Derby. (1969-1982).* Joined Wolves straight from school and scored their winning goal when they defeated Man City in the 1974 League Cup final. Now Head of Leisure for his local council in Staffordshire. This means he is responsible for a £3 million budget covering local theatres, sports facilities, museums and parks & gardens. Still a hero at Molineux, John was made a Director of the Club in 1995.

RICHARDS, Pedro. *Notts Co (1974-1985).* Played almost 400 league games as a right back with Notts County, ending in 1985. Pedro is now working as a builder in the Nottingham area.

RICHARDS, Tony. *Birmingham, Walsall, Port V (1951-1965).* Signed for Walsall in 1954 and went on to net more goals for them than anyone had done before including the legendary Gilbert Alsop. Helped Walsall's rise from the Fourth to the Second division, and topped their scoring list six times. Now working for A.T.S. in Walsall.

RICHARDSON, Damien. *Gillingham (1972-1980).* Republic of Ireland international, who after playing over 300 games for Gillingham has returned to Ireland to manage Cork City.

RICKABY, Stan. *Middlesboro, WBA. (1947-1954).* Capped once by England, Rickaby was a strong right back who retired in 1964. He went into insurance before emigrating to Australia . Now living in Perth, and works in accountancy.

John Ridley

RICKARD, Derek. *Plymouth, Bournemouth. (1969-1975).* Now a newsagent in Plymouth. Chairman of Oak Villa FC in the S.W. League.

RIDDICK, Gordon. *Luton T, Gillingham, Charlton Ath, Leyton O, Northampton T, Brentford. (1962-1976).* Gordon now lives in Watford where he used to run his own building company, then managed a builders merchants and kitchen company. Now employed as a sales executive, and has also worked freelance for BBCtv Match of the day since he finished playing in 1976.

RIDLEY, John. *Port V, Leicester, Chesterfield, Port V. (1973-1984).* Joined Port Vale from Sheffield University in 1973, then after 400 league appearances returned to Education to become a Maths teacher in the Stoke-on-Trent area.

RIMMER, Jimmy. *Man U, Swansea, Arsenal, Aston V, Swansea. (1967-1985).*Jimmy started as an apprentice ant Manchester United, but found his opportunities limited by the great Alex Stepney. However, went on to achieve success in his own right with Arsenal and Aston Villa, winning his one England cap in 1976. Now working as Youth team coach at Swansea City where he previously had enjoyed two spells as a player.

RIMMER, Warwick. *Bolton W, Crewe Alex (1960-1978).* Gave admirable service to Bolton Wanderers for fourteen years, during which time he was a permenant fixture in ther back four. Warwick has now returned to Tranmere Rovers, where he works as Youth development officer.

RIOCH, Bruce. *Luton, Aston V, Derby, Everton, Derby, Birmingham, Sheff U, Torquay. (1964-1983).* Bruce first came to prominence when cracking in 24 goals in 44 games to collect a Fourth division medal with Luton. He signed for Aston Villa and helped them to the 1970/1 League Cup final. Moved on to Derby County in 1974 for £200,000, and in his first full season with the club won a League Championship medal as an ever present. Later he played for Seattle Sounders in the States before coming home to play for, then manage Torquay United. Took over as Coach at Middlesborough in 1986. He then steered them to promotion from Division three to Division one after the club had seemed destined to fold. Managed Millwall from April 1990 until taking over at Bolton in May 1992. His hard work at Burnden Park culminated in the Club's promotion to the premiership via the play-offs in May 1995. However, this success co-incided with the end of his contract and within weeks he accepted the offer of the vacant managers job at Arsenal.

RITCHIE, John. *Stoke, Sheff Wed, Stoke. (1962-1974).* John scored an average of more than a goal every two games during his twelve years as a pro which included two spells at the Victoria Ground with Stoke City. He still lives in the town and runs his own business selling cups and saucers to hotels and restaurants.

RITCHIE, Tom. *Bristol C, Sunderland, Carlisle, Bristol C. (1972-1984).* Edinburgh born striker, made Bristol his adopted home having played over 400 games for Bristol City in his two stints. Now living in Clevedon, and is a Postman.

RITSON, John. *Bolton , Bury, (1967-1979).* Bolton's first choice right back for a decade from 1967. Now owns a newsagents in the Potteries.

RIX, Graham. *Arsenal, Brentford. (1976-1987).* Arsenal snapped Graham up from schools football in his home town of Doncaster and he preceeded to repay their faith by starring in their midfield in more than 300 matches.Won seventeen full England caps and spent a time in France with Caen before joining the coaching staff at Chelsea, where he now looks after the youth team.

ROBB, George. *Tottenham (1951-1958).* England international both as an amateur and professional, George was a teacher and only turned pro at the age of 25. After seven years with his only club, Spurs, he returned to teaching, firstly in Edgware, but now in Ardingley, Sussex.

ROBERTS, Brian. *Coventry, Hereford, Birmingham, Wolves. (1975-1990).* Manchester born full back who played over 400 games for three Midlands clubs. Brian is now working as Reserve Team Coach at one of them, Coventry City.

ROBERTS, Dave. *Aston V, Shrewsbury T, Swansea C. (1965-1974).* Played over 200 geames on the wing for Shrewsbury Town from 1967 until 1973. Now works as Commercial manager with Redditch FC, and is living in nearby Solihull.

ROBERTS, Dave. *Fulham, Oxford, Hull, Cardiff. (1968-1980).* Central defender who appeared for Wales in eighteen full international matches. Dave is now working as an Advertising representative for a newspaper in South Wales.

ROBERTS, Dudley. *Coventry, Mansfield, Doncaster, Scunthorpe. (1965-1975).* Forward who played the majority of his League soccer for Mansfield in the late sixties/early seventies is now a self employed Painter & Decorator in the town.

ROBERTS, Gary. *Brentford (1980-1985).* Now an Insurance consultant and has played for a number of non-league sides, currently Braintree.

ROBERTS, Gareth. *Hull, (1978-1990).* Welsh under 21 international who played over 400 league games for his only club, Hull City. Gareth now works for Humberside Leisure services.

(Courtesy: Southampton Evening Echo)

ROBERTS, Graham. *Portsmouth, Tottenham, Chelsea, Rangers, WBA. (1977-1993)* Despite failing to make the grade at both Portsmouth and Bournemouth, Graham's gritty determination ensured that he ultimately achieved success, noteably shoring up many a Tottenham defence. Starred for Rangers and then Chelsea. Won six England caps and a Cup winners medal with Spurs, and Scottish League and Cup winners medals. Joined Slough Town in the Summer of 1994, after a stint as Player/Manager at Enfield. Appointed Manager of Yeovil Town in January 1995

ROBERTS, John. *Swansea, Northampton, Arsenal, Birmingham, Wrexham, Hull (1965-1980).* After retiring through injury in 1981 he became a salesman for a stationery company, and is now a driving instructor in the Chester area.

ROBERTS, Phil. *Bristol R, Portsmouth, Hereford U, Exeter C. (1969-1981).* Welsh intenational defender, Phil became a self-employed builder in Whimple near Exeter, but now believed to be living in Bangkok, Thailand.

ROBERTS, Trevor. *Liverpool, Southend, Cambridge U. (1963-1971).* Welsh amateur intenational keeper, died in 1972 aged only 30.

ROBERTSON, Alistair. *WBA, Wolves. (1969-1989).* After 18 years and over 700 first team games, Ally became player/manager at Worcester City and then was made manager at Cheltenham Town in 1991/2. Now working as a Business manager in motor finance at Evans Halshaw.

ROBERTSON, George. *Plymouth (1950-1963).* First choice full back for Plymouth for 13 years George is now a milkman in the town, having previously been landlord the "Golden Hind" pub close to Argyle's Home Park Ground.

ROBERTSON, Jimmy *Tottenham, Arsenal, Ipswich, Stoke, Walsall, Crewe (1963-1978)* Jimmy won one Scottish cap whilst with Tottenham following his move from St Mirren in 1964. He finished in 1978 and now lives in the Potteries and is a director of the Task Force Group.

ROBERTSON, John. *Notts F, Derby, Notts F. (1970-1985)* Robertson began at Forest as a seventeen year old and went on to win Championships medal plus a Football League cup winners medal. He also scored the only goal of the game against S.V. Hamburg to win his second European Cup winners medal. John was at the centre of the rift between former best friends and colleagues Brian Clough and Peter Taylor, being the victim of a transfer swoop by Taylor, which deeply upset Cloughie . Finishing in 1985 while in his second spell at Forest, he then became a licensee, then an associate with Save & Prosper Insurance Group. Now works with his old team-mate Martin O'Neill at Wycombe Wanderers as Chief Scout.

ROBERTSON, Stuart. *Notts F, Doncaster R, Northampton T. (1964-1978).* Played over 200 games for each of his last two clubs, ending his career at Northampton in 1978. Stuart is now manager of a Sports Complex in the same town.

ROBERTSON, William *Chelsea, Leyton O. (1950-1962).*William was Chelsea's first team goalkeeper in 199 League matches during the 1950's. Sadly died in 1973 aged only 45.

ROBINS, Ian. *Oldham Ath, Bury, Huddersfield T. (1969-1981).* Veteran striker of over 400 League games, Ian who started out at Oldham Athletic in 1969, ended his playing days at Huddersfield Town some twelve years later, in 1981. He is now working for Port Petroleum, as well as being landlord of the 'Clowns Bar' in the centre of Wigan.

Bobby Robson in relaxed mood taking a "Yellow Pages" call !

ROBINSON, Mike. *Preston N.E. Man C, Brighton. & H.A., Liverpool, QPR. (1975-1986).* **Although Mike played relatively few league games, he became a star in the 1980's noteably with Brighton during their famous cup run and then later with Liverpool and Q.P.R. Won 23 full caps with the Republic of Ireland before quitting in 1986. Now a television pundit and commentator in Spain. His fluent Spanish can also be heard on the country's most popular nightly football radio programme.**

ROBSON, Bobby. *Fulham, WBA, Fulham (1950-1966).* After leaving Fulham for West Brom in 1956 Bobby was converted from a goalscoring inside-right to an international right-half. Going on to win 20 England caps (1957-1962) before returning to Fulham where he ended his League career in 1967 after 585 appearances. He coached Oxford University, Vancouver Royals, and was a scout for Chelsea before achieving real managerial success at Ipswich. A well documented eight year reign as England manager followed, where he was in charge for 90 matches before handing over to Graham Taylor in 1990. Despite many offers in this country, Bobby then accepted the challenge of managing P.S.V. Eindhoven in Holland, who he guided to League and Cup success before moving to Portugal to become manager of first division side Porto.

"Pop" Robson
(Courtesy: Newcastle Chronicle)

ROBSON, Bryan (Pop). *Newcastle U, West Ham, Sunderland, West Ham, Sunderland, Carlisle U, Chelsea, Carlisle U, Sunderland, Carlisle U. (1964-1985).* A small stocky forward, Robson turned professional in 1962 for Newcastle where he gained Under-23 honours. Became known as 'Pop' to the fans because of his shooting at the slightest chance of an opening. A prolific scorer, he had two spells at West Ham and Sunderland Joined Chelsea as player/coach for a while before returning to the north east where he owned a newsagency for a number of years. Now back at Roker Park Reserve Team Coach .

ROBSON, Bryan O.B.E *W.B.A., Man Utd (1974-1995).* Robson became the costliest player in Britain when he moved from West Bromwich Albion to Manchester United for around £2 million in 1981-2. Despite breaking his leg three times during his career, Bryan won 90 full caps for England and made a real impression on the game, being regarded by many as the best midfielder since the war. Was awarded the O.B.E. in the 1990 honours list. Appointed to his role as Middlesborough's player/manager in May 1994

ROBSON, Jimmy. *Burnley, Blackpool, Barnsley, Bury. (1956-1972).* Won an Under 23 cap while with Burnley in the late 1950's and went on to play over 450 league games before ending at Bury in 1972. Works for a small printing company and is part time coach at Rochdale.

ROBSON, John. *Derby C, Aston V (1962-1977).* Robson won seven England Under 23 Caps, Football League representative honurs and was a valuable member of the Aston Villa defence before sadly being forced to quit the game with multiple sclerosis in August 1978 at the age of 27. The illness means that he is still unable to work. John is now living in Sutton Coldfeld.

ROBSON, Tom. *Northampton T, Chelsea, Newcastle U, Peterborough U. (1961-1980).* Joined Peterborough United in 1968 and played 450 league games for them, still a regular at the ripe old age of 35. Tom now works as Property manager for a local free paper in Peterborough.

ROCHE, Paddy. *Man U, Brentford, Halifax. (1974-1988).* Republic of Ireland goalkeeper who won seven full caps, Paddy started at Manchester United, but played most of his 250 league games for Halifax Town. He is now based there as a Football in the Community officer.

RODAWAY, Billy. *Burnley, Peterboro. (1971-1982).* Liverpool born defender, who wore the Claret and Blue of Burnley during the 1970's, now works as a scaffolder living back on Merseyside and is Assistant manager at Runcorn FC.

RODRIGUES, Peter. *Cardiff, Leicester, Sheff Wed, Southampton. (1963-1976).* Captain of the Southampton side that beat Manchester United in the 1976 F.A. Cup final. A serious knee injury ended his career the following year, and he became a Publican outside Southampton. Still lives in the area, working in a Conservative club.

ROEDER, Glenn *Orient, QPR, Notts Co, Newcastle U, Watford, Orient. (1974-1995)* Appointed manager of Watford in 1993 after turning down the chance of travelling to Italy as Gazza's minder. Started and ended his pro playing career at Leyton Orient and spent a spell at Non-League Purfleet prior to becoming the Hornet's boss in 1993.

ROFE, Denis. *Leyton O, Leicester, Chelsea, Southampton. (1967-1983).* Was Reserve team coach at Southampton, before coaching at Bristol Rovers then Stoke City. Now runs a sports clothing business from his Midlands home.

ROGERS, Alan. *Plymouth A, Portsmouth, Southend U, Cardiff C, (1973-1986).* Nippy little winger who notched up close to 400 league appearances before returning to his home town of Plymouth in 1987. He has run the Swinton Hotel in the South Devon town, ever since.

(Photograph courtesy: Southampton Evening Echo)

Peter Rodrigues

(Courtesy: Evening Advertiser, Swindon)

ROGERS, Don. *Swindon, C Palace, QPR, Swindon. (1962-1976)* Former England Under 23 forward, Don ranks as one Swindon's all time greats, he starred in their League Cup victory in 1969 and played over 400 league games. Still living in the Wiltshire town today, where he has run his own sports shop for the past 26 years.

ROGERS, Martyn. *Bristol C, Exeter. (1973-1984).* Defender who spent five years at Torquay, Martyn is now Manager of Tiverton Town.

ROLLINGS, Andy. *Norwich, Brighton, Swindon, Portsmouth, Torquay, Brentford, (1973-1983).* Former Brighton central defender, Andy now plays for Newhaven in the Sussex League.

ROPER, Don. *Southampton, Arsenal, Southampton. (1946-1958).* Member of the great Arsenal sides who won the League title in 1947/8 and again in 1952/3. Don is now retired having worked in engineering, living in Southampton.

ROSENIOR, Leroy. *Fulham, QPR, Fulham, West Ham, Fulham, Charlton, Bristol C, (1982-1995).* Forward who played for a number of London clubs before venturing West in 1991 to sign for Bristol City. Leroy became the Club's Youth coach until May 1995, when he was released.

ROSS, Alan *Carlisle U (1963-1978)* Played 465 games in goal for Carlisle . Alan now works as a Housing worker for Carlisle City council.

ROSS, Ian. *Liverpool, Aston V, Notts C, Northampton, Peterboro, Wolves, Hereford. (1966-1982).* Captain of the Aston Villa side that won the league cup and promotion to Division One in 1975. In August 1989 moved into coaching, firstly with Wolves, and then Aston Villa. Posts followed in the Middle East, South Africa and Australia, before returning to assist Hereford United in 1982. Ross was appointed manager of the Icelandic Club FC Valur in 1983-4, more recently was Reserve Team Manager at Sunderland until June 1995.

ROUGVIE, Doug. *Chelsea, Brighton, Shrewsbury, Fulham, (1984-1988).* Scottish international defender who signed for Chelsea from Aberdeen in 1984. Doug is now back in Scotland, currently playing part-time for Huntly.

ROUSE, Victor *Millwall, C Palace, Oxford, Leyton O (1953-1966).* When capped by Wales in 1959, Victor became the first Fourth Division player to win full international honours. He was a reliable goalkeeper, with Crystal Palace and was ever present in their championship win of 1960. He ended up playing in America for Atlanta chiefs, where he also became coach for several years. On his return to England. Became Manager and Coach to Metropolitan Police F.C.

ROWLEY, Arthur. *WBA, Fulham, Leicester, Shrewsbury. (1946-1964).* Arthur was one of the the most prolific goalscorers of all time,netting a record 433 goals in a career stretching from 1946 to 1965. He played a leading role in getting Fulham, and then Leicester into the First division. Later became player/manager at Shrewsbury. Unfortunately has fallen on hard times and the prospect of him having to sell of his medals resulted in a testimonial match for him in 1995

ROWLEY, Jack. *Wolves, Bournemouth, Man U, Plymouth A (1935-1956).* Jack became one of Manchester Uniteds finest ever forwards following his move from Bournemouth in 1937. Scored over 200 league goals and won six full England caps. After a spell in Holland, coaching Ajax, he returned to manage Wrexham, Bradford and Oldham Athletic for a second spell. He is now retired and living in Shaw, near Oldham.

ROYLE, Joe. *Everton, Man C, Bristol C, Norwich. (1965-1981).* Joe scored over 100 goals for Everton in his 230 odd league appearances before a £200,000 move to Manchester City in 1974. Won six full caps to put in the cabinet with the ten that he had won at Under 23 level. Retired in 1982 because of a knee injury, and went into management later that year with Oldham Athletic. Resigned in November 1994 to take up the vacant managers seat at his former club Everton.

RUDGE, Dale. *Wolves, Preston, (1982-1985).* Former Wolves and Preston North End midfielder, Dale is currently Player/Coach at Stourbridge.

RUDGE, John. *Huddersfield T, Carlisle U, Torquay U, Bristol R, AFC Bournemouth. (1962-1976).* John's fourteen year career as a forward took in five clubs before retiring in 1976. He has been Manager of Port Vale since March 1984

RUSHBURY, Dave. *WBA, Sheff Wed, Swansea, Carlisle. (1974-1984).* Former Sheffield Wednesday defender, Dave now lives in Doncaster and is currently Physio/Coach at Chesterfield.

RUTTER, John. *Bournemouth, Exeter, Stockport, (1973-1985).* Commercial manager at Stockport County, where he had played over 400 games as a full back from 1976 until 1985.

RYAN, Gerry. *Derby, Brighton., (1977-1984).* Derby County spotted Irish international striker, Gerry, playing for Bohemians and signed him up in 1977. Now Player/Coach at Brighton & Hove Albion, where he has been since his move from the Baseball Ground in September 1978.

RYAN, John. *Arsenal, Fulham, Luton, Norwich, Sheff U, Man C, Stockport, Chester, Camb U. (1964-1984).* Spent time at nine league clubs, but is probably best remembered for his six years at Luton Town. Now runs a transport business in Maidstone. Managed Sittingbourne, but left to take over at Dover Athletic in February 1995.

RYAN, Jim. *Man U, Luton. (1965-1976).* Manchester United signed Jim from Scottish side for Corrie Hearts . Had a six year stay at Old Trafford before moving to Luton in 1970. Now back with the "Red Devils" working as Reserve team coach.

RYDEN, Hugh. *Bristol R, Stockport Co, Chester, Halifax, Stockport (1962-1972)* Hugh now lives in Stockport and works in Bolton as a Fleet Sales Manager for the Gordon Ford Dealership.

SABELLA, Alex. *Sheff U, Leeds (1978-1980)* Born in Buenos Aires and played for the River Plate club before signing for Sheffield United in August 1978, a month after Ossie Ardiles and Ricky Villa had signed for Spurs. Alex is now in business back in his homeland, Argentina.

SADLER, David. *Man U, Preston N.E. (1963-1976)* David spent eleven years at Old Trafford, winning four full England caps, a League Championship medal in 1967, then a European Cup winners medal the following year. Became a Branch Manager for a Building Society, but now runs his own corporate hospitality company in Manchester, as well as acting as secretary for the ex-Manchester United Players Association.

ST JOHN, Ian. *Liverpool, Coventry, Tranmere. (1961-1972)* In 1959 Ian set the record for the quickest hat-trick to be scored in Scotland, (2½ minutes), while playing for Motherwell. Liverpool snapped him up for £37,500 in 1961, and enjoyed his skill for the next nine years. Won 21Scottish caps and ended his playing days at Coventry where he became Assistant Manager in December 1971. Took over as Manager at Portsmouth in September 1974 until May 1977, then had a spell as Coach at Sheffield Wednesday before leaving to concentrate on television work.

SALMAN, Danis *Brentford, Millwall, Plymouth, Peterboro (1975-1991).* Cyprus born Danis served Brentford in over 300 matches. Became Commercial manager at Torquay United, but now helps ex-Plymouth Argyle Manager, Dave Smith with coaching courses for youngsters.

(Courtesy: Raymonds Press Agency)

SAMMELS, Jon. *Arsenal, Leicester. (1962-1977)* Jon made 212 league appearances for Arsenal and won nine England under 23 caps before moving to Leicester City in 1971. Now working as a driving instructor, living near Leicester.

SANCHEZ, Lawrie *Reading, Wimbledon (1977-1993).* Lawrie headed himself into the history books when he scored the winner in the 1988 FA Cup Final for Wimbledon. Returned to the "Dons" as Reserve team manager in 1995 after a time as manager of Sligo Rovers in Ireland.

SANDERS, Jimmy. *Charlton, WBA, Coventry. (1944-1958)* Played in goal for West Brom for close on a decade after signing pro terms in 1945. Now living in retirement in Tamworth.

SANSOM, Kenny. *C Palace, Arsenal, Newcastle U, QPR, Coventry C. (1974-1991).* Short but very effective defender, who was rewarded with 86 full England caps during the 1980's. Played over 300 games for Arsenal, having joined them in 1980 in a million pound deal, with Clive Allen taking the trip to Kenny's former club, Crystal Palace. Now lives in Bromley, Kent and became Assistant Manager at Watford in August 1994 after a brief spell with Chertsey Town.

SARTORI, Carlos *Man U (1968-1971)* **After leaving United in 1971, he played in Italian football for eleven years. Now runs a successful knife sharpening business, which has brought him the luxury of three homes in Italy and a comfortable house near Rochdale.**

SAUL, Frank. *Tottenham, Southampton, QPR, Millwall. (1960-1975)* Lives in Canvey Island and worked in building and decorating, but now runs a fashion business in the East End of London.

SAUNDERS, Derek. *Chelsea (1953-1958)* Chelsea wing half during the fifties and was an ever present in their Championship winning side of 1954-55.Was groundsman and Chief Soccer coach at Westminster School but is Derek is now Groundsman at Hampstead Cricket Club.

SAUNDERS, John. *Mansfield, Huddersfield, Barnsley, Lincoln, Doncaster. (1969-1980).* Was Chairman of Worksop Town, and owner of their "Tigers Club". The football club moved to a new ground, but John retained the old social club which he now runs as the "Riverside Club".

SAUNDERS, Ron. *Everton, Gillingham, Portsmouth, Watford, Charlton A. (1954-1966).* A much travelled man, both as player and manager. Ron was in charge of Yeovil Town, Oxford Utd, Norwich City, Manchester City and Aston Villa. In 1987, Saunders was dismissed as manager of West Bromwich Albion. When he left he had completed 36 years connected with professional football in a career which had encompassed eleven League clubs, highlighted in 1975, after Villa had won promotion and the League Cup, Ron was named "Manager of the Year". Now officially retired, but still acts as an advisor and scout.

SAWARD, Pat. *Millwall, Aston V, Huddersfield. (1951-1962).* Skippered Aston Villa and Huddersfield Town in the fifties and sixties . Won 18 caps for the Republic of Ireland. He was appointed player/coach by Coventry City in 1963, then took the managers job at Brighton in 1970. He was coach to the Saudi Arabian side, AL-NASR, and now he runs a holiday business in Minorca.

SAXTON, Bobby. *Derby, Plymouth, Exeter. (1964-1977).* Managed Blackburn Rovers and York City. Linked up with Peter Reid for the second time by accepting a coaching post at Sunderland in June 1995. They were previously together during Reid's short reign at Manchester City.

SAYER, Andy. *Wimbledon, Camb U, Fulham, Leyton O, Sheff U. (1983-1990)* Former Wimbledon forward, Andy is a player with Slough Town.

SAYER, Peter. *Cardiff C, Brighton & H.A., Preston N.E, Cardiff C, Chester C. (1973-1984).* Cardiff born winger who was capped by Wales on seven occasions, was forced to retire in 1984 aged 29. Peter now works as a Commercial & Community Assistant at Preston North End.

SBRAGIA, Ricky. *Birmingham, Walsall, Blackpool, York, Darlington. (1974-1985).* Former Birmingham apprentice who was a regular in the York City back four in the 1980's, now working at Bootham Crescent as Youth Coach.

SCHOFIELD, Johnny. *Birmingham, Wrexham (1952-1967)* Goalie who was on the books at Birmingham for fifteen years, during which time he notched up over 200 appearances. Now running his own Off License in Atherstone.

SCOTSON, Reg. *Sunderland, Grimsby T. (1946-1954).* Former Grimsby Town wing half, now works as an Arcade Manager in Cleethorpes.

SCOTT, Alex. *Everton (1962-1966).* Scottish international striker (16 caps), ventured South in a £39,000 move to Everton in 1963. However, after four successful years at Goodison Park, Alex returned back up to Scotland to join Hibernian. Now a publican in his home town of Falkirk.

SCOTT, Laurie. *Bradford C, Arsenal, C Palace. (1935-1952).* Full back who won fifteen caps for England, while with Arsenal. Spent three years as manager of Crystal Palace, before working for the Club's chairman, who happened to be a director of the national firm, GKN. Retired at the age of 64, and now lives in South Yorkshire.

SCOULER, Jimmy. *Portsmouth, Newcastle, Bradford P.A. (1946-1963)* Won nine England caps during his time at Portsmouth, before ending his playing days at Bradford P.A. Became the Yorkshire Club's player/manager from 1961 until 1964. Then took over at Cardiff City in June 1964, a post he held for over nine years. Later scouted for Aston Villa, Wolves, and managed Newport County. After spells in the jewellery trade and chemical industry, Jimmy finally retired to his home in Dinas Powys, near Cardiff.

SEACOLE, Jason. *Oxford U,(1976-1981).* Former Oxford United forward whose promising career ended at the age of only 21. Now working as a wood machinist at a furniture factory in Witney and lives in Highworth, Wiltshire.

SEALEY, Alan *Leyton O, West Ham, Plymouth Arg (1960-1967).* Alan played on the wing for West Ham during their successful years in the mid-sixties. He is based in Romford in Essex and advises on Greyhound tracks and betting.

SEALY, Tony. *Southampton, C Palace, Port V, Q.P.R, Port V, Fulham, Leicester, Bournemouth, Brentford, Bristol R, Brentford (1977-1993)* Laurie McMenemy's first apprentice signing at Southampton, Tony went on to serve a further ten league clubs before moving over to Hong Kong. He is now employed on the Island by the Hong Kong Football Club as Sporting Manager.

SEAR, Cliff. *Manchester C, Chester C. (1956-1969).* Full back who won his only Welsh Cap during his nine years at Manchester City. Ended his playing days at Chester, where he became Coach, Assistant Manager, then Manager. Now with Wrexham as Youth Decelopment Officer.

SELKIRK, Jack. *Rotherham (1946-1956).* Jack who played over 400 league matches at right back in his ten years at Millmoor, is now deceased.

SELLERS, John. *Stoke City (1946-1957)* A Stoke regular, who played 384 games in the wing half position from 1946 until 1957. Now deceased.

SENIOR, Steve. *York C, Darlington, Northampton T, Wigan Ath, Preston N.E. (1980-1993)* Defender with over 300 games experience. Now works with his father in law's building business.

SENIOR, Trevor. *Portsmouth, Aldershot, Reading, Watford, Middlesboro, Reading (1981-1991).* Goalscoring centre forward, moved "home" to Weymouth in May 1994 to become player/coach, and then had a brief spell as manager before re-joining Farnborough in May 1995.

SETTERS, Maurice. *Exeter, WBA, Man U, Stoke, Coventry, Charlton. (1953-1969).* A robust midfielder who won an FA Cup winners medal with Manchester United in 1963. After a career which took in six league clubs, Maurice went into management with Doncaster Rovers, then had stops at Sheffield Wednesday (Coach), Rotherham United (Assistant Manager), Newcastle United (Chief Scout.) Although English, with sixteen Under 23 caps to his name, he has been Assistant Manager of the Republic of Ireland National team since 1986. Lives in Tichill, Doncaster.

SEWELL, Jack. *Notts Co, Sheff Wed, Aston V, Hull. (1946-1960).* **Was once Britain's most expensive player, after Sheffield Wednesday had paid Notts County £34,500 in 1951. In 1960, went over to Rhodesia for three months but stayed for thirteen years! Later working as a coach-manager in Zambia and the Belgian Congo. Since 1973 had been working as a car salesman for Bristol Street Motors in Nottingham, now retired but still living in the city.**

SEWELL, John. *Charlton, C Palace, Leyton O. (1956-1971)* Full back who played over 400 games for his three clubs - all London based. However, he has now ventured substantially further away, to run his own teashop in America.

SEXTON, Dave. *Luton, West Ham, Leyton O, Brighton, C Palace. (1951-1959)* An Inside forward, he started his playing career in League football with Luton Town. Service with West Ham, Leyton Orient, Brighton and Crystal Palace followed, and when his playing days were over, he spent four years as coach at Chelsea. Dave next took over as manager of Leyton Orient, and after spells as coach to Fulham and Arsenal, he returned to Chelsea as manager. Also managed Q.P.R and Manchester United before taking over responsibility for the England Under 21side.

SHACKLETON, Len. *Bradford PA, Newcastle, Sunderland, (1946-1957).* The original "clown prince", started his career with Arsenal. However it was in the North-East that he made his name, moves to Newcastle and then Sunderland both broke the exsisting transfer records. Capped five times by England, Len became a journalist following his retirement through injury in 1957. Now lives in Grange-over-Sands, Cumbria.

SHANKLY, Bill. *Carlisle, Preston, (1932-1948).* **Died on 25th September 1981, just days after his 68th birthday. Capped five times by Scotland, Bill was appointed manager of Liverpool in 1959 after a spell with Huddersfield, leading them to promotion in his second full season after finishing third twice. Went on to become one of the greatest managers of all time before his surprising resignation in 1974 following their FA Cup victory. Awarded the O.B.E. in 1974, Bill is already part of Liverpool folklore and the "Shankly Gates" erected at Anfield will act as a permenant memorial.**

SHANNON, Les. *Liverpool, Burnley. (1947-1958)* Wing half who achieved international recognition with the England 'B' team, retired in 1958, but was briefly manager at Blackpool. Acted as Football advisor to the Channel 4 series 'The Manageress' and now works as a scout for Luton.

SHARP, Graham. *Everton, Oldham (1970-1995).* Former Everton and Scotland international striker, Graham took over as Manager of Oldham in 1994, having joined them as a player in 1991

SHAW, David *Huddersfield, Oldham, WBA. Oldham (1966-1977)* Scored a hatful of goals in his two spells at Oldham, ending in 1977. Now works for an engineering company in Yorkshire.

SHAW, Gary. *Aston V, Blackpool, Walsall, Shrewsbury. (1978-1990)* An England under 23 cap, he was voted 'Young Player of the Year' in 1981. Went over to Hong Kong where he worked as a sales executive and was Head Coach at the International school. Now a rep for Carlsberg Tetley and coaches at Villa park once a week.

SHAW, Graham. *Sheff U, Doncaster, (1951-1967).* A former ABA schools boxing champion, Graham later proved himself as an equally good footballer, winning five England Caps and a Sheffield United first team regular for fifteen years. Now works in business in the Sheffield Markets.

SHAW, Joseph. *Sheff U (1948-1965).* Played 629 matches for Sheffield United between 1948 and 1965, winning Football League representitive honours. Now retired living in the Sheffield area.

SHAW, Peter. *Charlton, Exeter, Gillingham. (1977-1985).* Former Charlton Athletic and Gillingham defender, now coaching at Bromley.

SHEPHERDSON, Harold. *Middlesboro (1936-1946)* Always will be remembered as a member of the England coaching staff which led the national side to victory in the 1966 World Cup. Harold now lives in Middlesborough and helps out as an Ambassador at Ayresome Park.

SHERWOOD, Alf. *Cardiff C, Newport Co. (1946-1960).* Made over 500 League appearances for his two clubs and achieved international recognition on 41 occasions for Wales. Alf died in March 1989 at his home in Cardiff aged 66.

SHERWOOD, Steve. *Chelsea, Millwall, Brentford, Watford, Grimsby (1971-1994).* Blond haired goalkeeper of the Elton John/Graham Taylor Watford side of the eighties. Now playing for Immingham Town in the N.C.E. League.

SHILTON, Peter. *Leicester, Stoke, Notts F, Southampton, Derby, Plymouth (1966-1995)* The Peter Shilton playing career seems likely to carry on for some time, with his services still in heavy demand since his very public and well documented departure from the Manager's post at Plymouth Argyle. The tabloid press's fascination with his private life should not take way from the fact that he ranks among the all time great goalkeepers, respected by players and fans alike.

Peter Shilton

(Courtesy: Southampton Evening Echo)

SHIMWELL, Eddie. *Sheff U, Blackpool, Oldham. (1946-1957).* England international (one Cap), who played in three FA Cup finals, scoring from the penalty spot in the winning final of 1948. Lived in retirement in Thornton Clevelys on the outskirts of Blackpool until his death in 1988.

SHINER, Roy. *Huddersfield, Sheff Wed, Hull. (1951-1959)* Former Sheffield Wednesday centre forward of the 1950's who scored 93 goals in 153 League starts. Had been living on the Isle of Wight for a number of years prior to his death in 1988.

SHINTON, Bobby. *Walsall, Camb U, Wrexham, Man C, Millwall, Newcastle, Millwall. (1971-1982)* Bobby's career included a brief spell with Manchester City in 1979, and a total of close to 400 league matches. Now a glazier in Cambridgeshire, and playing locally for Willingham

SHIPLEY, George *Southampton, Reading, Lincoln, Charlton, Gillingham (1979-1988)* Made only three appearances for Southampton before establishing himself as a Lincoln regular for five years. Was Assistant manager at Bradford City until 1995, when he became their first team coach.

SHIRTLIFF, Paul. *Sheff Wed, Northampton. (1980-1984).* Paul is now a Bank clerk living in Barnsley. A former England semi-pro international, and playing for Gateshead until 1994.

SHORTHOUSE, W.H. *Wolves (1947-1956)* Now retired after successful playing and coaching careers. Played 379 games for Wolves,winning FA Cup and Championship medals. Then coached Wolves and Birmingham before becoming manager of the England Youth team that woin the European Youth Cup in 1971.

SHOTTON, Malcolm. *Leicester C, Oxford U, Portsmouth, Huddersfield T, Barnsley, Hull C, Barnsley (1975-1995)* Familiar figure in the Oxford United back four throughout the 1980's. He then went on to give service to four more clubs before becoming Player/coach at Barnsley FC

SHOULDER, Alan. *Newcastle, Carlisle, Hartlepool (1978-1987).* Scored almost 100 league goals for his three North-Eastern based clubs. Now Poultry farming in Bishop Auckland and managing Crook Town in the Northern League.

SHOWELL, George. *Wolves, Bristol C, Wrexham. (1954-1967).* After over 200 league matches in the Wolves colours, George had a spell as Assistant manager at his last club, Wrexham.

SHOWERS, Derek. *Cardiff, Bournemouth, Portsmouth, Hereford (1970-1982).* Former Cardiff junior won six Under 23 caps and two full caps with Wales and appeared in almost 300 league matches between 1970 and 1982. Derek now works for the Royal Mail in South Wales

SHREEVE, Peter. *Reading (1958-1965).* Peter was an inside forward with Reading for seven years following his league debut in 1959. Then went on to Coach at Q.P.R. until July 1989. Now works as assistant to Glenn Hoddle at Chelsea.

SHUKER, John. *OxfordU (1962-1976)* A one club man, who was a permanent fixture at left back with Oxford United for the best part of fourteen years. Went on to run the Eagle Inn, in Bampton, where he still lives, from 1978 until 1984, since then has been a self empolyed haulier.

SIBLEY, Frank. *QPR. (1963-1970)* Chief Scout at Q.P.R.. He had previously played 150 league games as a wing half for the West London club.

SIDDALL, Barry. *Bolton W, Sunderland, Port V, Stoke C, Blackpool, Stockport Co, Hartlepool U, Carlisle U, Cheter C. (1972-1991).* Now using the considerable experience gained from his nomadic playing career, to help coach goalkeepers at a number of clubs including Burnley.

SILKMAN, Barry. *Hereford U, C Palace, Plymouth, Luton, Man C, Brentford, QPR, LeytonO, Southend , Crewe . (1974-1986).* Barry now acts as a football players agent; turns out regularly for the Showbiz XI; and trains greyhounds at Canterbury stadium in Kent. Also plays for Wingate & Finchley in the South Midlands League.

SILLETT, John. *Chelsea, Coventry C, Plymouth A. (1956-1967)* Jovial John was manager of Coventry City between 1987 and 1990, and guided them to their famous F.A. Cup victory in 1987. Most recently worked as Chief Scout at Portsmouth, until the shake up at Fratton Park in early 1995 following Jim Smith's departure.

SILLETT, Peter. *Southampton, Chelsea (1951-1961)* Former England international who won three England caps while with Chelsea. Peter now lives is Ashford, Kent, but arthritis of the knee prevents him from working. Elder brother of John, and son of Charlie, a 1930's Saints player.

SIMMONS, David. *Arsenal, Bournemouth, Aston V, Walsall, Colchester, Camb U, Brentford, Camb U. (1965-1975).* Now working as an insurance agent for the Prudential in Cambridge.

SIMONSEN, Allan. *Charlton (1982)* **Danish international striker Allan, enjoyed a brief spell in England, joining Charlton Athletic from Barcelona in 1982. Now working as Manager of the Faroes Islands national team.**

SIMPSON, Owen. *Rotherham U, Leyton Orient, Colchester U, Southend U, Darlington, Grimsby. (1964-1971).* Now working as a representative for an upholstery firm in Grimsby.

SIMPSON, Peter. *Arsenal (1963-1977).* A commanding central defender who during his fifteen years at Arsenal played 353 league games and was a valuable member of their famous League and Cup double winning team. Now working for a roofing materials firm in Hertfordshire.

SIMS, Steve. *Leicester C, Watford, Notts Co, Watford, Aston V, Lincoln C (1975-1990)* Midfielder who after finishing at Lincoln in 1990, Steve spent two years managing an indoor football and cricket stadium prior to his current job as Youth recruitment manager at Coventry City.

SIRRELL, Jimmy. *Bradford P.A., Brighton , Aldershot. (1949-1956)* Chief Scout at Notts County where he became a legend during three spells as Manager which totalled thirteen years.

SISSONS, John. *West Ham, Sheff Wed, Norwich, Chelsea (1962-1974).* Won ten Under 23 caps for England as an exciting winger during the 1960's. Played over 300 league games for West Ham and Sheffield Wednesday before retiring in 1974 while wit Chelsea. Now works for a motor products firm in Cape Town, South Africa.

Bill Slater
(Courtesy: Express & Star, Wolverhampton)

SITTON, John. *Chelsea, Millwall, Gillingham, Leyton O (1978-1990).* Became part of the management team at his last club, Leyton Orient, but departed in April 1995 following the club's takeover by famous Snooker impresario, Barry Hearn

SKEEN, Ken. *Swindon, Oxford. (1964-1973).* Former Oxford midfielder is now Golf secretary at a golf course in Cheltenham, Gloucestershire.

SKIRTON, Alan. *Arsenal, Blackpool, Bristol C, Torquay. (1960-1971).* Winger who played 144 games for Arsenal in the 1960's. Alan is now working as Commercial manager at Yeovil Town

SLATER, Bill. O.B.E. *Blackpool, Brentford, Wolves, Brentford. (1949-1963)* **An accomplished amateur Centre Half who played in the 1952 Olympic Games before turning professional with Wolverhampton Wanderers at the age of 27. Voted "Player of the Year" in 1959/60 and capped 12 times by England. Retired in 1963 having made over 300 appearances for Wolves. After holding posts at Liverpool and Birmingham Universities, Bill is now president of the British Amateur Gymnastics Association.**

SLATTER, Neil *Bristol R, Oxford, Bournemouth (1980-1989).* Although forced to retire at the age of 25, Neil had already made 22 international appearances for Wales. Now works in administration for a large supermarket chain.

SLEEUWENHOEK, John. *Aston V, Birmingham, Torquay U, Oldham Ath. (1961-1971).* Finished his career in 1972 to work as a joiner at an Aldridge firm with his former Aston Villa colleague, Alan Deakin. However, John sadly died in Birmingham in July 1989 at te age of only 45.

SLOUGH, Alan. *Luton, Fulham, Peterboro, Millwall, (1965-1981)* Alan is now a window cleaner living in Devon. Is player/manager of Torquay Christians in the South Devon League.

SMALL, Mike. *Luton, Peterboro, Brighton, West Ham (1981-1992)* Former Brighton and West Ham striker is now playing for Stevenage.

SMALLMAN, David. *Wrexham, Everton (1972-1976).* Welsh international forward, David was forced to quit in 1976 at the age of 23, shortly after joining Everton from Wrexham. Emigrated to Australia in 1982, but returned to Wales in 1988 and took a job with the local council.

SMART, Roger. *Swindon, Charlton. (1961-1973).* A first choice defender at Swindon Town for eleven years and 346 games, Roger now Runs the Plough public house in the Wiltshire town.

SMEE, Roger. *Chelsea, Reading, (1966-1973)* Went on to become Chairman of Reading FC for a spell and a successful businessman in the town.

SMETHURST, Derek. *Chelsea, Millwall (1970-1974).* **South African forward who signed up at Stasmford Bridge from Durban United in 1970. Now involved with Youth Soccer in Florida, USA. Derek is a born again Christian having experienced a vision whilst watching television in San Diego in 1978. His stay in England must have also made an impression as he has a daughter named CHELSEA.**

SMILLIE, Neil *C. Palace, Brighton, Watford, Reading, Brentford (1976-1993)* Former Palace, Brighton, and Brentford winger joined the coaching staff at Gillingham after his playing days.

SMITH, Bobby *Chelsea, Tottenham, Brighton (1950-1964)* Became a painter & decorator, but is now waiting for a double hip replacement operation and has to rely on crutches to get around.

Dave Smith

SMITH, Dave. Now organises coaching courses for youngsters in Devon. In March 1995, turned down the chance to return to League Management by declining an offer from Plymouth Argyle.

SMITH, Dennis. *Stoke C, York C. (1968-1982)* Former Stoke City central defender, who clocked up over 400 league appearances before ending at York City. Appointed manager of Oxford United in September 1993, having previously been boss at York, Bristol City and then Sunderland.

SMITH, Fred. *Burnley, Portsmouth, Halifax (1963-1974)* Works as a community worker with the Burnley Borough Council, having previously had a milkround; restaurant; and a newsagents.

SMITH, George. *Newcastle, Barrow, Portsmouth, Middlesboro, Birmingham, Cardiff, Swansea, Hartlepool. (1963-1979).* Was Assistant Manager at Doncaster until September 1994

SMITH, Gordon. *Brighton., Man C, Oldham. (1980-1985).* Immortalised by the words "and Smith must score", when Gary Bailey saved during the the 1983 FA Cup final. Gordon played in the First division of four countries including Switzerland and Austria. Now working as a financial consultant for a company which advises the S.F.A and S.P.F.A. Also writes two weekly newspaper columns, as well as summarizing on Radio Scotland and a panelist with S.T.V.

Jim Smith

SMITH, Granville. *Bristol R, Newport. (1958-1967).* Former Newport County winger, Granville is now working as a boiler attendant in Newport.

SMITH, Jim. *Sheff U, Aldershot, Halifax, Lncoln, Colchester. (1959-1972).* Jim is a Yorkshireman from Sheffield, who spent his playing days as a half-back. He acquired the rudiments of management at Boston United, before taking up his first League appointment with Colchester United. After a succession of clubs, became Manager of Portsmouth until February 1995, when he took up a post with the League Managers and Secretary's Association. However, within weeks he was back in League action, having accepted the job of Managing Derby County.

SMITH, Jimmy *Newcastle (1969-1974)* Nicknamed "Jinky" because of his tricky ball skills, Jimmy joined Newcastle from Aberdeen in 1969 but was forced to retire through injury in 1976. Unfortunately his love of gambling has cost him a fortune and he now drives a taxi on Tyneside.

SMITH, John. *West Ham, Tottenham, Coventry, Leyton O, Torquay, Swindon, Walsall. (1956-1971).* Former England Under 23 forward. Died aged 49 in February 1988 after a heart attack.

(Photograph courtesy: Liverpool Post & Echo)

Tommy Smith, tackling a rather unusual forward line.

SMITH, John. Managing Director at Luton Town until August 1989. He played for Orient at the age of 15, and became the youngest Secretary in the League when he joined Q.P.R. over 30 years ago. Spent seven years at Lotus Road before moving to New York Cosmos, and then Leicester City.

SMITH, Leslie. *Brentford, Aston V, Brentford (1936-1952).* Former Brentford and Aston Villa winger, is now retired, living in Litchfield, Staffs.

SMITH, Malcolm. *Middlesboro, Bury, Blackpool, Burnley, York. (1971-1981)* Malcolm's ten year League career ended in 1981 at York City. He is now working as a Vehicle Hire Manager.

SMITH, Steve. *Huddersfield, Bolton, Halifax T. (1964-1978).* Steve spent twelve years at Huddersfield Town, where he made over 330 League appearances. Now Youth Coach at Bradford City.

SMITH, Tommy. *Liverpool, Swansea. (1962-1978).* Tommy is remembered for his no-nonsense style of defending, which was the foundation stone of the great Liverpool sides of the sixties and seventies. In his fifteen years at Anfield, Smith collected winners medals for: European Cup, European Cup Winners Cup, UEFA Cup, the FA cup twice, and the League championship in 1966, 1973, 1976, and 1977. He joined Swansea City in 1978, becoming their player/coach the following year. When a knee injury eventually ended his career he briefly returned to Liverpool to coach the youth team. To this day, he is involved with the the 'Reds', in a public relations capacity.

Former Leicester City left back, **Bobby Smith.**
(Courtesy: Raymonds Press Agency.)

SMITH, Wilf. *Sheff W, Coventry, Brighton., Millwall, Bristol R, Chesterfield. (1964-1976).* Working in the insurance business in Coventry.

SNEDDEN, John. *Arsenal, Charlton A, Orient, Halifax (1959-1967)* Scottish centre half who finished playing at the age of only 25. Married a German girl and moved to her native homeland, where they still are believed to living today.

(Courtesy: Liverpool Post & Echo)

SOUNESS, Graham. *Tottenham, Middlesboro, Liverpool. (1970-1983).* Souness was initially an apprentice at Tottenham, but made his name at Middlesborough, as a masterful midfielder. Consistent performances encouraged Liverpool to shatter the existing transfer record by signing him for £352,000 in January 1978. Six very successful years followed, during which time he and his colleagues won the League Championship an incredible five times, and the European Cup on three occasions. A £650,000 deal then took him to Sampdoria in Italy before becoming player/manager of Rangers in 1986. The almost inevitable return to Anfield as manager was completed in March 1991. However, despite winning the FA Cup in 1991-2, his stay was relatively brief. In the summer of 1995, accepted the offer to take over as Manager of Turkish club, Galatasaray.

SPARROW, Brian *Arsenal, Wimbledon, Millwall, Gillingham, C. Palace. (1983-1986).* Former Crystal Palace left back, Brian has been Reserve Team Coach at Wimbledon since 1992

SPAVIN, Alan. *Preston. (1960-1978).* Played over 400 games for Preston North End between 1960 and 1973, then after a four year gap, put his boots back on to add a few more to his tally. Moved over to the United States to play for Washington, and is still believed to be living there.

SPENCE, Derek. *Oldham, Bury, Blackpool, Southend, Bury (1971-1983).* Irish international forward had spells in Greece and Hong Kong, ran an off license, but now coaches youngsters.

SPENCER, Tommy. *Southampton, York City, Workington T, Lincoln , Rotherham. (1965-1977).* Now area coach/community worker and is Manager of Worksop Town in the Unibond League.

SPOONER, Steve. *Derby C, Halifax T, Chesterfield, Hereford, York , Rotherham, Mansfield, Chesterfield (1978-1994)* Now plays for Rushden & Diamonds in the Beazer Homes League.

SPRAGGON, Frank. *Middlesboro, Hartlepool (1963-1976)* Frank now works as a Part time coach at Middlesborough's School of Excellence.

SPRAKE, Gary. *Leeds U, Birmingham C, (1961-1974).* Guarded the goal for Leeds United during ten of their most successful years and won 37 full Welsh international Caps. Gary ended his playing days at Birmingham City and still lives in Solihull. Briefly worked as a rep for a sports goods firm but now works for the local council as a training officer, responsible for placing business trainees and monitoring their progress.

SPRINGETT, Peter. *QPR, Sheff Wed, Barnsley. (1962-1979).* The younger of the two goalkeeping brothers (see Ron, below), Peter won six under 23 caps with England. He joined the South Yorkshire police from Soccer and for the past eleven years has been Community Constable at Sheffield United. Regularly attends United's games as a spotter in case of crowd trouble.

SPRINGETT, Ron. *QPR, Sheff Wed, QPR. (1955-1968).* In between two spells with Q.P.R., Ron played 345 League games for Sheffield Wednesday and was capped 33 times by England. He is now retired, although still only aged 60.

SPROSON, Roy. *Port V (1950-1971).* Now running a post office in Stoke-on -Trent. Played 756 league games for Port Vale in a career which included playing in their famous FA Cup run of 1953-4 when Port Vale reached the Semi-Final.

SPROSTON, Bert. *Leeds U, Tottenham H, Man C. (1933-1949).* Won eleven caps at full back with England and played for three of the Country's top sides. Retired after 30 years as Trainer & Physiotherapist at Bolton Wanderers. Now lives in Bolton and but still does some scouting.

STAINROD, Simon. *Sheff U, Oldham, QPR, Sheff Wed, Aston V, Stoke, (1975-1988).* After a thirteen year career in England, former QPR and Villa midfielder, Simon moved North of the Border, where he is now Manager of Ayr United

STANDEN, Jim. *Arsenal, Luton, West Ham, Millwall, Portsmouth (1957-1971)* **Former Hammers goalkeeper. As a player, Jim had a spell in the States with Detroit in the 1960's and now lives in Clayton, California where he works for a Honda Car Leasing company. He still plays cricket and coaches young goalkeepers. His car now bears the instantly recognisable registration. FA CUP 64, a reminder of cup winning success achieved as a West Ham goalkeeper**

STANIFORTH, Ron. *Stockport, Huddersfield, Sheff Wed, Barrow (1946-1960)* England international full back with eight caps to his credit. Played over 450 league games before coaching at Barrow and Sheffield Wednesday. Now deceased.

STANLEY, Garry. *Chelsea, Everton, Swansea, Portsmouth, Bristol. (1975-1988).* ex- Chelsea and Everton defender. Lives in the Portsmouth area, where he works for Nynex Communications.

STAPLETON, Frank *Arsenal, Man U, Derby, Blackburn, Aldershot, Huddersfield, Bradford C. (1974-1993).* Republic of Ireland international striker, Frank became Manager at Bradford City until May 1994, followed by brief spells at Brighton (as player) and Q.P.R (as reserve team coach. Now returned to his home in the North, seeking a coaching or managerial position.

STARLING, Ron. *Hull, Newcastle, Sheff Wed, Aston V. (1927-1946).* Played in FA Cup semi finals with four different clubs. In June 1950 Starling left football to open a newsagents/tobacconists business opposite the Sheffield Wednesday ground. He died in Sheffield in December 1991.

STATHAM, Derek. *WBA, Southampton, Stoke, Walsall. (1976-1991)* Derek was one of the finest left backs in the early 1980's who came to prominence during his eleven years with West Bromwich Albion. Won three England caps before ending at Walsall. Now plays for Kings Lynn.

STEAD, Mickey. *Tottenham, Swansea, Southend, Doncaster. (1975-1987).* Former Southend full back. Now coaching at Heybridge Swifts FC.

STEBBING, Gary. *C Palace, Southend, Maidstone (1983-1992).* Midfielder who appeared in the League for Palace and Maidstone as well as having a spell with K.V. Ostend in Belguim. Gary is now turning out for Dagenham & Redbridge.

STEEL, Jim. *Oldham, Port Vale, Wrexham, Tranmere (1977-1992)* After fifteen years as a player retired at the end of the 1991-2 season to join the Merseyside Police. Jim is stationed on the Wirral not far away from Tranmere Rovers Prenton Park and still plays for the Police side.

STEELE, Eric. *Peterboro, Brighton, Watford, Cardiff, Derby, Southend, Mansfield (1972-1987).* Full time goalkeeping coach at Leeds, Manchester City, Derby, Barnsley, and Grimsby, having previously spent four and a half years at Wolves. While he coaches, his wife runs a freehouse restaurant in Derby that they purchased in 1988.

STEELE, Jim. *Southampton (1971-1976).* Scottish central defender, became a Publican in Washington, U.S.A, and then foreman of an electrical plant. Has recently returned to the U.K.

STEIN, Brian. *Luton T, (1977-1993)* Brian won one England cap despite being born in Cape town, South africa. Scored over 125 League goals for Luon Town in two spells. Brian is now playing for Enfield FC in the GM Vauxhall Conference.

STEIN, Colin. *Coventry. (1972-1974).* Scottish international centre forward joined Rangers from Hibernian in October 1968 for £100,000, which was the first six figure fee between Scottish clubs. Had a spell South of the Border with Coventry from 1972 until 1974. Now back in his home town of Linlithgow working as a joiner. He and his wife are both local bowls champions.

STEPHENS, Kirk. *Luton T, Coventry C. (1978-1985)* Works as a director /owner of a building and civil engineering business and also had a spell as player/manager of Nuneaton Borough.

STEPNEY, Alex. *Millwall, Chelsea, Manchester U. (1963-1977)* **First choice keeper at Manchester United for over a decade. Only won one England Cap, and he was unfortunate to be playing at the same time as the great Gordon Banks, but never the less was still one of the greatest goalies of his time. In the Summer of 1995, Alex was apppointed goalkeeping coach at his old club's arch rivals, Man City. Until then he had run a van hire business in Rochdale. The most recent of a variety of jobs, which had included running a pub, working in a car body repair shop and a spell as Commercial manager at local club, Rochdale FC.**

STERLAND, Mel. *Sheff Wed, Rangers, Leeds (1978-1993)*Ex- England full back was appointed manager at Boston United in the Summer of 1994.

STEVENS, Dennis. *Bolton, Everton, Oldham, Tranmere. (1953-1967)* After finishing at Tranmere, where he played his last game against his old club, Everton. He opened a menswear shop in Bolton. Now retired but still living in the town.

STEVENS, Gary. *Brighton, Tottenham, Portsmouth, (1979-1993).* Joined Tottenham from Brighton for £350,000 following the South Coast Club's successful FA Cup run. An England International, Gary was forced to quit in 1990, while with Portsmouth. He has since had a brief spell as Manager of Petersfield, but is now Sales Director for Koolpak UK Ltd, a firm specialising in icepacks and heatpacks. Media interests include hosting a Saturday morning show on Sky Sports 2, and on Sundays he commentates on Dutch league matches for American channel ESPN.

STEVENS, Paul. *Bristol C (1977-1984)* Former Bristol City full back, who played 146 league games during his seven years at Ashton Gate. Is now a Sales Representative in the town.

STEVENSON, Alan. *Chesterfield, Burnley, Rotherham, Hartlepool. (1969-1984)* Ended in 1984 to become Hartlepool Commercial manager.

STEVENSON, Byron. *Leeds, Birmingham,, Bristol R (1974-1985).* Welsh international midfielder, now runs the 'Golden Lion' in Pudsey.

STEWART, David. *Leeds, WBA, Swansea, (1973-1980)* Joined Leeds United from Ayr United in 1973 as understudy to David Harvey. Played for two seasons in Hong Knog after finishing with Swansea City. David now lives on the Gower Coast and works as a goldsmith in Swansea.

Gary Stevens.

STEWART, Jim. *Middlesboro (1978-1980).* Now works as a Ministry of Defence Policeman.

(Courtesy: West Ham "Who's Who")

STEWART, Ray. *West Ham U,(1979-1990).* Ray is now assistant manager at Stirling Albion.

STILES, Nobby. *Man U, Middlesboro, Preston. (1960-1974).* Stiles became a national hero mainly due to the television coverage of the 1966 World Cup final, which highlighted his toothy grin and never say die spirit. He developed through the Manchester United juniors as a 'Busby Babe', and gained two League Championship medals and a European Cup winners medal in 1968. Was a Co-Director of Manchester United's School of Excellence until 1994.

(Photograph courtesy: Nottingham Evening Post)

STOREY-MOORE, Ian. *Notts F, Man U. (1963-1973)* Won one Enlgand cap and was Forest's top scorer for four years running (1969-1972), but was forced to retire the following year due to an ankle injury. However, Ian has since become a successful businessman in Nottingham where he is a publican and owns a bookmakers. Also employed by Nottingham Forest as a fully qualified FA Coach

STITFALL, Ron. *Cardiff (1947-1963).* Won two caps for Wales during his sixteen years at Cardiff City, for whom he made over 400 League appearances. Now works with the F.A. of Wales.

STOBART, Barry. *Wolves, Man C, Aston V, Shrewsbury. (1959-1968).* Barry now works as a window cleaner in Sedgley near Wolverhampton.

STOKES, Bobby. *Southampton, Portsmouth. (1968-1977)* A former England youth international who shot to fame after scoring the winner in the 1976 FA Cup final. Spent eight years at the Dell before making the short trip to Portsmouth in 1977. He worked at the Harbour View Cafe in Southsea until his shock death at his Portsmouth home in May 1995, aged only 44.

STOKOE, Bob. *Newcastle, Bury, (1950-1963).* Former Newcastle United centre half who won an FA Cup winners medal in 1955 with the "Magpies". He played over 250 league games at St James' Park before moving to Bury as player/manager. It was as a manager that Bob will probably be best remembered, having led Sunderland to their famous FA Cup victory over Leeds in 1973.

STONE, John. *Middlesboro, York, Darlington, Grimsby, Rotherham. (1971-1983)* Former full back, John now owns a Sports Shop in Grimsby.

Bobby Stokes

STOREY. Peter. *Arsenal, Fulham. (1965-1977).* Peter joined Arsenal in October 1962 and played 387 games in a career that lasted with the 'Gunners' until 1977. Won nineteen full caps with England. Now lives in Woodford, Essex and ran a market stall in the West End of London.

(Photograph courtesy: Evening Advertiser, Swindon)

Reunion of **Swindon Town's** League Cup winning side.

STONEYHOUSE, Steve. *Blackburn R, Huddesfield T, Blackpool, (1979-1994)* Returned to his native North-East to play for Bishop Auckland, South Bank and Northallerton Town. Currently player/coach and physio at Willington.

STOREY, Sydney. *York, Barnsley, Accrington St, Bradford PA, (1947-1959).* **Sydney played over 300 league games for York City, but was recently recognised at a cabaret concert by the star, Charlie Williams, who happened to an old team-mate at Barnsley!! Worked for many years as a bus driver before his retirement.**

STORTON, Stan. *Bradford C, Darlington, Hartlepool, Tranmere (1959-1969)* After many years in management, Stan now lives in Ellesmere Port and runs his own window cleaning business.

STORTON Trevor. *Tranmere R, Liverpool, Chester C, (1967-1983)* Former Chester City defender, veteran of over 500 League games, was Manager of Chorley FC until early 1995.

STRACHAN, Gordon. *Man U, Leeds, Coventry (1984-1995).* Edinburgh born midfield dynamo, Gordon enjoyed success both domestically and in Europe with Aberdeen, then Manchester United and Leeds United, before accepting the role as Ron Atkinson's assistant and manager-designate at Coventry City in early 1995.

STRATFORD, Paul. *Northampton (1972-1977)* Works for a publishing company in Duston.

STRINGER, Dave. *Norwich, Camb U. (1964-1980)* Dave lives in Great Yarmouth and is still working for Norwich, for whom he made over 400 league appearances. Now employed in an advisory capacity having previously held the posts of Youth Team and then First Team Manager.

STRONG, Geoff *Arsenal, Liverpool, Coventry (1960-1971)* Played 150 games for Liverpool following his move from Arseanl in 1964. Geoff now lives in Birkdale and is a successful businessman on Merseyside where he owns a thriving hotel furnishing company. Also co-owns a pub with his former team-mate, Ian Callaghan.

STRONG, Les. *Fulham, Brentford, C Palace, Rochdale. (1972-1984)* **Left back, who spent ten years at Craven Cottage before retiring in 1984. The profits from his successful pub in Mitcham, now allow him to travel the world. To add to the colour of his life, Les had a spell as manager of the Antiguan National Side.**

STUBBS, Brian. *Notts Co, (1968-1979).* While Brian is out at work as a painter, his wife is employed by Notts County, his one and only former club, for whom he appeared more than 400 times.

STUBBS, Robin. *Birmingham, Torquay, Bristol R, Torquay. (1958-1972).* **Former Torquay United Centre forward and one time husband to Anthea Redfern, Robin is now working as a Sales representative based in Paignton, Devon.**

STUCKEY, Bruce. *Exeter, Sunderland, Torquay, Reading, Torquay, Bournemouth. (1965-1976).* Bruce finished in 1976 to become a Child care Officer at Dawlish, and now lives in Torquay.

SUDDICK, Alan. *Newcastle, Blackpool, Stoke, Southport, Bury. (1961-1977).* England Under 23 international who played 310 League games forBlackpool, is now self-employed in the town.

Colin Suggett

SUGGETT, Colin. *Sunderland, WBA, Norwich, Newcastle. (1966-1978).* Retired in 1979. and became Youth Coach at Newcastle United.

SULLIVAN, Colin. *Plymouth, Norwich, Cardiff, Hereford, Portsmouth, Swansea, (1968-1985).* Plymouth and Norwich Left back who won England Under 23 honours in the1970's. Worked as a postman until 1992, when he became a Landscape gardener, based in Titchfield, Hants.

SUMMERBEE, Mike. *Swindon, Man C, Burnley, Blackpool, Stockport. (1959-1979)* **An exciting winger noteably with Manchester City, who also played eight times for England before finishing his career as Player/Manager with Stockport County. Mike now lives in an eighteenth century Cheshire vicarage and is Chairman of his own bespoke shirt making business. Clients have included David Bowie, Michael Caine and Sylvester Stallone. He also helps in the commercial office at Maine Road.**

SUNDERLAND, Alan. *Wolves, Arsenal, Ipswich. (1971-1985).* Former Wolves, Arsenal, Ipswich, and England striker Alan, ran a property rental company and sold insurance, before becoming Licensee of the 'Halberd Inn' near Ipswich.

SUTTON, Dave. *Plymouth, Reading, Huddersfield, Bolton, Rochdale (1973-1994)* Resigned as manager of Rochdale in November 1994 and was appointed Manager of Chorley in March 1995

Kenny Swain

SVARC, Bobby. *Leicester, Lincoln, Barrow, Colchester, Blackburn, Watford. (1964-1977).* Now owner of a Security company in Blackburn.

SWAIN, Ken. *Chelsea, Aston V, Notts F, Portsmouth, WBA, Crewe A. (1973-1994).* Former Chelsea, Villa and Forest defender. Joined Crewe in 1988 as player/coach, winning promotion from Division Four in his first season. However, a poor start in 1994 led to his dismissal, joining Grimsby as Assistant Manager only a few weeks later.

SWAN, Peter. *Sheff Wed, Bury. (1955-1973).* England international centre half (19 caps). Peter is now a publican in the Chesterfield area.

SWAN, Ron. *Oldham, Luton (1964-1966).* Has been in the Police force since 1971 and his duties include Policing the Oldham home games, but has plans to move to Spain upon retirement.

SWEENEY, Gerry. *Bristol C, York C. (1971-1981).* Bristol City veteran (over 400 games) finally ended at York City in 1981 and went on to have a spell as Assistant Manager at Walsall.

SWIFT, Frank. *Man City (1932-1949).* Was killed in the Munich Air disaster, when accompanying the United team as a newspaper reporter.

SWINBOURNE, Roy *Wolves (1949-1955)* Great centre forward who scored an average of more than a goal every other game during his time at Molineux. Worked for Goodyear tyres before setting up his own successful tyre distribution business. Now retired, living in Stourbridge.

SWINDLEHURST, Dave. *C Palace, Derby, West Ham, Sunderland, Wimbledon, Colchester , Peterboro. (1973-1988)* Lives in Kent, installs computer systems and helps out at former club Crystal Palace, in their School of Excellence.

SWORD, Tommy *Stockport , Hartlepool, Halifax, Stockport (1979-1987).* Popular goalscoring defender, Tommy now runs the "Powder Monkey" public house in Wallsend, Tyne & Wear.

SYDENHAM, John. *Southampton, Aldershot (1956-1971).* Made 341 appearances for the "Saints". Emigrated to Perth, Western Australia where he now runs an Insurance consultancy.

SYRETT, Dave. *Swindon, Mansfield, Walsall, Peterboro, Northampton. (1973-1983).* Dave is now a milkman living in Towcester, Northants.

TALBOT, Brian. *Ipswich, Arsenal, Watford, Stoke, WBA, Fulham, Aldershot. (1973-1990)* After a successful playing career which saw him win six full England caps, Brian became player/ manager at West Bromwich Albion for two years in 1988. Then had a spell as Manager of Aldershot, but is now managing Hibernians of Malta.

TALBUT, John. *Burnley, WBA. (1958-1970).* **Former Burnley centre half, John won seven England Under 23 international caps. He retired in 1974, to become a licensee in Belgium, taking over the 'Kup Winna' bar in Mechelen.**

TAMBLING, Bobby. *Chelsea, C Palace. (1958-1973)* Scored a record 164 League goals for Chelsea between (1958-1970). For many years ran a sports shop in Havant, but in 1994 was declared bankrupt in the County Court at Portsmouth, where he had been working as a hod carrier. Then moved over to the Republic of Ireland.

TANNER, Nicky. *Bristol R, Liverpool, Norwich, Swindon. (1985 -1994)* The former Liverpool centre half joined Bath City in 1994, having had to retire from the game early due to injury.

TARRANT, Ted. *Hull, Walsall (1950-1957).* Ted has moved over to Spain to live in Marbella.

TAYLOR, Alan. *Rochdale, West Ham, Norwich, Camb U, Hull, Burnley, Bury, Norwich. (1973-1988).* Striker who scored both of the goals in West Ham's FA Cup final victory of 1975. Alan once owned a Dairy Crest Milk franchise, but has now opened his own newsagency in Norwich.

TAYLOR, Brian. *Walsall, Birmingham, Rotherham, Shrewsbury, Port V, Barnsley. (1954-1967)* Winger who played over 400 matches for Walsall in two spells. Brian is now working as a painter and decorator, living near Stourbridge.

TAYLOR, Dick *Grimsby, Scunthorpe. (1938-1953)* Played for Grimsby Town and Scunthorpe United either side of World War Two, before retiring in 1954 to become Chief trainer/coach at the Old Show Ground. In 1956 he linked up with Joe Mercer at Sheffield United and followed him to Villa Park as his Assistant in 1958, taking over as manager when Mercer left in 1964. Dick became a successful businessman after leaving Aston Villa and in 1988 was still running his sports shop at Witton, 600 yards from Villa Park.

TAYLOR, Gerry. *Wolves, Swindon, (1966-1975)* **With the exception of a brief spell as a publican, former Wolves full back, Gerry has been a policeman since 1976. Currently a Sergeant serving with the Staffordshire force.**

TAYLOR, Gordon. *Bolton W, Birmingham C, Blackburn R, Bury. (1962-1979).* Gordon joined Bolton Wanderers in 1962 from non-league Curzon Ashton, and went on to play over 500 League games before ending his days at Bury, fifteen years later. He then took over from Cliff Lloyd as Secretary of the P.F.A. in December 1981. Now acts as a most influencial Chairman of the Union, which has developed into a very strong and supportive organisation covering all aspects of present and former players' needs.

Ex-Saints charity XI *(Courtesy: Bill Beaney)*

TAYLOR, Graham. *Grimsby, Lincoln. (1963-1972).* A full back, he joined Grimsby Town straight from school and turned professional in July 1962. He remained with Grimsby until July 1968 when he was transferred to Lincoln City. In the summer of 1972 he was appointed player-coach at Sincil Bank and later that year took over as manager. He quickly established himself as a leading manager and was snapped up by Watford in June 1977. In a colourful spell under Taylor's management and with Elton John's Support, they progressed from the Fourth to the First Division between. In 1983 they were runners up in the First Division and in 1984 reached the F.A. Cup final. After ten successful years he accepted the challenge of taking over at Aston Villa, and immediately steered them back to the top flight. Taylor left Villa Park in the Summer of 1990 to take over from Bobby Robson as England team manager. Despite his undoubted ability, after the disappointment of not qualifying for the World Cup, he bowed to public pressure and resigned in 1994. Was then linked with a number of top jobs before accepting the task of restoring the glory at Molineux, with Wolverhampton Wanderers.

TAYLOR, Les. *Oxford U, Watford, Reading, Colchester U (1974-1989)* Former Oxford United and Watford midfielder, Les ended Colchester United in 1988 after a fifteen year League career. Now works as a hospital porter in Oxford.

TAYLOR, Peter. *Southend U, C Palace, Tottenham, Leyton O, Oldham , Exeter. (1970-1983).* Former Tottenham and England winger (four caps). Peter became Manager at another of his former clubs, Southend United, until March 1995. He had previously managed non-league Dartford FC and worked in the Insurance industry.

Peter Taylor

TAYLOR, Steve. *Bolton, Port V, Oldham, Luton, Mansfield, Burnley, Wigan A, Stockport, Rochdale, Preston, Burnley, Rochdale. (1974-1988).* Lives in Shaw, helps out at Boundary Park with part time coaching for Oldham Athletic.

TAYLOR, Tommy. *Leyton O, West Ham, Leyton O, Charlton. (1967-1983).* Coached at Maidstone and managed Margate before joining Cambridge United. Initially he joined as Youth coach, but promoted to Manager in April 1995.

TAYLOR, Tony. *C Palace, Southend, Swindon, Bristol R, Portsmouth, Northampton. (1968-1979)* After working as Canada's national team Secretary became Youth Coach at Birmingham City.

(Courtesy: Liverpool Post & Echo)

TEMPLE, Derek. *Everton, Preston, (1956-1969)* Derek won one England cap and scored the winning goal for Everton in the 1966 FA Cup final, but left Goodison not much more than a year later. He went to Preston for £35,000 and had three years at Deepdale before finishing with Wigan Athletic. Now lives in Ormskirk and is in charge of the Merseyside branch of a national industrial cleaning company. He had previously worked in the glass industry for fifteen years.

TEES, Matt. *Grimsby T, Charlton A, Luton T, Grimsby T. (1963-1972)* Matt is now working for the Volvo Import Car Terminal in Grimsby.

TEMPLEMAN, John. *Brighton., Exeter, Swindon. (1966-1980)* Former Brighton and Exeter full back, now works as a District agent with the Prudential and lives in Pagham near Bognor.

TERNANT, Stan. *Burnley, Carlisle. (1966-1973)* Stan went on to coach at Crystal Palace, followed by a spell as Manager at Hull City (1990-91). Now working as Assistant Manager at Bury.

TERRY, Steve. *Watford, Hull, Northampton (1979-1993).* Watford's first choice defender for eight years, now playing for Walton & Hersham.

THIJSSEN, Frans. *Ipswich, Notts F (1978-1983)* Since leaving Nottingham Forest in 1983, this Dutch International has played in Holland for Fortuna Sittard, FC Groningen and Vitesse Arnhem - who now employ him as full time coach.

THOMAS, Danny. *Coventry, Tottenham. (1979-1986)* Former England Under 21 international defender signed as a professional in 1979 with Coventry City. Earning two full England Caps and a £650,000 transfer to Spurs before injury ended his career in 1986. Now works as the Club Physiotherapist at West Bromwich Albion.

THOMAS, Dave. *Burnley, QPR, Everton, Wolves, Middlesboro, Portsmouth. (1967-1984).* Former England winger now lives in Prinsted, Sussex and has set him self up as a Landscape gardener. Was Portsmouth's Youth Coach and helped out at Bognor Regis before accepting David Webb's invitation to coach at Brentford.

THOMAS, Geoff. *Swansea (1966-1975).* Geoff is now manager of a sports centre in Pontypool.

THOMAS, Mike. *Wrexham, Man U, Everton, Brighton., Stoke, Chelsea, W.B.A., Derby, Shrewsbury, Leeds, Stoke, Wrexham. (1971-1991).* Mickey played for ten League Clubs in a chequered career which was never short of excitement. High spots included winning 51 caps for Wales and a two year spell with Manchester United. Ended at Wrexham, ironically, where he had started over twenty years before. Having spent a short stretch at Her Majesty's pleasure, Mickey is now managing Konica League side, Portmadog

THOMAS, Rod. *Swindon, Derby, Cardiff, Newport. (1965-1981).* Welsh international right back, who was captain and a first choice for Swindon over eighteen years. After retiring in 1981, Rod worked for Francis Lee's paper company but now runs a pub near Stroud in Gloucestershire.

THOMPSON, Ian. *Bournemouth (1983-1985).* Former Bournemouth striker is teaching Mathematics at a school near his home in Swansea.

(Courtesy: Liverpool Post & Echo)

Mickey Thomas (right), part of an interesting forward line with **Ian Botham** and **Phil Thompson.**

THOMPSON, Peter. *Preston, Liverpool, Bolton (1960-1977)* Spent eight years at Anfield supplying incredibly accurate crosses for some of the era's greatest strikers, winning sixteen full caps. After seven years running two caravan parks, Peter moved to the Lake District where he has now run a Country Inn for the past thirteen years.

THOMPSON, Phil. *Liverpool, Sheff U (1971-1985)* A Merseyside lad who played 337 league games during his eleven years at Liverpool. Capped 42 times by England, he won almost every honour in the game before moving off to Sheffield United. Since ending his career in 1985, Phil has been involved in a number of D.I.Y related businesses which include a fireplace showroom, a Pine shop, and two units making conservatories. Spent six years coaching at Liverpool, but now writes for a local newspaper and works on Sky Sports' football programmes. In addition to all this, he is Chairman of the Vernons "Spot the Ball" panel, which also includes former Liverpool players, David Johnson and Alan Kennedy.

THOMPSON, Steve. *Bolton W, Luton T, Leicester C, Southend U (1982-1995)* Joined Southend as director of Football in early 1995 and appointed Manager in April of the same year. However, less than three months later, Steve accepted the post of Team Manager at Notts County.

Colin Todd

THOMSON, Bobby. *Wolves, Birmingham, Walsall, Luton, Port V (1961-1976).* Bobby was a full back with Wolves in the 1960's and won eight England caps. Spent several spells in America after finishing his League career at Port Vale. Now runs a sports shop in Sedgeley, near Dudley.

THOMSON, George. *Everton, Brentford (1960-1967).* Spent five years in the South with Brentford before returning to the North-West, where he had previously played for Everton following a move from Hearts. Now lives in Chester, where he runs a thriving salvage business.

THOMSON, Jim. *Chelsea, Burnley (1965-1980)* Played almost 300 games for Burnley, where he became Commercial manager. Now a Sales Executive with Ben Shaw's Soft Drinks Co in Huddersfield, but still lives in Burnley.

THORNE, Adrian. *Brighton & H.A., Plymouth Argyle, Exeter C, Leyton O. (1957-1965).* Former goalscoring winger, Adrian is now teaching P.E. to pupils at a school in Ealing, West London.

TILER, Brian. *Rotherham, Aston V, Carlisle. (1962-1973)* Spent four years in the heart of the Villa defence following his move from Rotherham in 1968. Became Managing Director at AFC Bournemouth before dying in a tragic car accident in Spain during the 1990 World Cup Finals.

TINDALL, Ron. *West Ham, Reading, Portsmouth (1955-1969)* Was an all rounder who also played cricket for Surrey. Emigrated to Australia in the 1980's and Ron now lives in Perth.

TODD, Colin. *Sunderland, Derby, Everton, Birmingham, Notts F, Oxford, Luton. (1966-1984).* Although making his debut for Sunderland in 1966-7, he did not get the first of his 27 England caps until Derby splashed out £170,000 in 1971 to take the 22 year old to the Baseball Ground. A key member of Brian Clough's side, he formed a brilliant centre back partnership with Roy McFarland, at international as well as club level. He gained a Championship medal in his first season and collected another in 1974-5. Became Assistant manager at Middlesborough and now holds the same post at Bolton Wanderers.

TOPPING, Chris. *York, Huddersfield. (1968-1980)* Played over 400 games for York City including an amazing run of 378 consecutive appearances, now runs a Market Garden in Selby.

TOSHACK, John. M.B.E. *Cardiff, Liverpool, Swansea. (1965-1983).* A natural goalscorer who formed a deadly partnership with Kevin Keegan at Liverpool. He had moved to Anfield in a £110,000 deal from Cardiff in 1970 and in his seven year stay, scored 74 goals in 174 appearances. His move into management was equally impressive, inspiring Swansea City's dramatic rise from the Fourth to First division. When things started to go wrong at Vetch Field, his departure opened the door to a new challenges abroad, notably in Spain, where he managed Real Sociedad, then the mighty Real Madrid, winning the championship in his first season. Despite this, the club sacked him shortly afterwards, and in 1991 he returned to Real Sociedad as General Manager. In March 1994, a spell as Welsh national team boss lasted a mere 44 days before John returned to Spain to take over at Deportivo La Coruna.

TOWNER, Tony *Brighton, Millwall, Rotherham, Wolves, Chalrton, Rochdale, Camb U (1972-1986).* Drives a van for furniture giants "Courts", but is still involved in football as coach of Saltdean in the Unijet Sussex County League.

TRAIN, Ray. *Walsall, Carlisle, Sunderland, Bolton, Watford, Oxford, Bournemouth, Northampton, Tranmere, Walsall. (1968-1986)* Ray is now Coach and Chief Scout at Middlesborough.

TRAUTMANN, Bert. *Man C (1949-1963)* **The 'Footballer of the Year' title was bestowed upon Trautmann, and was followed by a wonderful display in the winning 1956 Cup final, when he sustained a broken neck but insisted on completing the match. The tall powerful goalkeeper had been a paratrooper and was in a P.O.W. Camp when spotted. The German went on to represent the League and to play over 500 games whilst at Maine Road. Owns a house in Germany, but lives in Valencia, Spain.**

TRAYNOR, Tommy. *Southampton (1952-1965).* Played 434 games for the 'Saints' and eight times for his country, the Republic of Ireland. Still lives in Southampton and works in the docks.

TREACY, Ray. *WBA, Charlton A, Swindon T, Preston N.E., Oldham A, WBA.(1964-1976).* Managed of the Northern Irish side Crusaders. Ray is now working as a travel agent in Dublin.

(Courtesy: Manchester Evening News)

"Past meets present", **Bert Trautmann** with current Man City keeper, **Tony Coton**

TREBILCOCK, Mike *Plymouth, Everton, Portsmouth, Torquay (1962-1972).* Helped Everton pull off one of the most dramatic comebacks in FA Cup final history in 1966. The Merseysiders were trailing 2-0 to Sheffield Wednesday, but won 3-2 thanks to two goals by Trebilcock and a Derek Temple winner. Now lives in Australia at Lake Macquarie, sixty miles north of Sydney. Mike works as a storeman and helps coach a local semi-professional side at weekends.

TREWICK, John. *WBA, Newcastle, Oxford, Birmingham, Hartlepool (1974-1989).* John became Reserve Team Manager at West Brom, and briefly took over as Caretaker Manager during 1994 following Keith Burkenshaw's dismissal.

TROLLOPE, John. *Swindon (1960-1980)* A long serving single club man, Trollope made his debut in 1960, before going on to play 770 league games for the 'Town'. The highlight of his marvellous career came in 1968-9 when as a Third Division club, Swindon beat the mighty Arsenal to win the Football League Cup. John is still at the County Ground, and now runs the Youth team.

TRUSSON, Mike *Plymouth, Sheff U, Rotherham, Brighton, Gillingham (1976-1994)* Mike is playing for Stamco in the Sussex League.

TUDOR, John. *Coventry, Sheff U, Newcastle, Stoke (1966-1976.)* Scorer of over 100 League goals for his four clubs before finishing his career at Stoke in 1976. John is now a publican.

(Courtesy: Manchester Evening News)

TUEART, Dennis. *Sunderland, Man C, Stoke, Burnley (1968-1983)* Dennis started his career at Sunderland and was a member of their F.A. Cup winning side of 1973, before a £250,000 transfer took him to Manchester City the following year. Now runs his own corporate promotions company in Manchester and can be regularly seen back at Maine Road, where he leases an executive box.

TUNKS, Roy. *Rotherham, York, Preston, Wigan, Hartlepool, Preston. (1967-1989)* After a twenty year career, playing in goal for six clubs and appearing in close to 700 League games, Roy now works as a coach for the Lancashire F.A.

TURNBULL, Fred. *Aston V, Halifax. (1967-1973).* He had to retire due to injury at the age of 28 having played 160 games in central defence for Aston Villa. Fred now lives in Northumberland and is involved in business based in Blyth.

TURNER, Gordon. *Luton (1950-1963).* Prolific former Luton Town goalscorer who netted 243 times from 406 appearances. Died in 1976.

TURNER, Graham. *Wrexham, Chester, Shrewsbury (1964-1983)* Turner was a midfielder who made over 700 league and cup appearances in a playing career from 1965 to 1984. Became manager at Shrewsbury and took them from the Fourth Division to the Second. A two year stint at Aston Villa preceded a move to Wolves where he repeated the feat of climbing from the Fourth to the Second Division. Despite this pressure mounted, and was dismissed in 1994. Then worked as a scout for several clubs before being appointed director of Football at Hereford United.

TURNER, Ian. *Huddersfield, Grimsby, Walsall, Southampton, Newport, Lincoln, Walsall, Halifax. (1970-1980)* Southampton's goalkeeper in their 1976 F.A.Cup victory over Man United. Now a mechanical supervisor, living in Southampton.

TURNER, John. *Derby, Doncaster, Huddersfield, Reading, Torquay, Chesterfield, Torquay, Burnley, Peterboro. (1972-1985)* Now Landlord of the 'Fortune of War' public house in Torquay.

TWENTYMAN, Geoff. *Carlisle, Liverpool, Carlisle. (1946-1963).* Former Carlisle and Liverpool centre half, was Chief Scout at Anfield for many years, is now retired, still living in the City.

TYDEMAN, Dick. *Gillingham, Charlton Ath, Gillingham, Peterborough U. (1969-1983).* Long serving Chatham born midfielder who made over 500 League appearances during his four club career. The majority of them were played during two spells at Gillingham. Dick is now working for the Prudential Assurance Company.

TYNAN, Bobby. *Tranmere, Blackpool (1972-1978)* Quit at the age of 22, having already played close to 200 games for Tranmere Rovers. Now lives in Birkenhead and runs a Shop/post office.

UGOLINI, Rolando *Middlesboro, Wrexham (1948-1959)* Italian born Rolando played over 300 games in goal for Middlesborough. Then established his own chain of betting shops which he sold in 1984, before returning to Scotland where he had previously played for Glasgow Celtic.

UPRICHARD, Norman. *Swindon, Portsmouth, Southend. (1949-1959)* Irish international keeper who won eighteen caps for his Country. Was Portsmouth's first choice for six years, before ending at Southend in 1959. Moved over to Ireland to run the bar at Queens University after his playing days. Returned to England after twelve years to retire in Hastings, East Sussex.

(Photograph courtesy: Raymonds Press Agency)

A veritable "Who's Who" of former footballers, gathered to honour **Gordon Banks** (front)
(Back L to R): Cohen, Ball, Wilson, Hurst, Peters, Jennings, Chivers, Birchenall, McGee

Norman Uprichard
(Courtesy: Portsmouth News)

URE, Ian. *Arsenal, Man U. (1963-1970)* Retired through injury during the 1973-4 season. Managed East Stirling for a year. Then coached in Iceland before returning to Scotland in 1977 to become a social worker based in Kilmarnock.

VAESSEN, Paul. *Arsenal, (1978-1981)* Scored a goal which took Arsenal into the 1980 Cup Winners Cup final. Has had a bad run since injury ended his career, having had numerous jobs including building work and a spell as a postman.

"Scribes West" owned by **Terry Venables**

VAN BREUKELEN, Hans. *Notts F (1982-1983).* Dutch international keeper Hans, who had a 61 game stay at Notts Forest. Only recently hung up his boots, back in his home country, Holland.

VASPER, Peter. *Leyton O, Norwich, Camb U. (1963-1973).* Former Norwich and Cambridge goalkeeper, Peter now works an insurance agent for the Prudential and lives in Birmingham.

VAUGHAN, Nigel. *Newport, Cardiff, Reading, Wolves, Hereford, (1976-1992).* Lives in Telford and works as a production controller for Bundy U.K. Welsh international with ten caps, Nigel is still playing, in non-league soccer, for Newport, who were his first club during their League days.

VEALL, Ray. *Doncaster, Everton, Preston, Huddersfield. (1960-1966).* Played for four clubs before the age of 23, now lives in New Zealand.

VENABLES, Terry. *Chelsea, Tottenham, QPR, C. Palace, (1959-1974).* **'El Tel' seems to have occupied a high profile position in the game ever since first signing professional terms at Chelsea in 1960. As a player, he appeared for four London Clubs and won two full caps. Has since held managerial positions at Crystal Palace (with his "team of the eighties"); Queens Park Rangers (where hebecame a Director and second largest shareholder); Barcelona (with Gary Lineker and Mark Hughes); Tottenham Hotspur (with Alan Sugar!). Commercial ventures have included owning a West London night club, and co-writing the "Hazell" books which were made into a successful television series. Having appeared for England at every level, Terry was the perfect choice for the vacant National Team Managers job.**

VERNON, Roy. *Blackburn, Everton, Stoke, Halifax. (1955-1969).* Welsh international with with a great knack of scoring, netting 172 times from 395 games. Ran an Antiques business in Blackburn before his death in December 1993.

VILLA, Ricardo. *Tottenham. (1978-1982).* Joined Tottenham Hotspur in July 1978 for £375,000 from Racing Club of Buenos Aires, having been a member of the Argentinean World Cup winning squad. After leaving Spurs, he spent a year in America, and then Columbia, before finishing his playing days in the Argentinean second division at the age of 36. Now owns a 740 acre ranch in Argentina, south of Buenos Aires.

Mick Wadsworth

VINEY, Keith. *Portsmouth, Exeter, Bristol, (1975-1988).* Now an insurance agent for the Britannic Assurance Company in Exeter. His sister is married to Portsmouth keeper, Alan Knight.

VINTER, Mick. *Notts Co, Wrexham, Oxford, Mansfield, Newport. (1972-1986).* Ex-Notts County striker is now a salesman in Nottingham.

VIOLLET, Dennis. *Man U, Stoke, (1952-1966).* Spent thirteen successful years at Man United. In 1967 moved to the United States as one of the pioneers of the sport in America. He is still over there now directing the Dennis Viollet Dolphin Soccer Camps in addition to his duties as Head Coach of Jacksonville University.

VOWDEN, Geoff *Notts F, Birmingham, Aston V. (1959-1973).* Left competitive football in December 1974 and concentrated on coaching youngsters in the Kettering area after service with Kettering Town and in Saudi Arabia - Geoff can still be found playing in Sunday league soccer.

WADE, Joe. *Arsenal (1946-1954).* **Upon leaving Arsenal in 1956, Joe ended his career at Hereford United, as player and manager for six years. Remaining in the area, he then opened two sports shops in Hereford and Leominster, a business which was to last thirty years. Now retired, Joe still lives in Hereford in a house named "Highbury", a permenant reminder of,the great times he had enjoyed at Arsenal. He recently went on the Ashes Tour with the England Cricket team to Perth and Brisbane, where he was reunited with his old team mate Denis Compton, who was their host.**

WADSWORTH, Mick. *Scunthorpe U (1976)* Former Scunthorpe winger, is now enjoying success as Director of Coaching at Carlisle United.

Terry Venables. *(Courtesy: Yellow Pages)*

(Courtesy: Hull Daily Mail)

WAGSTAFF, Ken. *Mansfield, Hull. (1960-1975)* One of Hull City's greatest goal scorers, Ken struck up a great partnership with Chris Chilton. Returned to the U.K. after a spell in the sunshine of Australia, where he was Manager/ Player/Coach for George Cross of Melbourne. Now owns Waggy's club in Hessle, Humberside, and as well as writing a column for the local newspaper Ken helps out as an after lunch speaker in the sponsors lounge at Hull City home games.

WAGSTAFFE, Dave. *Man C, Wolves, Blackburn, Blackpool, Blackburn. (1960-1978).* Played in over 550 league games, most of them in the gold and black of Wolverhampton Wanderers. The connection with the club continues, as he now runs Waggy's Bar inside Molineux.

WAINMAN, Harry. *Grimsby, Rochdale (1964-1972)* Harry now owns the Saxon House Hotel in the Cleethorpes. He had previously been first choice keeper at Grimsby for nearly thirteen years.

WAINWRIGHT, Eddie. *Everton, Rochdale. (1946-1958).* Former Everton and Rochdale inside forward, Eddie went on to become landlord of 'The Acorn' public house in Bebington.

WAITERS, Tony. *Blackpool, Burnley. (1959-1971)* Won five England caps while playing in goal for Blackpool in 1964-5. Retired in 1967 to become FA regional coach. Held coaching posts at Liverpool, Burnley, Coventry and was Manager at Plymouth Argyle. Tony then moved over to Canada to assist Vancouver Whitecaps and was named "Coach of the Year" in 1978. Now runs his own successful soccer school and in 1984 was Coach to the Canadian Olympic Games team.

WALDEN, Richard. *Aldershot, Sheff Wed, Newport Co. (1964-1981).* Played over 400 games for Aldershot. Now manages a sports wholesale business, Midas Leisure Ltd based in Hampshire.

WALDRON, Colin. *Bury, Chelsea, Burnley, Man U, Sunderland, Rochdale. (1966-1979).* Former Burnley central defender (308 apps) Colin now runs a bookmakers in Nelson, Lancs.

WALDRON, Malcolm. *Southampton, Burnley, Portsmouth. (1974-1984)* Malcolm became an Advertising representative in Portsmouth but now believed to be selling Double Glazing in the area.

WALFORD, Steve. *Tottenham, Arsenal, Norwich, West Ham, Huddersfield, Gillingham, WBA, (1975-1988).* Steve, who played for three of biggest London clubs as a defender, is now Youth Team manager at Wycombe Wanderers.

WALKER, Clive. *Chelsea, Sunderland, QPR, Fulham, Brighton (1976-1993).* Chelsea enjoyed Clive's skills on the wing for seven years before he moved on to play for four more League clubs, ending at Brighton. Now playing for Woking FC.

WALSH, Bradley. *Brentford* Once best known as a footballer with Brentford, Bradley is set to become a household name in a different profession, as he already has a major TV series under his belt. Appearances as a guest on several major shows have ensured that his unique brand of humour is reaching an ever wider audience. He is tipped for an exciting future, having been described as "the best guest on the Des O'Connor show, who had Des crying tears of laughter all over his new suit."

WALKER, Clive. *Leicester, Northampton, Mansfield, (1963-1974)* Clive played over 225 games for Mansfield as a left back, was Assistant Manager at Kettering Town until February 1995.

WALKER, David *Burnley, Southampton (1960-1973).* After completing almost 200 League games for Southampton, defender David finished his career in South Africa, playing for Cape Town. When he eventually returned to England, set up his own successful antiques business.

WALKER, James. *Derby, Hartlepool, Brighton, Peterboro, Chester. (1967-1980).* Has been physiotherapist at Aston Villa since 1987.

(Courtesy: Mike Jones)

WALKER, Len. *Newcastle U, Aldershot, Darlington. (1963-1977).* Len became Manager of Aldershot, where he had played 440 league games between 1964 and 1975. Now working at Fulham as Assistant Manager to Ian Branfoot.

WALKER, Mike. *Reading, Shrewsbury, York, Watford, Charlton, Colchester U. (1963-1982).* An extremely competent goalkeeper who made over 700 League appearances after starting out with Reading in January 1963. He signed for Colchester United in June 1973 becoming a mainstay of the club. Mike worked wonders as Manager of the Layer Road outfit, and then achieved more success during a two year spell at Norwich City. This led to his appointment to the Everton hot seat. However, his stay at Goodison Park was a remarkably brief one, leaving with a healthy pay-off only a few months later, in November 1994

WALKER, Nigel. *Newcastle U, Crewe A, Sunderland, Blackpool, Chester C, Hartlepool (1977-1986)* Nigel, who had a six club League career, is now teaching at St Bedes School in Chester.

WALKER, Tommy. *Newcastle, Oldham, Chesterfield, Oldham. (1946-1958).* Outside right who plied his trade on the wing for Newcastle United and Oldham Athletic in the late 1940's and 1950's Tommy is now living in retirement in Edinburgh.

WALLEY, Tom. *Arsenal, Watford, Leyton O, Watford (1965-1976).* For a long time, Welsh international midfielder Tom, was Youth Team Coach at Watford and was responsible for developing many youngsters including a certain John Barnes. His team won the 1991 F.A. Youth Cup.

WALLINGTON, Mark. *Walsall, Leicester, Derby, Lincoln. (1971-1990).* England Under 23 goalkeeper, who played over 400 games between the sticks for Leicster City. Mark is now working as a P.E. teacher in the Midlands and also holds the post of Assitant Manager at Grantham FC.

WALSH, Dave. *W.B.A., Aston V, Walsall. (1946-1955).* Dave won 29 caps, playing for both Northern Ireland and the Republic of Ireland. Played twice for the Irish League and was named reserve for the Great Britain side. Walsh continued running a sports-shop and newsagents in Droitwich before retiring to Torquay in 1984.

(Photograph courtesy: Evening Post, Nottingham.)

WATSON, Dave. *Notts Co, Rotherham U, Sunderland, Manchester C, Southampton, Stoke C, Derby Co, Notts Co. (1966-1984).* Dave began with Notts County, then moved to Rotherham United, Sunderland (with whom he won an F.A. Cup winners medal in 1973) and then Manchester City. They transferred him to West German club Werder Bremen for £200,000 in June 1979, but he did not settle and within four months was back in England with Southampton before he left to play in quick succession for Stoke City, Vancouver Whitecaps in the U.S.A., and Derby County. Now back in the Midlands, living in West Bridgeford and runs his own marketing business, Dave Watson International.

WALSH, Ian. *C Palace, Swansea, Barnsley, Grimsby, Cardiff. (1976-1988).* Lives and works in Cardiff, where he sells Insurance and can often be heard on BBC Radio Wales. In his playing days, Ian won eighteen full Welsh caps during his successful five year stay at Crystal Palace.

WALSH, Jimmy. *Leicester. (1956-1962).* Now runs a newsagency in the centre of Leicester, where he played as a centre forward for the local side, following his transfer from Celtic in 1956.

WALSH, Mike. *Bolton, Everton, Norwich, Burnley, Man C, Blackpool, Bury. (1974-1989).* Former Republic of Ireland defender (5 caps), has been Manager of Bury since December 1990, having signed for them as a player in July 1989.

WALSH, Micky *Blackpool, Everton, Q.P.R. (1971-1979)* Micky attracted attention from top clubs whilst playing for Blackpool. Went on to play for Everton and Q.P.R. but was forced to quit at the age of 26, having already won 22 caps for the Irish Republic. He went on to become manager of Chertsey Town in the Diadora League.

WALTERS, George. *Shrewsbury, Newport Co. (1956-1965).* Ex-Shrewsbury right back, is now a maintenance supervisor in Newport, Gwent.

WALTON, Ronnie. *Northampton, Crewe, Carlisle, Aldershot, Camb U, Aldershot. (1964-1976).* Now a Chain store owner in his home town of Newcastle. Played 300 League matches for Aldershot in two spells during the 1960's and 1970's.

WANT, Tony. *Tottenham, Birmingham. (1967-1977).* Tony is now a warehouse manager for a frozen food department in Birmingham, the City where he ended his playing career in 1977.

WARBOYS, Alan. *Doncaster, Sheff Wed, Cardiff, Sheff U, Bristol R, Fulham, Hull, Doncaster. (1966-1981).* Scored bags of goals during his career, striking up a great partnership with Bruce Bannister. Alan is now Landlord of 'The Ring O' Bells' in Swinton which he took over when he retired from the game with a back injury.

WARD, Gerry. *Arsenal, Leyton O. (1953-1964).* Former Arsenal and Orient wing half, Gerry died in January 1994 at the age of 57.

WARD, John. *Lincoln, Workington, Watford, Grimsby, Lincoln. (1970-1981).* John scored nearly 100 league goals for Lincoln City, Workington, and Watford before moving into coaching and then management with York City and now in his current post at Bristol Rovers.

John Wark (left) with fellow Ipswich coach, **Paul Goddard.**

(Photograph courtesy: Lancashire Evening Telegraph)

WHELAN, David. *Blackburn R, Crewe Alex. (1956-1965).* Bradford born defender who signed for Blackburn Rovers in 1953 and played 78 League games for the Lancashire club before moving to Crewe Alexandra, where he ended his playing days in 1965. Upon retirement, set up his own sports shop business, JJB sports, which blossomed to become a chain of 115 stores. The company was floated on the Stock exchange in 1994, making him an estimated £13.5 million! David took over as Chairman of Wigan Athletic in 1995, but still attends Blackburn Rovers matches, sharing his executive box with a number of the Club's former stars such as Ronnie Clayton and Bryan Douglas.

WARK, John. *Ipswich, Liverpool, Ipswich, Middlesboro, Ipswich (1974-1995)* P.F.A. "Player of the Year" in 1991, John is still enjoying his football, more than twenty years after first signing for Ipswich as a youngster. As well as 29 Scottish Caps, he also won UEFA Cup and F.A. Cup winners medals. Joined Liverpool in 1984 for £450,000 before returning to Portman Road four successful years later. Now in his third spell with the Suffolk club where he is their Firs team coach.

WARNOCK, Neil. *Chesterfield, Rotherham, Hartlepool, Scunthorpe, Aldershot, Barnsley, York, Crewe. (1967-1978).* Manager of Huddersfield Town until he resigned shortly after guiding the club to victory in the play-offs earning promotion to the First Division. However, within weeks he was back in work, relishing the challenge of restoring pride at Plymouth Argyle who had just had to endure the torment of relegation.

WATERHOUSE, Ken. *Preston, Rotherham, Bristol C, Darlington. (1953-1964).* Wing half who played for Rotherham, is now an enforcement officer for the North-West Water Authority.

WATSON, Graham *Doncaster, Rotherham, Doncaster, Camb U, Lincoln, Camb U (1966-1979).* Graham's 400 plus game career took in two stops a piece at Cambridge United and Doncaster Rovers. He is now Landlord at 'The Three Horseshoes' in Comberton in Cambridgeshire.

WAYMAN, Charlie. *Newcastle, Southampton, Preston., Middlesboro, Darlington.. (1946-1957).* Centre forward who was a most prolific goalscorer for all his clubs, scoring 254 goals in 382 league games. Charlie now works as a Brewery representative in his home town of Bishop Auckland.

WATSON, Willie. *Huddersfield, Sunderland, Halifax T. (1937-1955)* One of a rare bunch of players who played both Cricket and Football for England. Now retired and living in South Africa.

WEALANDS, Jeff. *Wolves, Darlington, Hull C, Birmingham C, Man Utd, Oldham A, Preston N.E.. (1968-1984).* Jeff is now a property developer living in Wilmslow, Cheshire and helps coach the goalkeepers at Bury. Also a director of Altrincham F.C., for whom he had played after his seven club League career finished in 1984.

WEBB, David. *Leyton O, Southampton, Chelsea, QPR, Leicester, QPR, Leicester, Derby, Bournemouth,, Torquay. (1964-1984).* Scored the winning goal for Chelsea in the 1970 F.A. Cup final. After leaving the Blues in 1974, having played 230 games in their defence, David served three more clubs before progressing into Soccer management with Torquay United, Bournemouth, and Southend United. He has held his current position as Manager of Brentford since 1993.

WEBB, Dougie. *Reading, (1956-1966).* Played as an Inside Forward with Reading for a decade before becoming a painter and decorator in the same area. Father of former England player, Neil.

WEBSTER, Malcolm. *Arsenal, Fulham, Southend, Camb U. (1969-1983).* Recently started up his own goalkeeping schools to add to his duties coaching keepers at various League Clubs.

WEBSTER, Ron. *Derby (1961-1977).* Long serving Derby County right back, who played over 450 matches for the Rams in his sixteen years at the Baseball Ground. Ron is now minding cattle on a 100 acre beef farm north of Nottingham.

WEBSTER, Barry. *Rotherham, Bradford. (1956-1963).* Former Rotherham winger, now works for an engineering company in Sheffield.

WELBOURNE, Duncan. *Grimsby, Watford, Southport. (1957-1975).* Started as a defender at Grimsby, but played over 400 games for Watford having joined them from the "Mariners" in 1963. Delivers potatoes for a living, and has had a variety of jobs since finishing playing, including digging a tunnel under London's Albert Dock !

WELLER, Keith. *Tottenham, Millwall, Chelsea, Leicester C. (1964-1978).* **Skillful striker who had success with Millwall and then Chelsea. However, it was during his seven years at Leicester City that he was finally rewarded with four England caps. A £40,000 transfer to New England Teamen took him to the States, where Keith still lives toady. His home is in Seattle, where he was coach to Tacoma Stars. Although a qualified pilot, he now drives a massive television outside broadcast lorry for a locally based American Television company.**

WENT, Paul. *Leyton O, Charlton, Fulham, Portsmouth, Cardiff, Leyton O. (1965-1979).* Paul started and ended his thirteen year career at Leyton Orient where he also had a disastrous 20 day spell as Manager. Retired in 1979 after almost 500 League appearances. Most of his playing days were based in London and he is still living in the Capital, now working as a representative for the Courage Brewery Company.

WEST, Alan. *Burnley, Luton, Millwall (1969-1982).* Former England Under 23 midfielder who played close on 300 League games for Luton Town. Managed Hitchin Town for a spell, lives in Luton and is a Pastor as well as being actively involved in the Christians in Sport organisation.

WEST, Gordon. *Blackpool, Everton, Tranmere. (1960-1978).* Won two championship medals and three Enlgand caps during his eleven years in goal for Everton. Later played for Tranmere Rovers, where he went on to work on the ground staff at Prenton Park. Gordon is currently employed in Security on Merseyside.

WESTON, Don. *Wrexham, Birmingham, Rotherham, Leeds, Huddersfield, Wrexham, Chester. (1958-1968).* Don now works as a senior salesman in a Vauxhall dealership in Wrexham.

WHATMORE, Neil. *Bolton , Birmingham, Bolton, Oxford, Bolton, Burnley, Mansfield, Bolton, MansfieldT. (1972-1987).* Played consistently for Bolton Wanderers in the 1970's before leaving for Birmingham City in 1981. However, Neil returned to Boundary Park for three more spells before retiring in 1987. Now works as a milkman in the Mansfield area and manages Rainworth MW in the Notts Alliance League.

WHITAKER, Colin. *Sheff Wed, Bradford P.A., Shrewsbury, Q.P.R., Rochdale, Oldham Ath, Barrow (1951-1964).* **After managing Stalybridge and then Buxton, former goalscoring winger Colin, purchased a 46 acre farm and transformed it into a golf course. He is now retired and manages to escape from the British weather by living part of the year over in Spain.**

WHITE, Dick. *Scunthorpe U, Liverpool, Doncaster R, (1950-1963).* Scunthorpe born central defender, who joined Liverpool from his home town club in 1955 (Sixteen years before a certain Kevin Keegan took the same route). Went on to play over 200 games for the "Reds" before ending at Doncaster Rovers in 1983. Dick is now a garage proprietor in Nottingham and keen golfer who is a past Captain and President of Scunthorpe Golf Club - but can often now be found on the links of the Chilwell Manor Club in Beeston.

WHITE, Ian. *Leicester, Southampton, (1959-1966).* Former Leicester and Southampton wing half opened his own Sports shop in Totton, Hants.

WHITE, John. *Tottenham (1959-1963).* **Scottish international (22 caps) who made 183 appearances for Tottenham. Died 1964 aged only 27 when struck by lightening on a golf course.**

WHITE, Len. *Rotherham, Newcastle, Huddersfield, Stockport. (1950-1965)* Died in the June 1994 after a long fight against cancer, aged 64

WHITE, Winston. *Leicester C, Hereford U, Chesterfield, Port V, Stockport Co, Bury, Rochdale, Colchester, Burnley, W.B.A. (1976-1993).* Winston purchased a pub/restaurant in Padiham after hanging up his well travelled boots.

WHITEFOOT, Jeff. *Man U, Grimsby, Notts F. (1949-1967).* Former England Under 23 wing half, became licensee of a pub after a career which took in three clubs and over 350 appearances, 255 of them in Nottingham Forest's colours.

WHITEHEAD, Clive. *Bristol C, W.B.A., Wolves, Portsmouth, Exeter. (1973-1990).* Played 256 games for Bristol City prior to joining W.B.A. for £100,000. He had helped City win promotion to the first division in 1975-6, scoring the promotion winning goal against Portsmouth, ironically a club he was to join later. Became manager of Yeovil Town. Clive was with Bristol City as Reserve/Youth coach but departed in May 1995.

WHITEHOUSE, Brian. *W..B.A., Norwich, Wrexham, C.Palace, Charlton, Orient (1955-1967).* Played most of his football in the lower divisions but, since ending his playing career, he has made a name for himself as a top class coach working at Arsenal, West Bromwich Albion, Manchester United and most recently Aston Villa.

WHITEHURST, Billy. *Hull C, Newcastle U, Oxford U, Reading, Sunderland, Hull C, Sheffield U, Stoke C, Doncaster R, Crewe Alex. (1980-1993)* Powerful forward,who led the line for Hull City in the early 1980's, before touring the Country with his boots. Nine stops later, Billy went abroad, to play in Hong Kong. However, he has now returned home to manage Frickley Athletic.

WHITESIDE, Norman. *Man Utd, Everton (1981-1990).* **Although forced to retire in 1990 at the age of 25, Norman had already proved himself to be one of the most exciting players of his day, and had won 38 caps for his Country, Northern Ireland. Now a full time student at Salford University studying Podiatry (feet!). He plays in occasional charity matches and undertakes regular after dinner speaking.**

WHITTLE, Alan. *Everton, C Palace, Leyton O, Bournemouth. (1967-1980).* The blond bombshell who took Everton by storm when he scored eleven goals in fifteen games in 1969-70. He was only 20 at the time, but the early success petered out and he was sold to Crystal Palace for £100,000 in 1972. Subsequently he played for Orient and Bournemouth before going to Australia. Now lives on the Wirral and works for the Football in the Community programme, based at Goodison Park.

WHITTLE, Maurice. *Blackburn, Oldham, Wigan (1966-1980)* Played over 300 games for Oldham Athletic, then spent three years in the States with Fort Lauderdale Strikers, followed by a spell in Finland. Now lives in Wigan and is manager of the JJB Sports shop in Chorley.

WHITTON, Steve, *Coventry, West Ham, Birmingham, Sheff Wed, Ipswich. (1979-1993)* Former Coventry City junior, who played professionally for six League clubs including Colchester United, where he is now Player /coach.

WHYMARK, Trevor. *Ipswich, Derby, Grimsby, Southend, Peterboro, Colchester. (1969-1985).* Trevor won one England cap while starring at ipswich Town in the late 1970's. After spells with Vancouver in Canada and Sparta Rotterdam in Holland, Grimsby Town broke their transfer record to take him to Humberside. Became Coach at Blundell Park and later held the same post at Southend United. Went on to coach youngsters and ran courses at holiday camps for four years, but now works as a van salesman.

WICKS, Steve. *Chelsea, Derby, Q.P.R, C.Palace, Q.P.R., Chelsea. (1974-1987).* Won England Under 23 honours as a Chelsea player in the 1970's. He both started and ended his career at Stamford Bridge before becoming Assistant manager at Portsmouth until August 1989. Steve then linked up with Paul Mariner to run an agency handling player's affairs. Returned to League management at Scarborough but held the post for less than a season, leaving in August 1994

WIGGINGTON, Clive. *Grimsby, Scunthorpe, Lincoln, Grimsby, Doncaster, Torquay, Doncaster. (1968-1982).* Experienced defender who spent nine years at Grimsby Town in two spells. Now a manager for a pipework company in the town.

WIGLEY, Steve. *Notts F, Sheff U, Birmingham, Portsmouth, Exeter. (1982-1993).* Former Nottingham Forest winger, Steve was appointed Manager of Aldershot Town in January 1995

WIGNALL, Frank. *Everton, Notts F, Wolves, Derby, Mansfield. (1959-1972).* Winner of two England caps in 1965, former Nottingham Forest centre forward Frank had a stint as National Coach to Qatar in the Persian Gulf. Now owns a garage and car showroom back in Nottingham.

WIGNALL, Steve. *Doncaster R, Colchester U, Brentford, Aldershot. (1972-1990).* Managed Aldershot Town until January 1995, when he returned to his former club, Colchester United, as Manager. He had previously been a commanding defender at Layer Road between 1977 and 1983.

WILE, John. *Sunderland, Peterboro, W.B.A., Peterboro. (1966-1985).* Played 500 games for West Bromwich Albion before leaving to take over as Player/Manager of Peterborough United in 1983. Later became involved in indoor cricket at Walsall and Solihull. John now lives in Litchfield.

WILKINS, Ray. *Chelsea, Man U, QPR, C. Palace, Q.P.R. (1973-1995)* A real thouroughbred footballer who oozed class. Played top level soccer in Britain with Chelsea, Manchester United, Q.P.R. Crystal Palace and Rangers, as well as succeeding abroad with Paris St Germain in France and AC Milan in Italy. This glorious career began at Chelsea, with a debut in 1973 at the age of 17. Twenty one years, a cupboard full of silverware and 84 England Caps later, 'Butch' finally hung up his boots to take over as player/manager at Queens Park Rangers in November 1994. His father George (Brentford), and brother Graham (Chelsea), both played professionally.

Ray "Butch" Wilkins

WILKINSON, Howard. *Sheff Wed, Brighton (1964-1980).* Howard played as a winger, intitially with Sheffield Wednesday, (where he later returned as Manager in 1983), then for Brighton & Hove Albion. He spent five years in command at Hillsborough until October 1988, when he accepted the offer to take the helm at Leeds United.

WILKINSON, Norman. *Hull, York. (1952-1965).* Goalkeeper who played his entire career as a part timer and was given time off from his job as a shoe repairer to play. He has worked in a Newcastle-Under -Lyne Shoe factory for the past eleven years and will retire in February 1996.

WILLIAMS, Bert. *Walsall, Wolves. (1937-1956).* Played 381 matches in goal for Wolverhampton Wanderers and won 24 England caps. Retired in 1957 and worked in a Sports Clothing business in Bilston. However, Bert now lives in Saifrial, Salop and works in an engineering firm.

WILLIAMS, Bobby. *Bristol C, Rotherham, Bristol R, Reading. (1958-1970).* Former inside forward who played for both Bristol clubs. Now working as a courier, but since 1972 has worked with the youth team at Reading, which has produced the likes of Neil Webb and Lawrie Sanchez.

WILLIAMS, Danny. *Rotherham. (1946-1959).* Was the manager who guided Swindon to League Cup and promotion in the same season. He made 459 league appearances for Rotherham where he also managed. Retired, living in Bournemouth.

WILLIAMS, Graham. *W.B.A.. (1955-1970).* Made 308 appearances for West Brom and earned 26 Welsh Caps. Retired as a professional player in 1972 and became Manager at Weymouth then Sports Club Kuwait , OFI (Greece, coach), Poole (Manager), Cardiff City (Coach, then Manager), Newport County (Scout), Leopards FC Nigeria (coach), FC Rovaniemen, Finland (Manager). Based in Oswestry but now coaching in Kuwait.

WILLIAMS, Graham. *Bradford C, Everton, Swansea, Wrexham, Tranmere, Port V (1955-1968)* Former Welsh international outside left, Graham now works as a carpenter in Wrexham.

WILLIAMS, Herbie. *Swansea. (1958-1974).* Loyal servant to his only club, Swansea. Became player-coach to Woollongong in Australia in 1975 after sixteen years at the Vetch Field. However he and his family could not settle, so returned to Port Talbot, where he now works as a postman.

WILLIAMS, John. *Watford, Colchester (1964-1977)* Held the left back position at Watford for ten years before ending at Colchester in 1977. John now lives in Great Horksley near the same Essex town and works for a local electrical firm.

WILLIAMS, Oshor *Man U Southampton, Exeter, Stockport, Port V, Preston. (1976-1987).* Ex-Stockport County winger. As well as being assistant manager at Hyde United, Osher has been a full time student at Salford Universtity studying History and Politics. Also lectures in Sports studies on a part time basis at Trafford College.

WILLIAMS, Stuart. *Wrexham, W.B.A, Southampton. (1947-1965).* After more than 350 League games Stuart became trainer at West Bromwich Albion in 1967, then held coaching posts at Aston Villa , Payhaam (Holland), Morton, Southampton (Assistant Manager) and Stavanger, Norway (Manager). Now works as a financial controller with a transport company, having spent twelve years as a commercial tyre salesman.

WILLS, Len. *Arsenal (1953-1960).* Former Arsenal full back, lives in Chigwell, Essex, and worked in the D.I.Y. retail trade before retiring.

WILLIAMS, Charlie. *Doncaster R. (1949-1958).* "Hello, me old flower!" The unmistakeable words of Charlie Williams, one of Britain's best loved comedians. Charlie never intended to become a comedian. He had his sights firmly set on a career in professional football. Indeed, he played 158 League games as a centre half with Doncaster Rovers for twelve years. But he enjoyed singing, particularly Nat King Cole - he sang in the dressing room, in the showers, in the coach on the way home, or to a game... and told funny stories too. Encouraged by his mates, he started entertaining in the Working Men's Clubs in Yorkshire on Saturday evenings - and the rest as they say - is history! In spite of his fame and fortune, Charlie still lives a simple life in a little village near Barnsley. His main hobby is golf when he can get away from work and he also gives much of his time to charity shows.

WILSHAW, Dennis. *Wolves, Walsall, Stoke C. (1948-1960).* Fearsome goalscorer with Wolves in the 1950's, Dennis won twelve England caps before retiring in 1961. Became a school teacher, and is now living in Newcastle-under-Lyme.

WILSON, Billy. *Blackburn, Portsmouth. (1964-1978).* The fair haired defender who played over 200 times for Portsmouth after signing from Blackburn Rovers in 1972. Has been a publican for many years, currently licensee of the "Horse & Jockey" pub in Curbridge, Hampshire.

WILSON, Bob. *Aston V, Cardiff, Bristol C, Exeter C. (1963-1975).* Played in goal for Cardiff City in the 1960's and Exeter City through until his retirement in 1975. Bob now works for the Post Office and still lives in the Devon town.

WILSON, Bob. *Arsenal (1963-1973).* Member of Arsenal's double winning side retired in 1973 to concentrate on his television work. He also runs a successful goalkeeping school and his expertise is often called upon by League Clubs to help coach their young goalies. In 1994, a lucrative offer and the opportunity of a new challenge persuaded Bob to switch channels to Carlton Television after over twenty years with the BBC.

WILSON, Danny. *Bury, Chesterfield, Notts F, Scunthorpe, Brighton, Luton T, Sheff Wed, Barnsley (1977-1995)* Experienced Northern Ireland international midfielder. Danny took over as manger of Barnsley when Viv Anderson chose to join up with Bryan Robson at Middlesborough.

Danny Wilson

WILSON, Glen. *Brighton, Exeter. (1949-1961).* After playing over 400 games for Brighton, ended his career at Exeter City before returning to the Sussex town where he now lives and works.

WILSON, Harold. *Burnley, Brighton., Preston, Darlington, Hartlepool (1971-1983).* Reserve team coach at Burnley, who were his first club as a player. Appeared for four more League clubs as a left back before making his return to Turf Moor.

WILSON, Kevin. *Derby C, Ipswich T, Chelsea, Notts Co, Walsall (1979-1995)* Goalscoring Northern Ireland forward, who found the net for four League clubs before joining Walsall, where he is now Assistant Manager to Chris Nicholl.

WILSON, Ray. *Huddersfield, Everton, Oldham, Bradford C. (1955-1970).* **Played over 400 league games and won 63 England caps including one for the victorious 1966 World Cup final. Now one of the most famous undertakers in Britain, running the family Funeral Directors business from its base near Oldham.**

WILSON, Robert. *Fulham, Millwall, Luton, Fulham, Rotherham, Huddersfield. (1979-1993)* Former Fulham midfielder, Robert went on to play soccer for Vauxhall conference side Altrincham.

WILSON. Tom. *Millwall, Hull. (1961-1969).* After running his own shops for five years, decided to persue a career in law, joining a fim of Solicitors in 1972. In 1986 Tom re-joined one of his former clubs, Hull City, where he worked as coach, Assistant Manager, and Caretaker Manager no less than four times! Following two years as Company Secretary at Boothferry Park, returned to the legal profession in October 1993,

WINFIELD, John. *Notts F, Peterboro. (1961-1974).* Now runs a newsagency in Woollaton, having played over 350 League games as a left back for Nottingham Forest from 1971 until 1973

WINSTANLEY, Eric. *Barnsley, Chesterfield (1961-1976).* Became first team coach at Barnsley, where he had played over 400 matches as a player.

Peter Withe

WITHE, Peter. *Southport, Barrow, Wolves, Birmingham, Notts F, Newcastle, Aston V, Sheff U, Birmingham, Huddersfield. (1970-1989).* A full England international, and a much-travelled player. He won Championship medals with Nottingham Forest and then again at Aston Villa in 1988. Withe was appointed player/coach of Huddersfield Town, followed by a brief spell as Assistant Manager to Josef Venglos at Villa Park before taking over as Manager of First Division Wimbledon. In February 1992 he signed as a player for Evesham United, but now works back at Aston Villa as a Youth Development Director.

WITHERS, Colin. *Birmingham, Aston V, Lincoln. (1957-1969)* In 1975 he became a hotelier in Blackpool, and later ran a pub in Bridgenorth.

WOMBLE, Trevor. *Rotherham, Crewe, Halifax. (1968-1972).* Works in the catering trade in Rotherham, where he played most of his career.

WOOD, Alf *Man C, Shrewsbury, Millwall, Hull, Middlesboro, Walsall. (1963-1977)* **Alf's six club career came to an end at Walsall in 1997. Now runs his own promotions company in the Midlands which he set up after three years as promotions manager at Birmingham City. The firm used to supply theTrophies for the Barclays League and the Autoglass Trophy.**

WOOD, George. *Blackpool, Everton, Arsenal, C Palace, Cardiff, Blackpool, Hereford U. (1971-1990)* Former Arsenal and Everton goalkeeper, George is now an ornithologist with Glamorgan Wildlife Trust and Manager of Inter Cardiff FC.

WOOD, Ian. *Oldham, Burnley.(1965-1980).* Full back who made 517 league appearances for Oldham Athletic, is now a self employed butcher.

WOOD, Ray. *Darlington, Man U, Huddersfield, Bradford C, Barnsley (1949-1967).* **Goalkeeper who won three full England caps and was a survivor of the Munich air disaster. Played over 450 League games, 178 of them between the posts for Manchester United. Retired in 1967 after seventeen years as a professional, and qualified as an F.A. Coach. Ray has since had jobs in Greece, Kuwait, Canada, United Arab Emirates, and Cyprus. In Kenya he won the League title three times and their National Cup once. Also won the Eastern Central National Championship of Africa with Kenya in 1975. Based in Bexhill, Sussex.**

WOODCOCK, Tony. *Notts F, Lincoln, Doncaster, Arsenal. (1973-1985)* **Former Forest and Arsenal star, Tony won 42 England caps, but has now made Germany his adopted home. Lives in Cologne, where he had previously spent two spells with the local club as a player. His intial £650,000 move in 1982 broke the German transfer record. Now a qualified coach, his most recent appointment was as Manager of East Geman side VfB Leipzig until mid 1995.**

WOODHEAD, Dennis. *Sheff Wed, Chesterfield, Derby Co, Southport.* Former Sheffield Wednesday outside left who scored 73 goals in his 213 League games for the "Owls". Dennis is now retired, but still living in the Yorkshire town.

WOODS, Charlie. *Newcastle, Bournemouth, C Palace, Ipswich, Watford, Colchester. (1960-1971).* Brought his career to a close in 1971 and went on to become First Team Coach at Ipswich.

WOODS, Clive. *Ipswich, Norwich. (1969-1981).* Played over 200 League games for Ipswich but finished at neighbours Norwich in 1981. Lives near Norwich and still turns out for Newton Flotman in the Anglian Combination League.

WOODS, Matt. *Everton, Blackburn R, Luton T, Stockport Co (1952-1967).* Long serving centre half who made in excess of 380 League appearances, the majority of them in the colours of Blackburn Rovers. Matt left football after an 18 month spell as manager of Stockport County, to run his own haulage company, and could still be found behind the wheel well into his 60's.

WOODWARD, Alan. *Sheff U. (1963-1978).* Wingman Woodward played 550 games for Sheffield United and broke their scoring record with 158 goals before finishing in 1978/9. Now lives in Oklahoma and has worked for American Airways maintenance section for the past six years.

WOOLLETT, Alan. *Leicester , Northampton T. (1966-1978).* Alan is now a Prison Officer.

WOOSNAM, Phil. *Man C, Leyton O, West Ham, Aston V. (1952-1965).* **In 1969-70, Phil, who is a cousin to golfer Ian Woosnam, coached the USA World Cup side. He appeared in 358 League games and scored 68 goals and in 1965 he was widely tipped to become player/manager at Aston Villa, but chose instead to move to America, where he was given the task of developing Soccer as a national sport. He was US Soccer league Commissioner until 1982, when he became M.D. of Kick Enterprises, the marketing arm of the US Soccer Federation.**

WORTHINGTON, Frank. *Huddersfield, Leicester, Bolton, Birmingham, Leeds, Sunderland, Southampton, Brighton, Tranmere, Preston, Stockport. (1966-1987).* A colouful forward who has been through more clubs than Nick Faldo. Brought a smile and plenty of goals to all of them during a career that spanned more than twenty years. Lives in Shelf, near Halifax and now entertains an after dinner speaker. His recent autobiography 'One Hump or Two?' served as an amusing written account of his experiences.

WORTHINGTON, Bob. *Halifax, Middlesboro, Notts Co, Southend, Hartlepool (1964-1974)* Notts County's first team left back of the late 1960's and early 70's. Bob is now running a sports promotion firm based in Halifax.

WRAGG, Peter. *Rotherham, Sheff U, York, Bradford C. (1948-1964).* Inside Forward who played most of his League Soccer for York City. Managed Macclesfield Town until the Summer of 1994, when he took over at Halifax Town.

WRIGHT, Billy. *Wolves. (1946-1958).* **Star of the immediate post-war soccer scene. Billy had begun with Wolves straight from school. He became an inspiring captain for both club and country, making his international debut for England in 1946 and going on to make a then record 105 appearances, including a run of 46 consecutive matches. Holder of three League Championship medals, he retired in 1959, becoming England Youth Team Manager, then taking over at Arsenal from 1962 until 1966. Voted Player of the Year in 1951-2 and awarded the C.B.E. in 1959, his later years were spent working for A.T.V., and Central Television Sports departments. Married to Joy of the Beverley sisters. Died September 1994.**

WRIGHT, Charlie. *Workington, Grimsby, Charlton, Bolton. (1958-1972).* Glasgow born goalkeeper, whose smiling face and undoubted ability entertained the fans of four League clubs during his fourteen year career. Charlie now runs his own transport cafe in Greenwich, S.E.London.

WRIGHT, Mick. *Aston V (1963-1972).* Full back, who played for Aston Villa in ten seasons before having to retire through injury in May 1973. He now works for an engineering firm.

WRIGHT, Pat. *Birmingham, Shrewsbury, Derby, Southend, Rotherham (1959-1970).* Now back in Birmingham as M.D. of P & E Sports Ltd. His coaching talents have been in demand all over the world and has been National Coach in Zambia; U.A.E.; Saudi Arabia; and Malaysia.

WRIGHT, Peter. *Colchester (1951-1963)* Long serving winger who appeared for Colchester United more than four hundered times, now works as a steward at a leisure club in the town.

WRIGHT, Tommy. *Everton (1964-1972).* With Ball, Labone and Newton gave Everton a four man involvement in the Mexico World Cup. Made 308 appearances before retiring at the age of 29. Still a regular attendee at Goodison park and is now working in the docks at Garston.

WYLDE, Roger. *Sheff Wed, Oldham, Sunderland, Barnsley, Rotherham, Stockport Co. (1972-1988).* Now Physiotherapist at Stockport County.

WYLIE, Ron. *Notts Co, Aston V, Birmingham. (1951-1969).* He finished with Birmingham at the age of 36, after playing nearly 550 League games. Coached at Aston Villa, Coventry, in Cyprus, then in Hong Kong. Managed West Brom (1982-1984). Now in his fourth spell at Villa Park as their "Football in the Community Officer".

YEATS, Ron. *Liverpool, Tranmere. (1961-1973).* Made his name in his ten years with Liverpool after joining them from Dundee United in 1961 Became player./assistant manager at Tranmere Rovers in 1971, and manager until April 1975. Ron went into the haulage business, and then the catering trade. He still lives in Liverpool and is now back at Anfield as Chief Scout.

YORATH, Terry. *Leeds, Coventry, Tottenham, Bradford C, Swansea. (1967-1986).* A Welshman with midfield duties instilled under Don Revie. Terry was capped over 50 times by Wales. He later played for Coventry City and Spurs before a lengthy spell in the U.S.A, with Vancouver Whitecaps. In 1982 became player/coach at Bradford City. Terry was general manager at Cardiff City until 1995, when he resigned following an unsuccessful takeover bid by his consortium.

(Courtesy: John Cocks)

Ron Yeats at Liverpool's training ground, before setting off on a Scouting mission.

YOUNG, Alex. *Everton, Stockport. (1960-1968).* Scottish international who was a crowd favourite at Goodison Park in the 1960's. Briefly became player/manager of Glentoran, but soon returned to play for Stockport. Alex retired in 1969 through injury, returned back to Scotland and now runs a wholesale business in Edinburgh.

YOUNG, Gerry. *Sheffield Wed (1956-1970).* Played over 300 games for Sheffield Wednesday and was capped once by England. Took up coaching positions firstly at Hillsborough and then at nearby Barnsley before running a Sports Shop in Sheffield with former team-mate John Quinn.

YOUNG, Kevin. *Burnley, Torquay U, Port Vale, Bury (1978-1986).* Kevin was a left winger with Burnley for a number of years in the 1970's and 80's, but is now working as a prison officer.

YOUNG, Neil. *Manchester C, Preston N.E., Rochdale (1961-1974).* A regular fixture on the Manchester City team sheet for ten years, Neil now runs his own soccer school in Wilmslow and also helps coach youngsters in Cheshire schools.

YOUNG, Tommy. *Tranmere R, Rotherham U. (1972-1978).* Lives in Maltby, and from 1979 until 1993 worked in the local colliery before being made redundant. Now employed as a platelayer.

YOUNG, Willie. *Tottenham H, Arsenal, Notts F, Norwich C, Brighton, Darlington. (1975-1984).* A solid central defender, Willie started his playing career with Aberdeen, and won his first Scottish Under 23 caps before being signed by Terry Neill for Tottenham Hotspur. Then followed his manager across London, to join rivals Arsenal in March 1977 for £80,000. He now owns a picturesque country pub on the outskirts of Nottingham, called the'Bramcote Manor' in Bramcote.

Alan Young
(Courtesy: Raymonds Press Agency)